W0259645

Knitting Stitches

STEP BY STEP

Knitting Stitches

STEP BY STEP

Jo Shaw

Contents

Introduction

Knitting as we know it today has a long history: the earliest pieces of knitwear, found in Egypt, date back to at least the 5th century. Until the invention of the knitting frame by William Lee in 1589, hand-knitting was commonly used in most households to make clothing. After this point, machine-knitted textiles became more commonly available and knitting moved to become a pastime, rather than a necessity of life.

WHAT IS KNITTING?

Knitting is created with a continuous length of yarn, with interlocking loops made by knitting needles that results in a stretchy, non-woven fabric. Knit and purl (see p.36) are the two basic stitches upon which the entire foundation of knitting stitches and patterns are based. Using different combinations of stitches and yarn colours, a whole myriad of designs can be created.

PROCESS OR PRODUCT KNITTER

The reasons why we knit can differ. For me, it is very much about the process: I find the rhythm and creativity of knitting is relaxing, yet inspiring. For that reason, I like to use yarns and colours that are comfortable and soothing. I find myself making items for the love of the stitch pattern or yarn first and foremost, and will find a happy recipient for them afterwards. For others, the main reason is to create that finished object for themselves or a loved one, to clothe them beautifully and warmly. These product knitters are led more by the pattern choice, though none of us fit neatly into a category and we are more likely to be a bit of both. Whichever reason you lean more towards, knitting can provide comfort and warmth in many ways.

SOCIAL KNITTING

Knitting can seem like a solo occupation – you sit with your yarn and needles and create beautiful projects. However, there is a large knitting community out there, which can bring fulfilment in itself. Yarn shops can be a hub of activity, acting as workshops in which you can learn new techniques, and social hubs, where you can "knit and natter" with like-minded people about your latest projects. There are numerous knitting shows around the world, where designers, makers, and yarn dyers share wares and inspiration. And then, of course, there is social media. There is a strong knitting community online where you can

discuss your projects, ask for advice, or just wax poetic about your love of knitting. Every month brings with it another wave of "knit-a-long" (KAL) opportunities, where a group of knitters work on similar projects. Knitting might at first seem like a solitary hobby, but there is a whole web of social connections to find.

MY KNITTING JOURNEY

We all have a start to our knitting journey. This may be with a family member teaching us, a knitting class, or as self-taught knitters. My formative years were spent living in the Midlands of England, an area that has been synonymous with textiles for centuries. My grandparents all worked in the textile industry and my father was a successful lace designer and draughtsman. That combination of art and maths that are the foundations of lace design happen to be the same as knitting design, so it must be in my genes.

My love for knitting had a few false starts at a young age, when knitting didn't really click. That changed in my early twenties. I decided to try my hand at knitting socks. With encouragement from a good friend, who supplied me with my first sock yarn and needles, it finally clicked, and I haven't put my knitting needles down since.

Knitting is a huge part of my life. For a time, I worked in a local yarn shop and started designing knitting patterns. I began publishing these patterns myself, and later in collaboration with magazines and yarn companies. I spent three years working on a knitting qualification, wrote a knitting book, and now another. Knitting fits my personality down to the ground, from the creativity of textures and colours, to the detailed maths and grading required to work out how to share those patterns with other knitters.

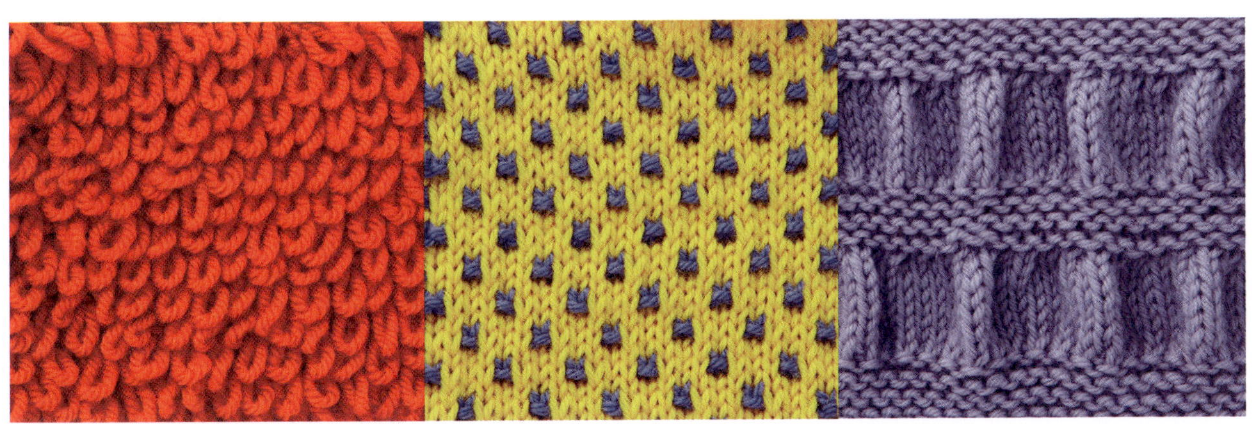

Tools, Materials, and Techniques

Knitting Needles

Knitting needles come in different forms. The three main types are straight, double-pointed, and circular. All come in a range of different materials – metal, wood, bamboo, carbon, and plastic. Metal needles tend to be cheaper, but bamboo and wood needles are a better option for those with arthritis or other hand issues, as they warm to body temperature quickly.

NEEDLE SIZE

Knitting needles vary in width. The standard range is 2–12mm, though sizes outside of this range are available. Generally, the thickness of the yarn helps determine the size of the needle used. A fine lace-weight yarn will require a thinner needle to create a closed knitted fabric. However, a closed knitted fabric isn't always the desired result: a shawl, for example, would need more drape to hang nicely, so a larger needle would be used. Other projects require a dense and hard-wearing fabric, so a smaller needle is needed. For example, a sock would require a dense fabric to tolerate the wear. Always knit a test swatch with the needles you plan to use, to make sure that the finished size is fit for purpose (see p.19).

STRAIGHT NEEDLES

Straight needles are usually the first needles knitters learn to knit with, and are used to create a flat piece of knitting. They are limited in scope as they only allow you to work backward and forward. They are typically available in lengths of 15–40cm (6–16in); the choice of length depends on personal preference and the size of the project that will be knitted, as the needles need to be long enough to contain all the stitches.

DOUBLE-POINTED NEEDLES

Double-pointed needles come in sets of four or five needles. They are typically 15–20cm (6–8in) long, and are best suited for small circumferences in the round, such as socks. The stitches are shared across three or four needles and the empty needle is used to knit.

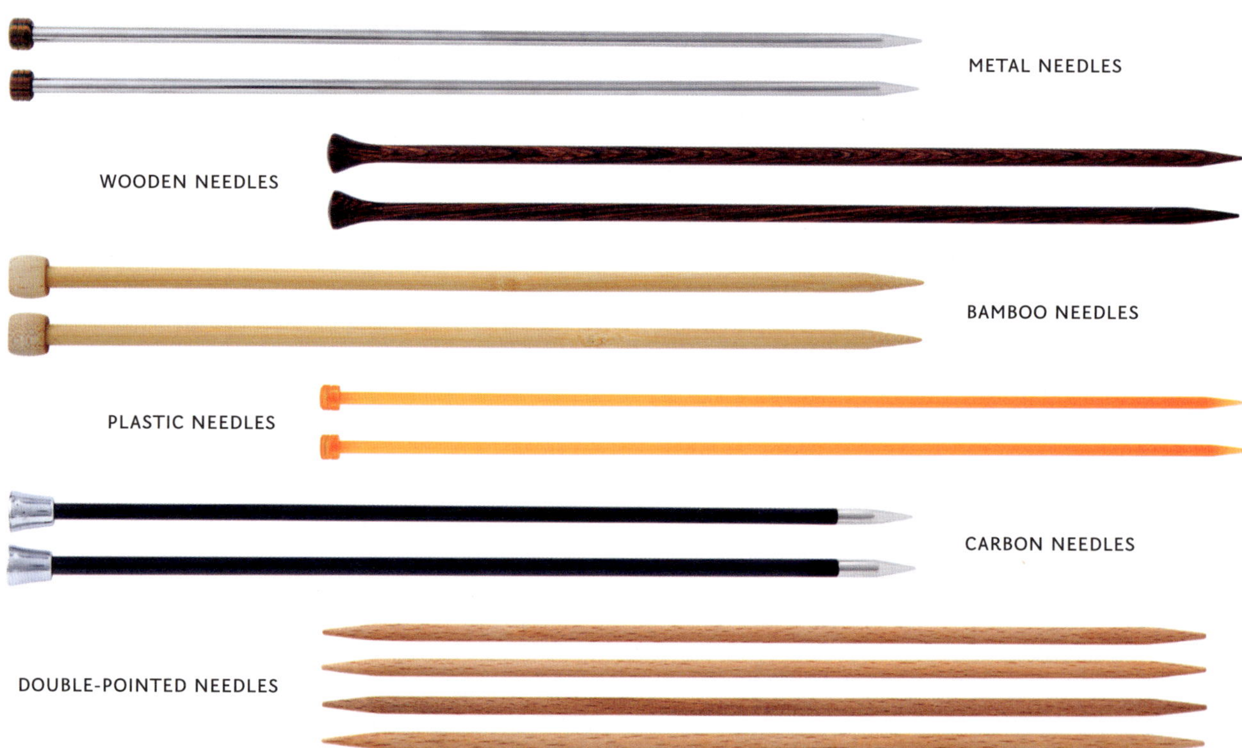

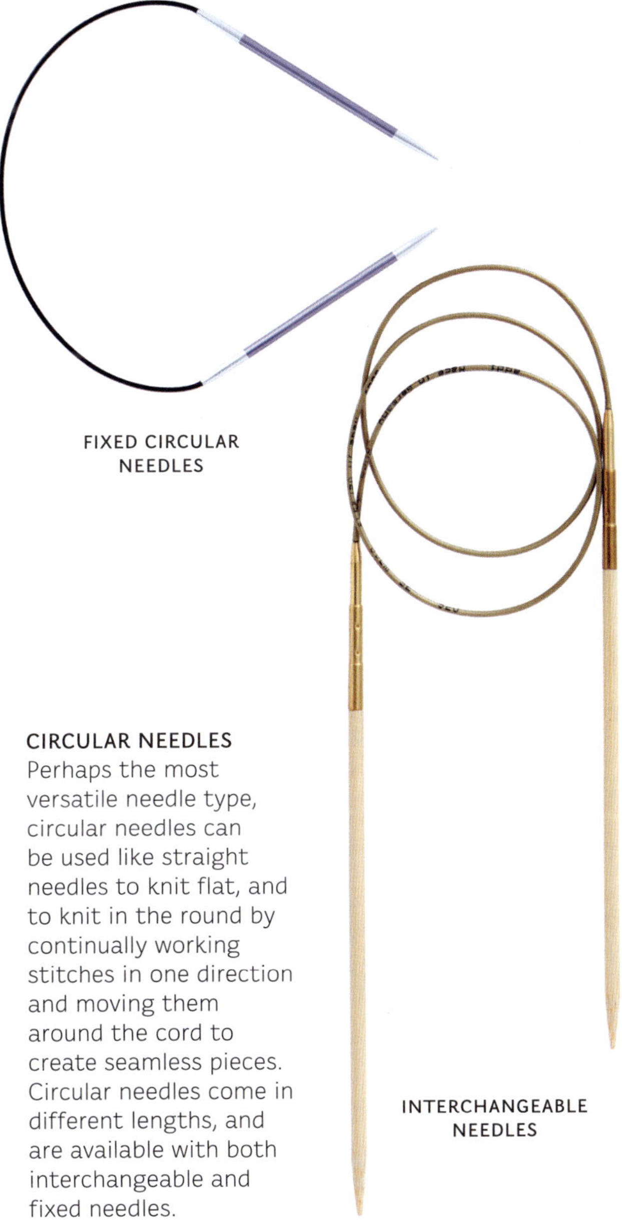

FIXED CIRCULAR NEEDLES

INTERCHANGEABLE NEEDLES

CIRCULAR NEEDLES

Perhaps the most versatile needle type, circular needles can be used like straight needles to knit flat, and to knit in the round by continually working stitches in one direction and moving them around the cord to create seamless pieces. Circular needles come in different lengths, and are available with both interchangeable and fixed needles.

NEEDLE SIZE CONVERSION CHART

EU METRIC	OLD UK	US
1.5mm	N/A	000 00
2mm	14	0
2.25mm 2.5mm	13	1
2.75mm	12	2
3mm	11	2.5
3.25mm	10	3
3.5mm	N/A	4
3.75mm	9	5
4mm	8	6
4.5mm	7	7
5mm	6	8
5.5mm	5	9
6mm	4	10
6.5mm	3	10½
7mm	2	N/A
7.5mm	1	N/A
8mm	0	11
9mm	00	13
10mm	000	15
12mm	N/A	17
15mm	N/A	19
20mm	N/A	35
25mm	N/A	50

FIXED CIRCULAR NEEDLES

Fixed circulars are a pair of needle tips attached to a flexible cord. They are available in different standard lengths varying from 23cm (9in) to 150cm (60in). For traditional fixed working in the round, a length is chosen that is smaller than the finished ircumference. It is possible to use an advanced knitting technique (the magic loop method) to work smaller circumferences than the length of the circular.

INTERCHANGEABLE NEEDLES

These are similar to fixed circulars, except that the needles can be detached from the cable. This allows more versatility as the cable length can be changed when needed. It can be a more cost-effective option too – instead of buying multiple circular needles in different lengths, you can just buy one pair of needles and a variety of cable lengths.

Yarn

There is a huge variety and combination of yarns. Yarn construction can vary, with the most common type being plied yarn, which contains multiple single plies that are spun together. Plies can be worsted or woollen: worsted plies (the more common form) create a smoother yarn that shows textured stitches clearly, while woollen plies are hairier and more textured, and are more suited for stranded colourwork. Other yarn styles are available including chain, single ply, encased, corespun, bouclé, fur, and eyelash yarn.

YARN WEIGHT	SYMBOL	RECOMMENDED NEEDLE SIZES metric	US
Thread, cobweb, lace, light fingering, 1–3-ply	0 Lace	1.5mm	00
		2mm	0
		2.25mm	1
Superfine, fingering, baby, sock weight, 4-ply	1 Superfine	2.25mm	1
		2.75mm	2
		3mm	2.5
		3.25mm	3
Fine, sport, baby,5/6-ply	2 Fine	3.25mm	3
		3.5mm	4
		3.75mm	5
Double-knit (DK), light worsted, 8-ply	3 Light	3.75mm	5
		4mm	6
		4.5mm	7
Aran, medium, worsted, Afghan, 10/12-ply	4 Medium	4.5mm	7
		5mm	8
		5.5mm	9
Bulky, chunky, craft, rug, 12/14-ply	5 Bulky	5.5mm	9
		6mm	10
		6.5mm	10½
		7mm	N/A
		8mm	11
Super bulky, super chunky, bulky, roving, 14/16-ply	6 Super Bulky	8mm	11
		9mm	13
		10mm	15
		12.75mm	17

THICKNESS

There are seven main thicknesses of yarn. Most knitting patterns are written with a specific yarn weight in mind. The samples shown in this book are worked in worsted weight (medium/size 4). However, the stitches shown can be used with any thickness of yarn but will have a different finished look depending on the yarn used. Yarn thicknesses and types can be known by different names, depending on the country. 4-ply yarn is referred to as "fingering weight" in the US; it may also be referred to as sock weight.

One convention was to name the yarn after the number of plies that it had because, originally, this determined the thickness, such as 1 ply, 2 ply, 3 ply, etc. Yarn thickness is no longer determined by ply, but in certain countries the naming conventions have stuck.

FIBRE

There are many different types of fibre available, and these can be produced entirely in a single fibre or a blend of multiple fibres. There are three main types: animal, plant, and synthetic.

Animal Fibres
Animal fibres tend to be warm with some elasticity. Wool is the most versatile animal fibre and creates a stretchy and warm fabric. It blocks crisply too.

Plant Fibres
Plant fibres are cooler than animal fibres, but tend to have no stretch. Cotton is the most common plant fibre – it is good for hot weather but has very little elasticity.

Synthetic Fibres
Acrylic is the most common human-made fibre as it can be constructed to resemble any other type of fibre and is cheaper to produce. Since acrylic is essentially plastic, it doesn't block very well to create crisp lines. Although cost-effective, synthetic fibres can negatively impact the environment. Many are made from fossil fuels and produce toxic by-products.

Other Useful Tools

Along with yarn and needles, there are other tools that can make your knitting easier to manage. Some can be very project specific; cable needles, stitch holders, bobbins, and embellishments will only be needed sporadically. However, there are several tools, such as scissors and stitch markers, that can be useful in all projects.

SCISSORS

Scissors are needed to cut the yarn when you've finished using it. These are used more frequently when working with multiple colours in a project.

TAPE MEASURE AND RULER

Most projects will be worked to a particular size. Often, the pattern will instruct you to work until a certain length, so a tape measure is vital for an accurate measurement. It can be used to measure your gauge swatch too, though a ruler would be more accurate.

STITCH MARKERS

Stitch markers are a very helpful knitter's tool, and are used either on the needle or attached to the fabric. They can be used to indicate a change in pattern, mark stitch pattern repeats, indicate the beginning of the round, mark the right side (RS) of the work when a knitted fabric is reversible, plus many other uses. Many published patterns include stitch marker guidance (for example, "knit to marker, kfb, slip marker"). When slipping the marker, insert the RHN into the hole in the marker and move it from the LHN to the RHN.

STITCH COUNTER

Stitch counters help to keep track of your position in your knitting. They are clicked to mark when a row has been completed, or when an increase or decrease takes place. They can be either mechanical or electronic. Alternatively, you can use a pen and paper.

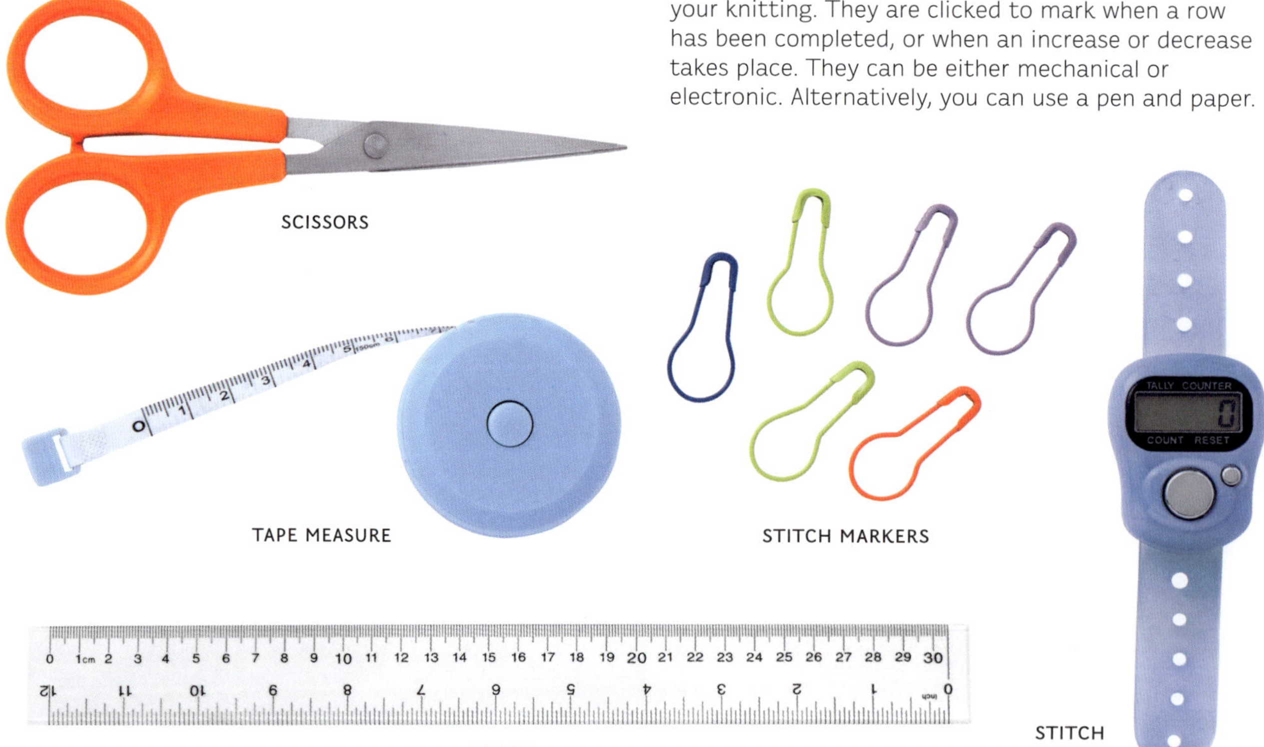

SCISSORS

TAPE MEASURE

STITCH MARKERS

RULER

STITCH COUNTER

CROCHET HOOK

A crochet hook can be used to fix mistakes by pulling up a stitch from below (see p.21). They can be used with other knitting techniques too, such as adding beads (see p.150).

CABLE NEEDLES

When working with cables (see pp.125–33), some of the stitches are slipped to a cable needle and held to the front or back of your work until needed. These are double-ended needles, either straight or with a V- or U-shaped middle, designed to hold the stitches without them falling off and unravelling.

DARNING NEEDLES

These are used to sew in the ends of the yarn. A darning needle needs to have a blunt end and a large enough eye for the yarn to be threaded through.

STITCH HOLDER

Some patterns require the stitches to be put on hold until a later stage. These can be slipped to a stitch holder, which closes to prevent the stitches from unravelling.

BOBBINS

When working intarsia designs (see p.83), bobbins can be used to hold lengths of different coloured yarns to keep them out of the way and prevent them from getting tangled. They can also be used for managing scraps of yarn.

EMBELLISHMENTS

Embellishments can be added to the knitted fabric. Beads and sequins are the most common. Beads need to have a large enough hole to fit the yarn through. For beads, the suitable sizes are 8/0 for 4 ply weight and thinner, and 6/0 for DK weight and thinner.

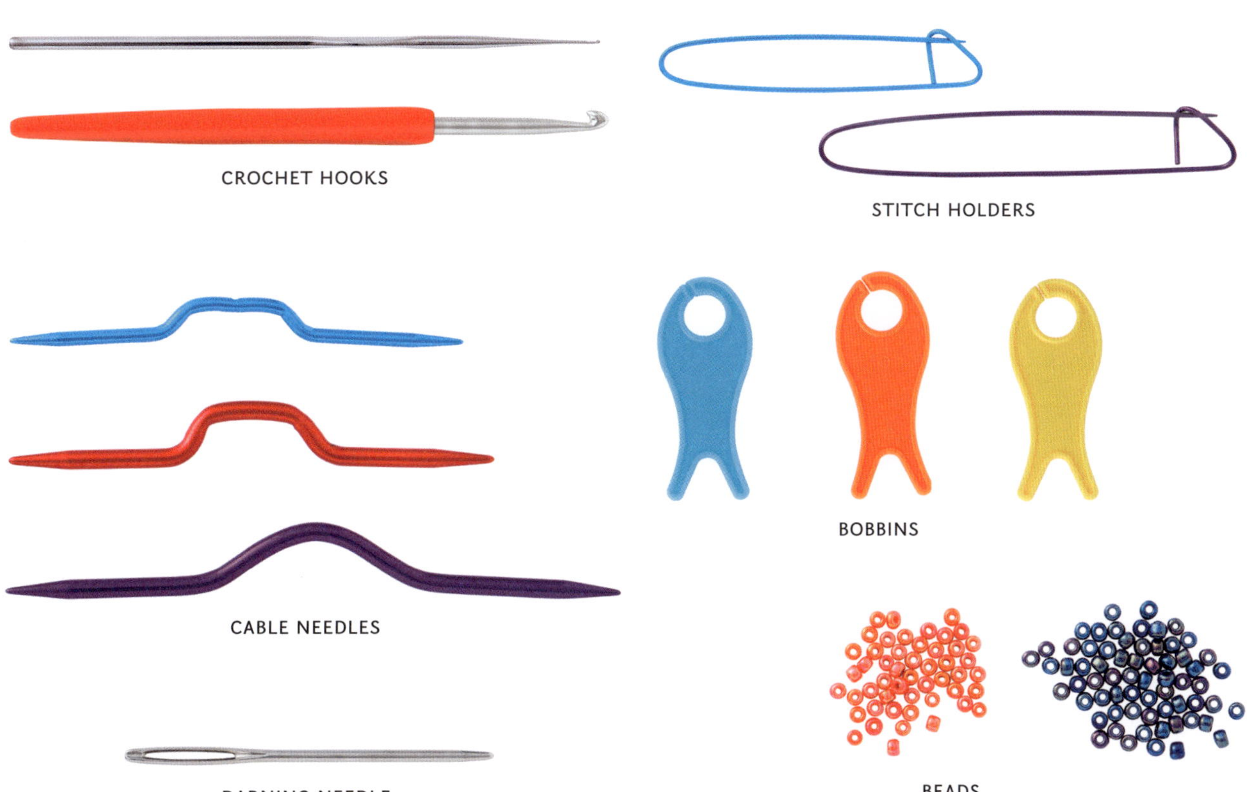

CROCHET HOOKS

STITCH HOLDERS

CABLE NEEDLES

BOBBINS

DARNING NEEDLE

BEADS

Understanding Patterns

Knitting patterns could be excessively long if every step was written out long-form. They have evolved into more succinct instructions that use abbreviations and repeats. Though this makes them shorter, so it becomes quicker to follow patterns, there is a learning curve when it comes to mastering the "translation" of these instructions.

READING A PATTERN

The format of knitting patterns depends upon the author. A good knitting pattern will contain certain information, including the type and amount of yarn used, the finished measurements and available sizes, the needle size, tension gauge (see p.19), other tools you may need, and a list of any abbreviations used.

Trying to read knitting abbreviations can feel like learning a new language. It is. Knitting abbreviations should be listed clearly, such as in those shown opposite. You can "translate" the knitting instructions by referring to this list.

PATTERN REPEATS

Pattern repeats can be a confusing part of knitting instructions. In this book, asterisks (*) are used to indicate a point from which instructions need to be repeated: for example "*k2, p2, repeat from * until the end" indicates that you would alternate two knit stitches and two purl stitches until the end of the row.

Brackets can be used in the same way. For example, the instruction (k2, p2) across means that you repeat everything within the brackets across the row.

WORKING THE ROWS

If the row starts with a knit stitch, hold the working yarn at the back of the work (see p.36). Conversely, if the row starts with a purl stitch, keep the working yarn at the front of the work (see p.36).

When you have completed a row and have an empty needle, turn the work, so that the needle with the stitches is in your left hand. A bold row number (e.g. **Row 3**) indicates the start of a new row, meaning that the work needs to be turned.

Selvedges

Many knitting fabrics will curl in at the edge on a flat fabric. If these edges will remain visible in the finished project, add selvedge stitches to your work. These are one to three garter stitches (see p.36), or any stitch that does not curl, added to either side of the knitted piece.

USING THE PATTERNS IN A PROJECT

Each stitch pattern in the book is accompanied by guidance on how it can be used in a project. To use a stitch multiple of "5 (+2)", for example, you could cast on 62 stitches (12 x 5 stitches, plus 2), or 37 stitches (7 x 5 stitches, plus 2), and so on. If incorporating a selvedge (see opposite), remember to factor in these extra stitches as well. If the rows are "8 (+2)", there are 8 rows plus 2 setup rows. This means to work complete repeats you will work sets of 8 rows. The 2 setup rows are only worked on the first repeat. If you are substituting one of the stitches into another pattern, make sure to adjust for the stitch multiple. You can always add extra plain border stitches too.

Each stitch pattern includes details about the appearance of the knitted fabric. Many of these fabrics are single-sided, meaning the right side (RS) is the only side with a pattern. However, there are several fabrics that are reversible, so both sides will have the same appearance. Some do not have identical patterns on both sides, but the wrong side (WS) also has an appealing appearance and so can be used as the right side (RS) of the fabric.

ABBREVIATIONS

(k, p, k) in 1 stitch knit 1, purl 1, knit 1 into 1 stitch
1/1 LPC 1 over 1 left purl cross
1/1 RPC 1 over 1 right purl cross
1/3 LC 1 over 3 left cross
1/3 RC 1 over 3 right cross
2/1 LPC 2 over 1 left purl cross
2/1 RPC 2 over 1 right purl cross
2/2 LC 2 over 2 left cross
2/2 RC 2 over 2 right cross
3/3 LC 3 over 3 left cross
3-to-3 3 stitches into 3 stitches
brk brioche knit
brp brioche purl
C4B cable 4 back
C4F cable 4 front
CC contrast colour
k knit
k1b knit into centre of stitch 1 row below
k2tog knit 2 stitches together
k3b knit into centre of stitch 3 rows below
k3togtbl knit 3 stitches together through the back loop
kfb knit front and back
kfbfb knit into the front and back twice
k-tbl knit through the back loop
kyok knit, yarnover, knit into 1 stitch
LHN left-hand needle
LT left twist
m1l make 1 left
m1r make 1 right
mb make bobble
MC main colour
p purl
p2tog purl 2 stitches together
p3tog purl 3 stitches together
p4tog purl 4 stitches together
p-tbl purl through the back loop
rep repeat
RHN right-hand needle
RS right side
RT right twist
s2kpo slip 2 stitches, knit 1, pass slipped stitches over
sk2po slip 1, knit 2 stitches together, pass slipped stitch over
skyp slip 1, knit 1, yarnover, pass slipped stitch over
sl 1-k2-psso slip 1 knitwise, knit 2 stitches, pass slipped stitch over
sl1yo slip 1 purlwise, yarnover
ssk slip, slip, knit 2 stitches together
ssp slip, slip, purl 2 stitches together
st(s) stitch(es)
wyib sl with yarn in the back slip
wyif sl with yarn in the front slip
yfrn yarn forward around needle
yfsl1yo yarn front, slip 1 purlwise, yarnover
yfwd yarn forward
yo yarnover
yon yarn over needle
yrn yarn round needle

Understanding Charts

Once you've mastered the stitches that make up the stitch pattern you want to make, it is often easier to read a chart (usually accompanied by abbreviated notes for each row) than to follow long-form written instructions. Charts are made up of symbols representing each stitch (see table below).

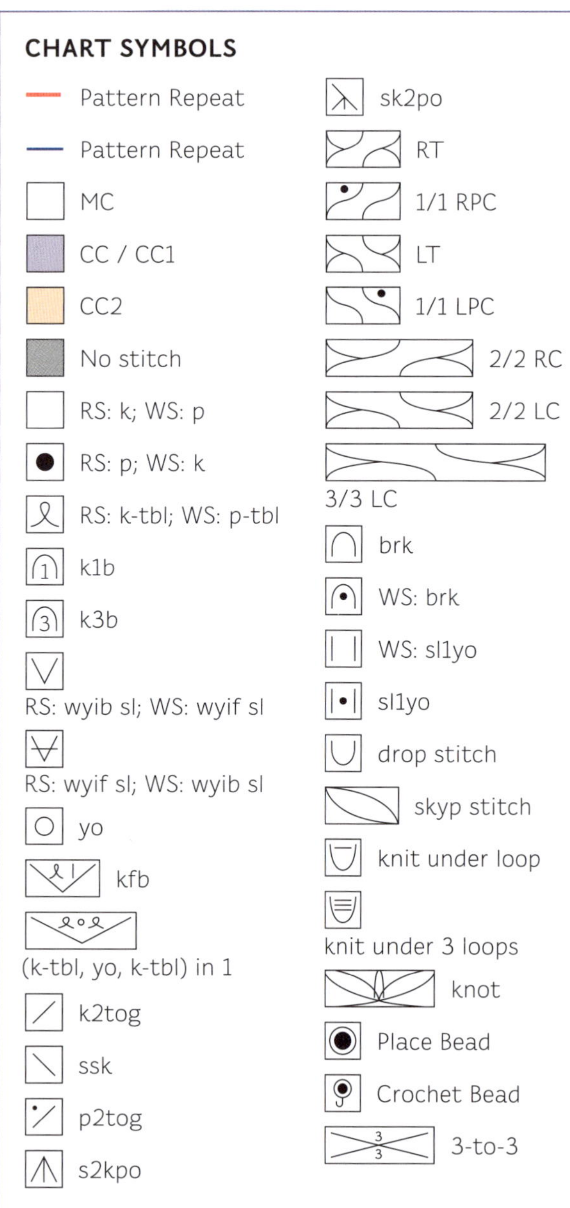

READING A CHART

Charts are read from bottom to top. Work each stitch as you come to it. Occasionally, you may see a dark grey box (not to be confused with a coloured box, which indicates the use of a contrasting colour (CC)). This means that no stitch is worked here; it is just there to allow the chart to line up correctly. Skip this square and move onto the next stitch.

Some symbols are grouped across multiple squares since the stitch being created uses all these stitches. All the samples are worked flat, so the charts are read from right to left for right side (RS) rows and left to right for wrong side (WS) rows. The positioning of the number at the side of the chart represents the starting point. If the number is to the right, this is a right side row and should be read right to left, and vice versa.

A red box around a section of a chart indicates the area to be repeated, corresponding with the stitch multiple information (see p.17). Stitches outside of the red square are not repeated.

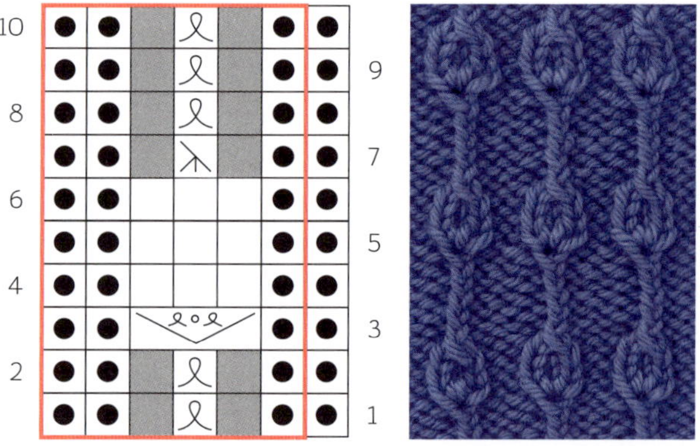

Mini Leaf Rib chart and swatch
This chart includes the no stitch symbol, which allows the chart to line up. Ignore these stitches when following the chart. The red box indicates the pattern repeat, so repeat the pattern within the lines only. There are some stitches, including an increase, that cover 3 squares.

Basic Techniques

There are seemingly endless techniques involved in knitting - which ones you focus on depends on the type of knitting that you enjoy most and would like to explore further. However, there are a few basic skills that every knitter should master, such as casting on and finishing techniques such as casting off and blocking.

WORKING IN THE ROUND

The stitch patterns in this book are worked flat; after completing one row, the knitting is turned and the subsequent row is worked in the opposite direction. This creates a flat piece of knitting. These flat pieces can be sewn together to create different shapes or used flat, such as in a scarf.

However, many projects can be knitted in the round instead; a piece is worked in a continuous spiral meaning that the work is not turned and the right side is always facing the knitter. This allows the knitter to avoid seams in the work. Also, as there is no wrong side to the knitting, the stitches do not need to be reversed. To knit in the round, different types of knitting needles are used such as circular or double-pointed needles (see pp.10–11).

Should you wish to convert stitch patterns to working in the round, follow the charts from the right-hand side for every round. Make sure that you use the right-side version of the chart symbol for the even rounds (for example, swapping a knit stitch for a purl stitch and vice versa).

Working small circumferences

Small circumferences can be knitted in the round with double-pointed needles (see p.10). The work is shared out over 3 or 4 needles and the extra needle is used to work the stitches.

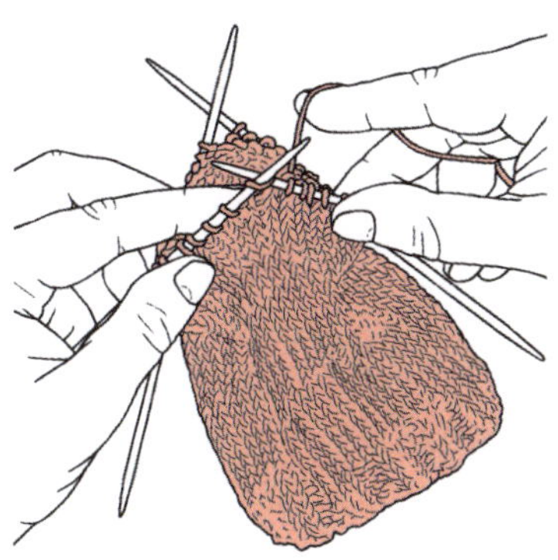

GAUGE

Published patterns will usually specify a desired gauge. This is the number of stitches and rows the designer expects that the item will need in order to be the right size once finished and blocked. Checking the gauge is essential before embarking on a project; otherwise, you might finish knitting a jumper only to find that it is two sizes smaller than you thought it would be.

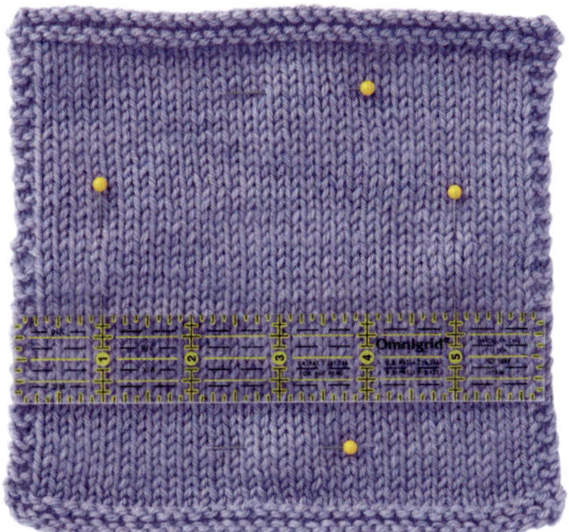

Checking the gauge

Knit a sample square, at least 15x15cm (6x6in), for each stitch pattern you plan to include in your project. Block it (see p.21) and leave to dry. Measure 10cm (4in) across the centre of the swatch, mark the distance with pins, and count how many stitches fall within the area. Do the same in the other direction, counting the number of rows.

If the stitch and row count does not match the gauge specified in the pattern, reknit the swatch again in a larger or smaller needle size (see pp.10–11), until you achieve a gauge as close as possible to the one you need. For example, if you are aiming for 22 stitches and your swatch measures 20 stitches, try again with needles 1–2 sizes smaller.

SLIP KNOT

Most cast-ons require a slip knot to start.

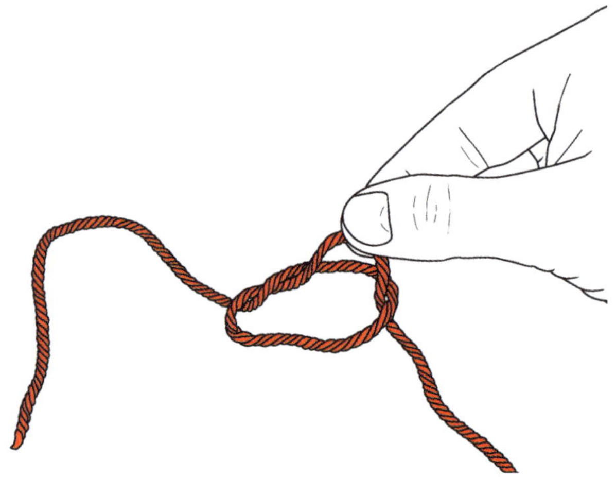

1 Create a loop with the yarn, with the ball end over the top. With your fingers in the loop, pull the working yarn through to create another loop.

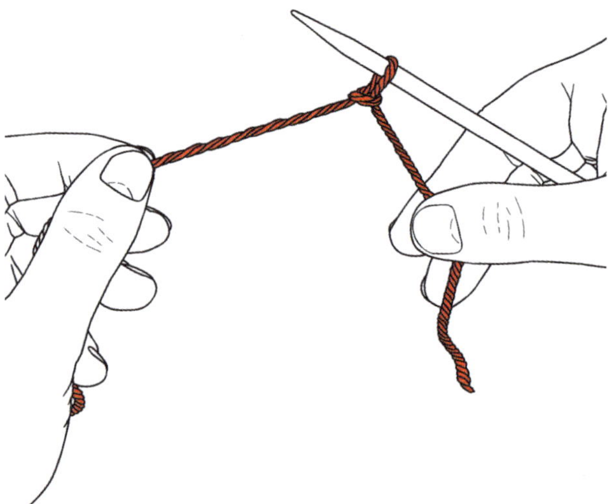

2 Insert the knitting needle into this loop. Pull both ends of the yarn tight, until the loop is snug against the needle.

CASTING ON

There are hundreds of different cast-ons. They can be decorative, practical, double-sided, or very stretchy. The cable cast-on shown below is the neatest and simplest method.

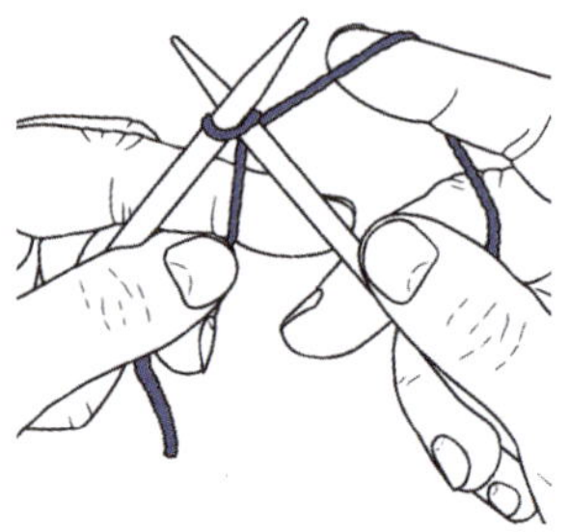

1 Place a slipknot on the LHN. Insert the RHN from left to right into the slipknot. Wrap the yarn anticlockwise around the RHN.

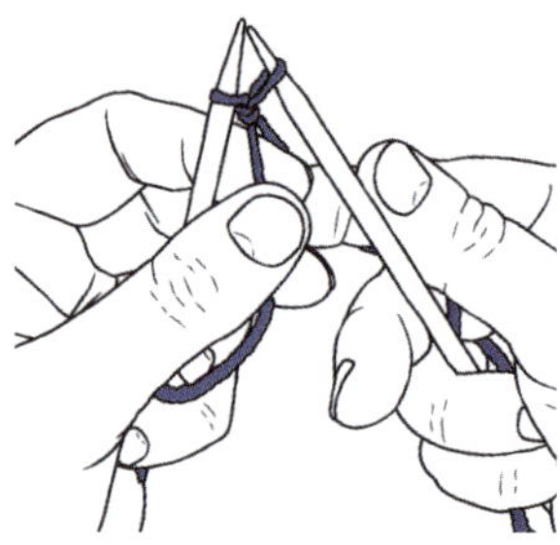

2 Keeping tension on the yarn, scoop the working yarn back through the stitch to the left.

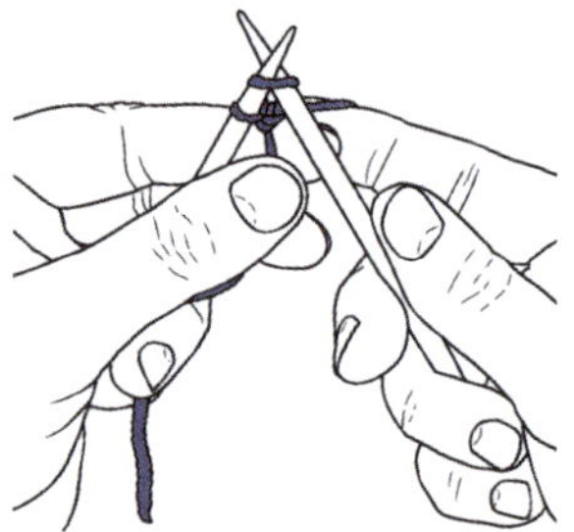

3 Place the new stitch onto the LHN by inserting the LHN from right to left into the loop on the RHN. (Note: this can also be done from left to right and gives a slightly flatter edge. Just stick with one method throughout the cast on.)

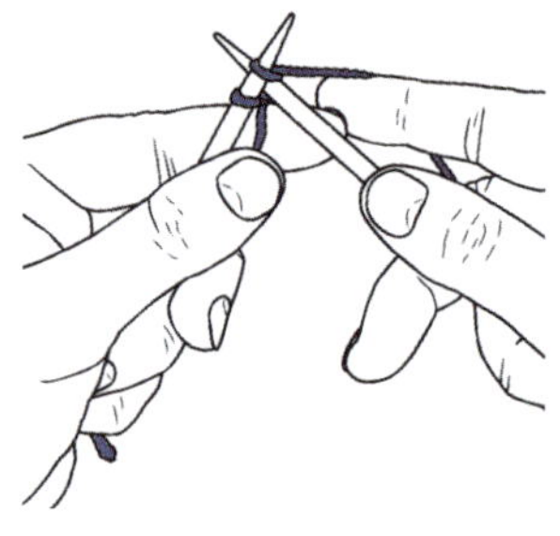

4 Insert the RHN from front to back between the first and second stitch on the LHN. Do not pull the yarn tight until the RHN has been inserted. Wrap the yarn anticlockwise around the RHN and scoop a stitch through to the front. Repeat steps 3 and 4 until the required number of stitches has been cast on.

CASTING OFF

There are several methods for casting off; the suspended cast-off shown below is a good option for beginners.

1 Knit 2 stitches. Insert the LHN from left to right into the second stitch on the RHN.

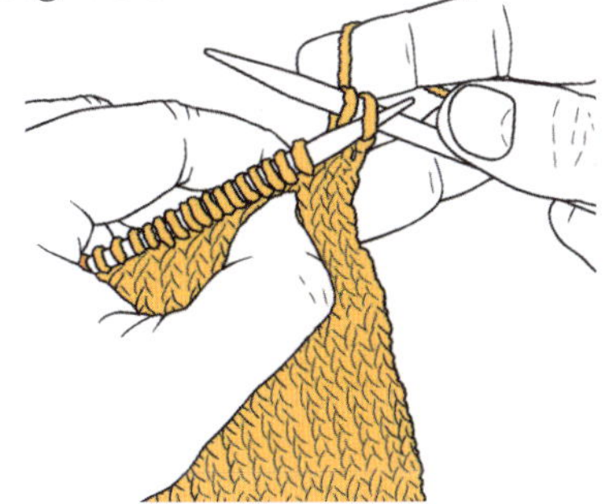

2 Lift this over the top of the first stitch and then off the RHN. Drop from both needles.

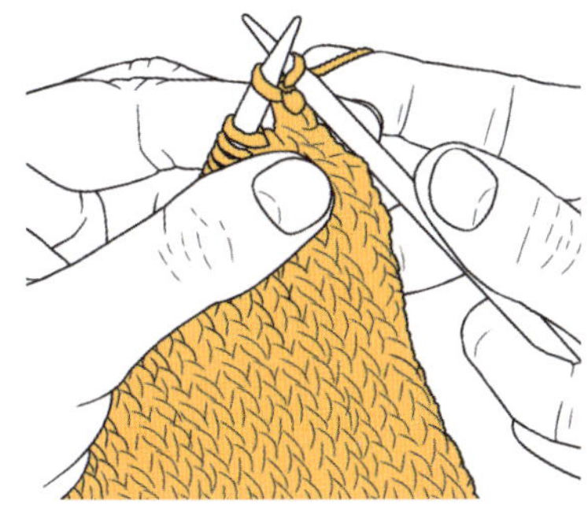

3 Repeat until 1 stitch remains. Cut the yarn and then pull this loop until the end comes out of the stitch.

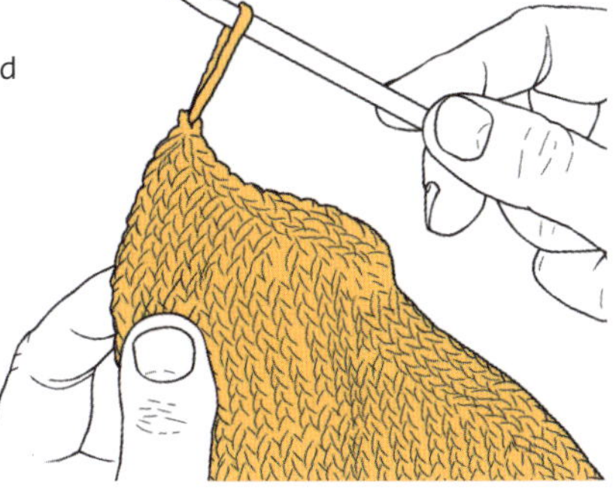

STRANDED KNITTING

When working stranded colourwork (see pp.95–103) flat, knit any selvedge stitches in both yarns to avoid holes. To achieve the best finish when working stranded colourwork, keep the position of the yarns consistent throughout. For example, always keep the main colour at the bottom and the contrast colour at the top. Do not swap positions or twist the yarns. This principle is known as colour dominance.

PICKING UP A DROPPED STITCH

It is relatively simple to pick up an accidentally dropped stitch in stocking stitch using a crochet hook. Insert the hook from front to back into the loop of the dropped stitch. Then insert the hook under the horizontal bar of the row above, and scoop through the dropped stitch. This strand will now be on the hook and you can place the live stitch back onto the needle with the right leg at the front. Repeat for as many rows as have dropped.

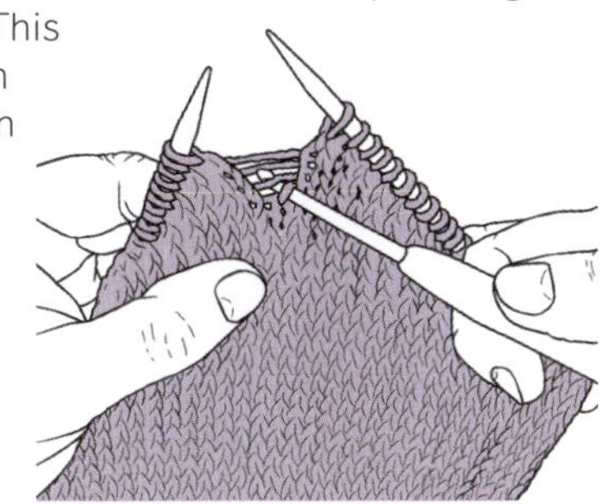

DARNING IN ENDS

Thread one of the ends onto a darning needle, then weave it into the fabric. If the yarn is at a seam, weave it in and out of this raised seam. If it emerges from the middle of the fabric (for instance, in intarsia designs), either follow the path of the stitches on the wrong side or skim along the top. Reverse direction at least once so that the end won't easily come loose.

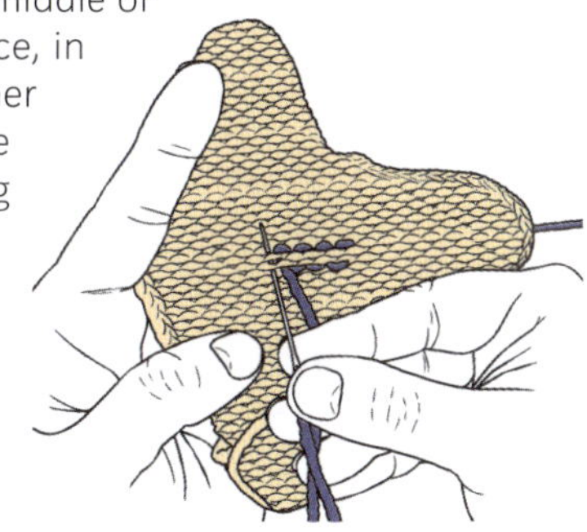

FINISHING AND BLOCKING

Wet the knitted piece, either by hand-washing or by spraying with a water mister until the fabric is soaked. Treat it gently as many fibres will felt with water and agitation. Once wet, lay the piece out to dry, pinning it onto a foam board if necessary in order to keep the item in its desired shape. Let it dry thoroughly before moving it.

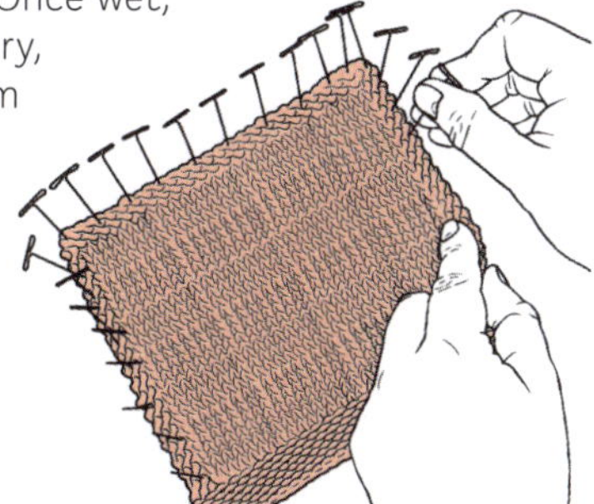

Gallery of Stitches

Knit Stitch (p.36)

Purl Stitch (p.36)

Knit Through the Back Loop (p.37)

Purl Through the Back Loop (p.37)

Knit 2 Together (p.38)

Slip, Slip, Knit 2 Together (p.38)

Purl 2 Together (p.39)

Slip, Slip, Purl (p.39)

Make 1 Left (p.40)

Make 1 Right (p.40)

Knit Front and Back (p.41)

Knit, Yarnover, Knit Into One Stitch (p. 41)

Knit to Knit Yarnover (p.42)

Purl to Purl Yarnover (p.43)

Knit to Purl Yarnover (p.43)

Purl to Knit Yarnover (p.43)

Slip 1, Knit 2 Together, Pass Slipped Stitch Over (p.44)

Double Moss Stitch (p.49)

Basketweave (p.50)

Slip 2 Stitches, Knit 1, Pass Slipped Stitches Over (p.44)

Garter Ridges (p.49)

Textured Honeycomb (p.51)

With Yarn in Front Slip 1 (p.45)

Foundations (p.50)

Checkerboard Stitch (p.51)

With Yarn in Back Slip 1 (p.45)

Horizontal Dash (p.50)

Stepping Stones (p.51)

Moss Stitch (p.49)

Mock Rib (p.50)

1 x 1 Ribbing (p.53)

2 x 2 Ribbing (p.53)

Broken Rib (p.54)

Twisted Rib (p.54)

Ropewalk Rib (p.55)

Skyp Rib (p.56)

Twisted and Knit Rib (p.57)

Beaded Rib (p.57)

Garter Rib (p.57)

Garter Chevrons (p.61)

Stocking Stitch Chevrons (p.62)

Herringbone Stitch (p.63)

Ridge Stitch (p.63)

Faux Increase Cable (p.64)

Mock Cable (p.65)

Ruching (p.65)

Mini Leaf Rib (p.66)

Thorn Stitch (p.67)

Eye of Partridge (p.69)

Linen Stitch (p.69)

Slipped Stitch Ladder (p.70)

Woven Texture (p.71)

Little Tent Stitch (p.72)

Lattice (p.73)

Speckled Rib (p.74)

Alternating Ladders (p.74)

Honeycomb Slip Stitch (p.74)

Half Linen Stitch (p.75)

Reverse Brick Stitch (p.75)

Garter Stripes (p.79)

Contrast Garter Ridges (p.79)

Two-row Garter Stitch (p.80)

Two-colour Moss Stitch (p.80)

Basic Mosaic Dots (p.85)

Contrast Bow Tie Stitch (p.89)

Tricolour Garter Rib (p.81)

Slip Garter Columns (p.86)

Stepped (p.90)

Contrast Welts (p.82)

Ridge Check (p.86)

String of Pearls (p.82)

Triple Tweed (p.87)

Corner Square (p.91)

Intarsia Diamond (p.83)

Fish Scale (p.88)

Chain Link (p.92)

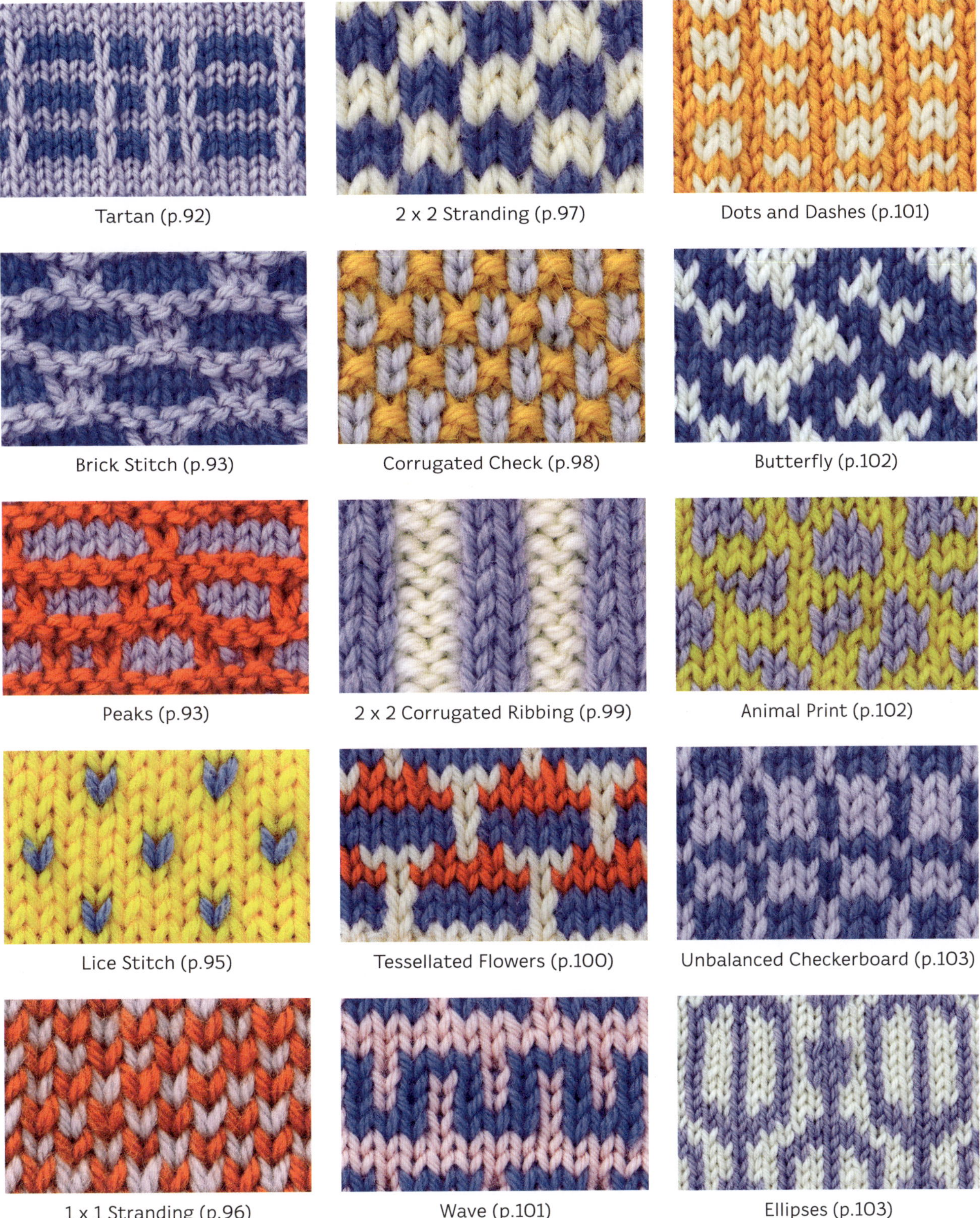

Tartan (p.92)

2 x 2 Stranding (p.97)

Dots and Dashes (p.101)

Brick Stitch (p.93)

Corrugated Check (p.98)

Butterfly (p.102)

Peaks (p.93)

2 x 2 Corrugated Ribbing (p.99)

Animal Print (p.102)

Lice Stitch (p.95)

Tessellated Flowers (p.100)

Unbalanced Checkerboard (p.103)

1 x 1 Stranding (p.96)

Wave (p.101)

Ellipses (p.103)

Basic Eyelet (p.107)

V Eyelets (p.108)

Punchwork (p.108)

Contrast Eyelet Band (p.109)

Clover Lace (p.110)

Purl Eyelet Rib (p.110)

Elongated Lace Rib (p.111)

Eyelet Meander (p.111)

Openwork Hourglass (p.112)

Woven Lace (p.112)

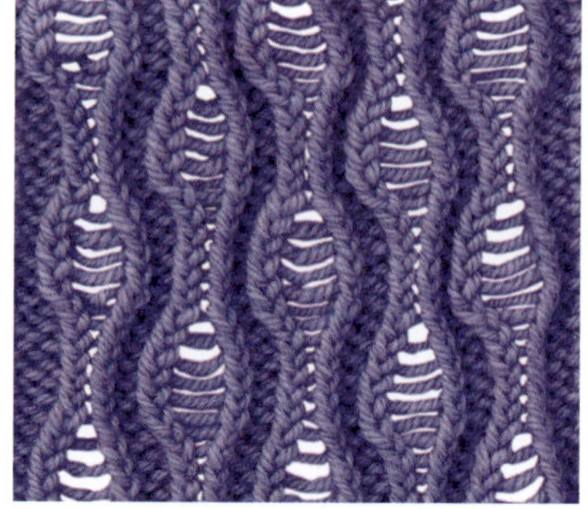
Ladder Stitch (p.113)

Contrast Garter Column (p.115)

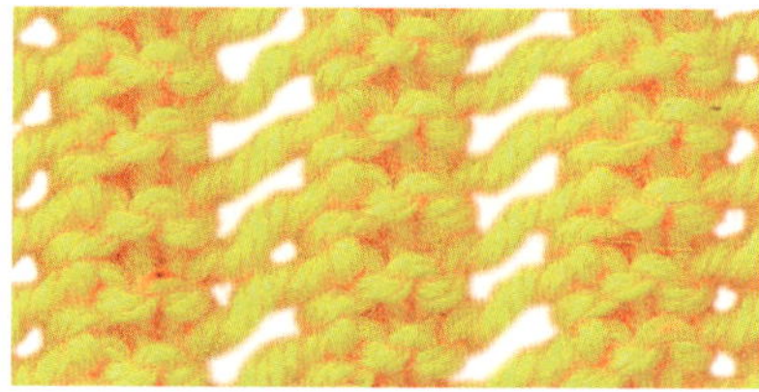
Lapwing Lace (p.116)

Mesh Lace (p.116)

Mariposa (p.117)

Miniature Leaf (p.118)

Merinette Eyelet (p.119)

Thistles (p.120)

Fine Old Shale (p.120)

Garter Chevron Lace (p.120)

Lattice Lace (p.121)

Arrowhead Lace (p.121)

Wandering Leaves (p.121)

Left Twist (p.125)

Right Twist (p.126)

Twisted Ladder (p.126)

Right Cross (p.127)

Left Cross (p.127)

Meandering Purl Cross (p.128)

Wide Horseshoe (p.128)

Crossed Rib (p.129)

Wave of Honey (p.130)

Lightning (p.130)

Simple Twisted Braid (p.130)

Chain Twist (p.131)

Honeycomb Column Twist (p.131)

Honeycomb (p.132)

Shadow Plaited (p.132)

Small Horseshoe Cable (p.132)

Large Cable with Garter (p.133)

Wandering Cable (p.133)

Basketweave Cable (p.133)

Basic Popcorn Stitch (p.135)

Cluster Stitch (p.135)

Basic Bobble (p.136)

Loop Stitch (p.137)

Trinity Stitch (p.138)

Tuck Stitch (p.139)
Tuck Rib Column (p.145)
Beaded Column (p.149)
Fisherman's Rib (p.141)
Knot Stitch (p.146)
Crochet Beading (p.150)
Bee Stitch (p.142)
Star Stitch (p.147)
Smock Ribbing (p.151)
One-colour Brioche (p.143)
Lice Stitch Beading (p.148)
Indian Cross Stitch (p.152)
Two-colour Brioche (p.144)
Beaded Row (p.149)
Armour Stitch (p.153)

Basic Stitches

Knit Stitch

ABBREVIATION
k

SKILL LEVEL
Easy

STITCH RESULT
Basic stitch

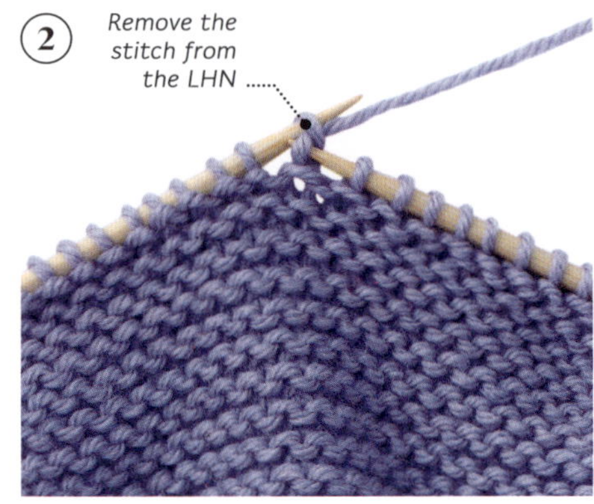

1 With the yarn at the back of the work, insert the RHN from left to right into the first stitch on the LHN. Wrap the working yarn anticlockwise around the RHN.

2 Keeping tension on the yarn, scoop the yarn back through the stitch to the left. Remove the stitch from the LHN, leaving a new stitch on the RHN.

Garter Stitch

This is the most basic knitted fabric, which produces an identical texture on both sides. When worked flat, it is made by working rows of knit stitch, as shown in the images above. To achieve garter stitch while working in the round, alternate knit and purl rows.

Purl Stitch

ABBREVIATION
p

SKILL LEVEL
Easy

STITCH RESULT
Basic stitch

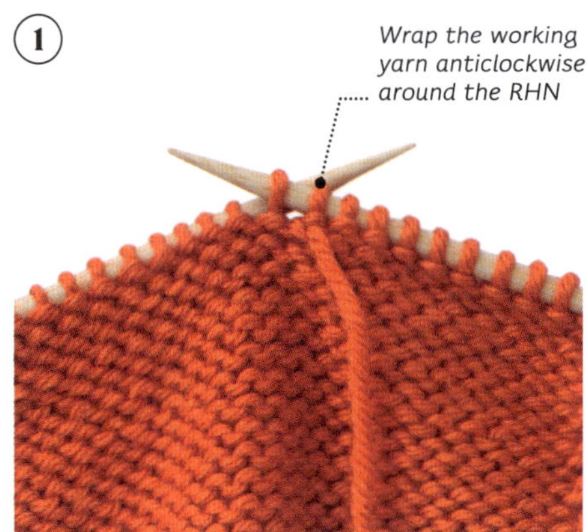

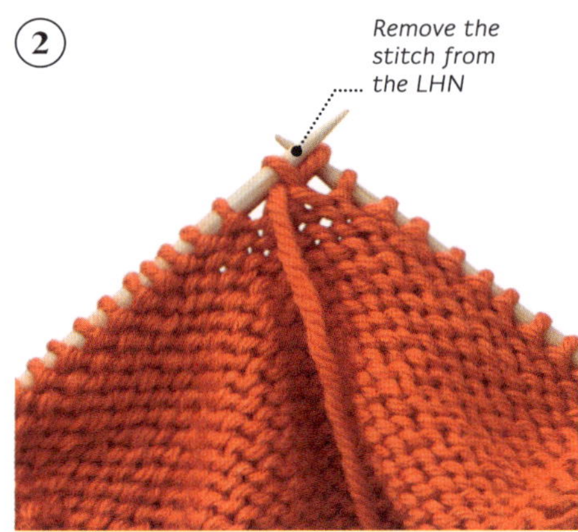

1 With the yarn at the front of the work (if at the back, bring to the front between the needles), insert the RHN from right to left into the first stitch on the LHN. Wrap the working yarn anticlockwise around the RHN.

2 Keeping the tension on the yarn, scoop the yarn back through the stitch to the right.

Stocking Stitch

When worked flat, stocking stitch is made up of alternate rows of knit and purl stitches. This creates a smooth surface on one side, and a textured surface (see right) on the other.

Knit Through the Back Loop

ABBREVIATION
k-tbl, ktbl

SKILL LEVEL
Easy

STITCH RESULT
Twisted version of knit stitch

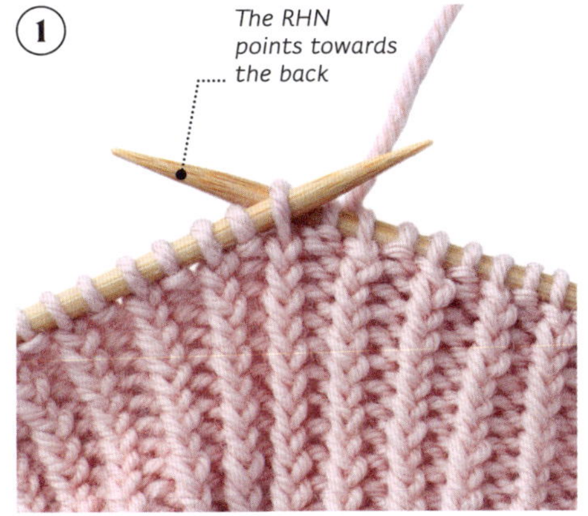

1 With the yarn at the back, insert the RHN from right to left and towards the back into the first stitch on the LHN. Wrap the working yarn anticlockwise around the RHN.

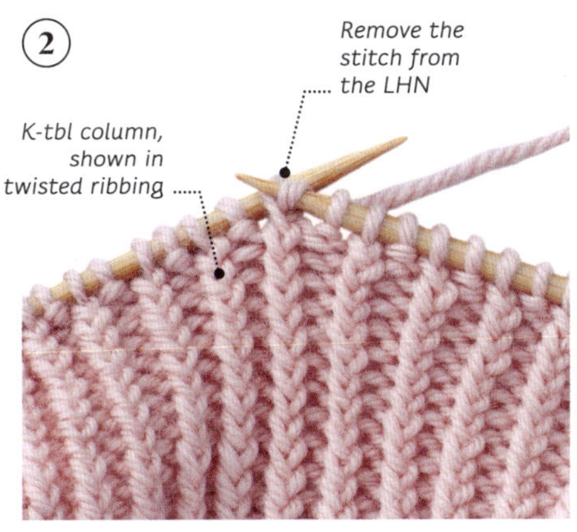

2 Keeping tension on the yarn, scoop the yarn back through the stitch to the right and towards the back.

Purl Through the Back Loop

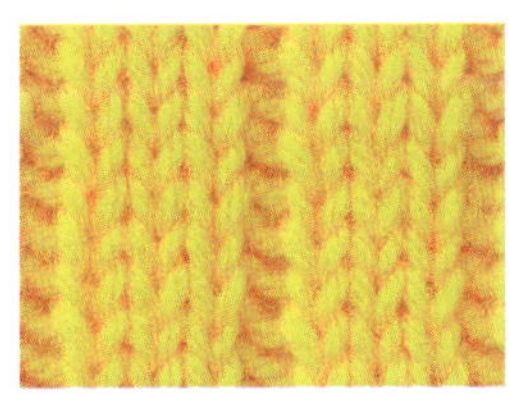

ABBREVIATION
p-tbl, ptbl

SKILL LEVEL
Intermediate

STITCH RESULT
Twisted version of purl stitch

1 With the yarn at the front of the work, starting with the RHN behind the work, insert the RHN from left to right into the back loop of the first stitch on the LHN. Wrap the working yarn anticlockwise around the RHN.

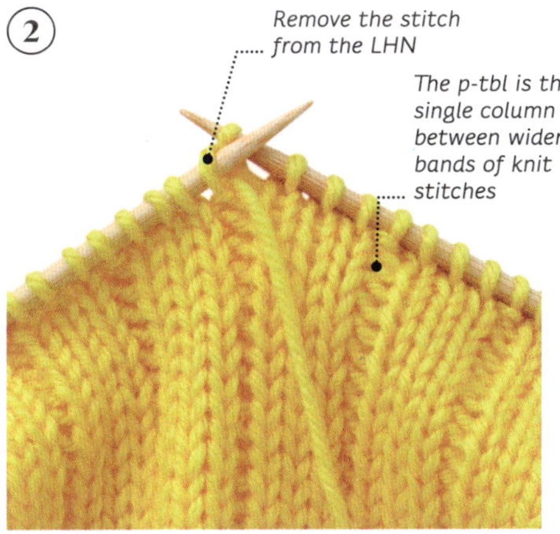

2 Keeping tension on the yarn, scoop the yarn back through the stitch to the left and towards the back.

Knit 2 Together

ABBREVIATION
k2tog

SKILL LEVEL
Easy

STITCH RESULT
Single decrease

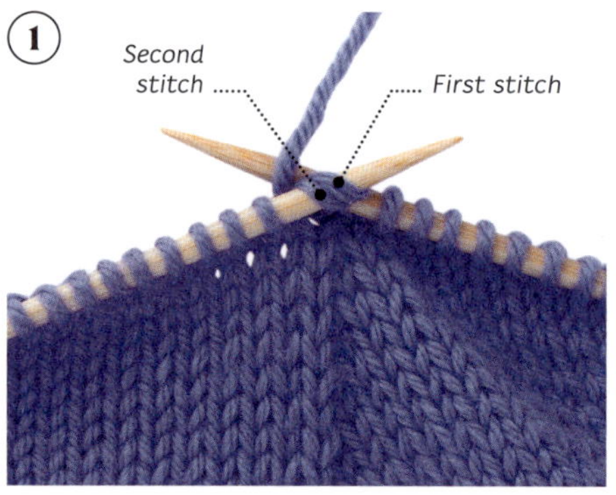

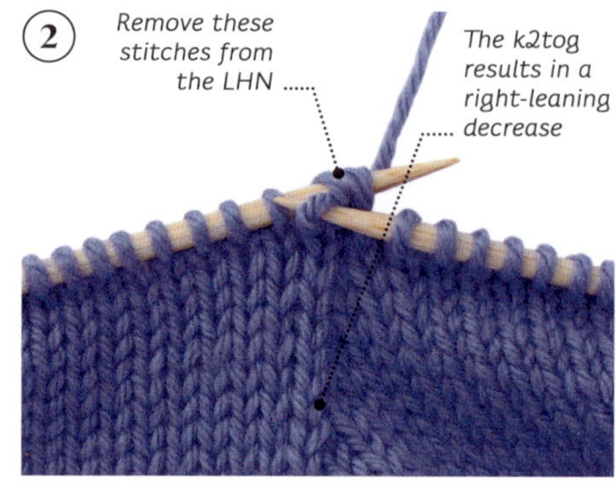

1 With the yarn at the back, insert the RHN from left to right into the second stitch, and then the first stitch on the LHN. Wrap the working yarn anticlockwise around the RHN.

2 Keeping tension on the yarn, scoop the yarn back through both stitches to the left. Drop both stitches on the LHN, leaving just one new stitch on the RHN.

Slip, Slip, Knit 2 Together

ABBREVIATION
ssk

SKILL LEVEL
Intermediate

STITCH RESULT
Single decrease

1 With the yarn at the back, insert the RHN into the first stitch from left to right and slip from the LHN to the RHN. Repeat for the second stitch.

2 Insert the LHN from left to right and towards the front into both stitches just slipped. Wrap the working yarn anticlockwise around the RHN.

3 Keeping the tension on the yarn, scoop the yarn back through both stitches to the right.

Purl 2 Together

ABBREVIATION
p2tog

SKILL LEVEL
Easy

STITCH RESULT
Wrong side single decrease

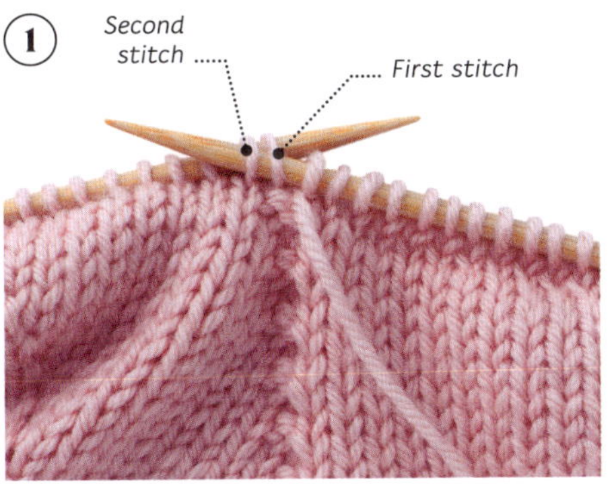

1 With the yarn at the front of the work, insert the RHN from right to left, towards the front into the first stitch, then the second stitch on the LHN. Wrap the working yarn anticlockwise around the RHN.

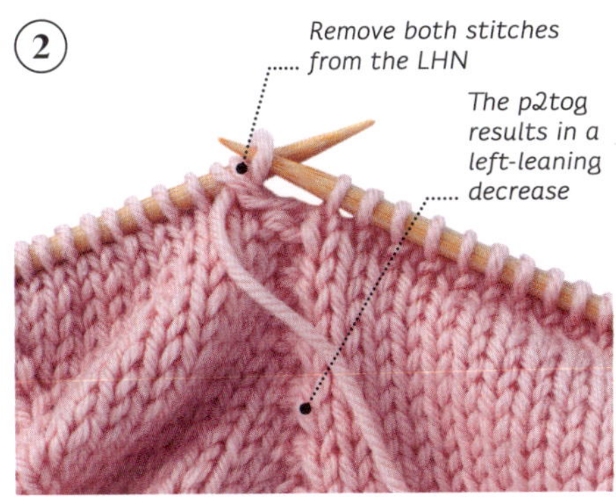

2 Keeping tension on the yarn, scoop the yarn back through both stitches to the right.

Slip, Slip, Purl

ABBREVIATION
ssp

SKILL LEVEL
Advanced

STITCH RESULT
Wrong side single decrease

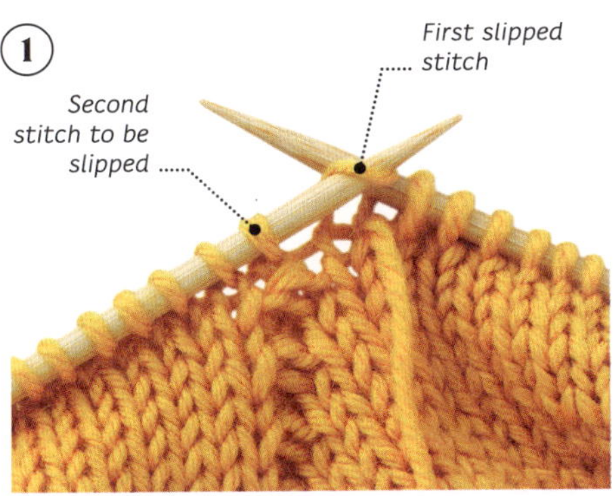

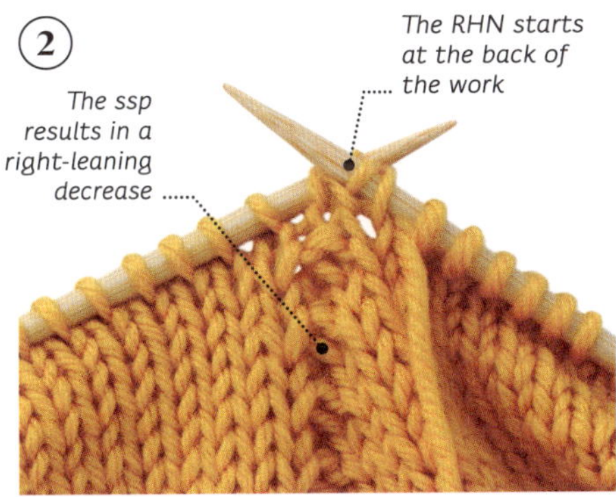

1 With the yarn at the front of the work, insert the RHN into the first stitch from left to right and slip from the LHN to the RHN. Repeat for the second stitch.

2 Slip both stitches from the RHN tip back to the LHN tip. With the RHN tip starting at the back of the work, insert from left to right into the second stitch then the first stitch on the LHN. Wrap the working yarn anticlockwise around the RHN.

3 Keeping tension on the yarn, scoop the yarn back through both stitches to the left and towards the back of the work.

Make 1 Left

ABBREVIATION
m1l

SKILL LEVEL
Intermediate

STITCH RESULT
Lifted increase

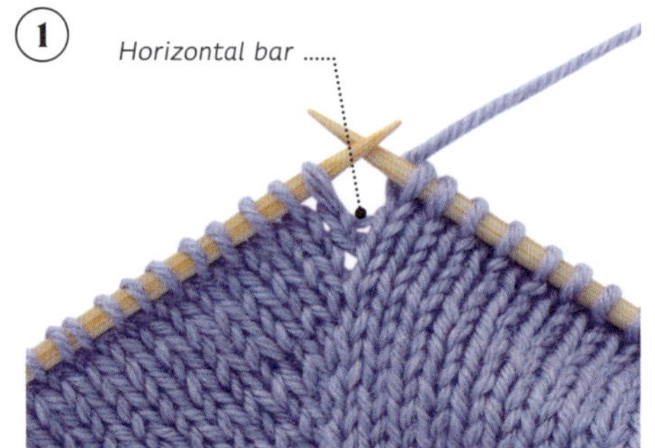

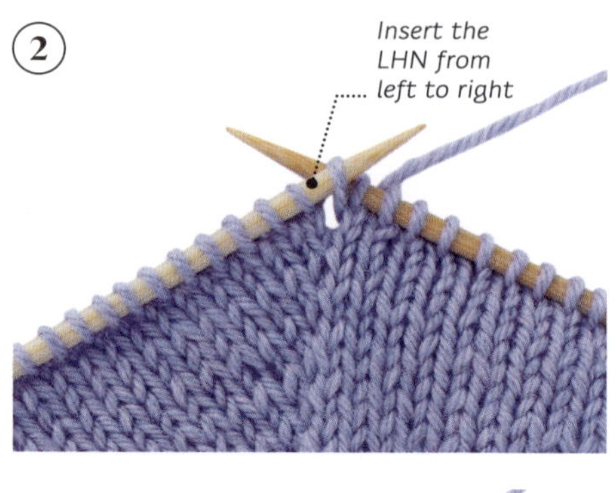

1 Insert the RHN from back to front into the horizontal bar between the stitches.

2 Insert the LHN from left to right into the front loop of this strand, making sure that the LHN finishes in front of the RHN. Wrap the working yarn anticlockwise around the RHN.

3 Keeping tension on the yarn, scoop the yarn back through the stitch to the right.

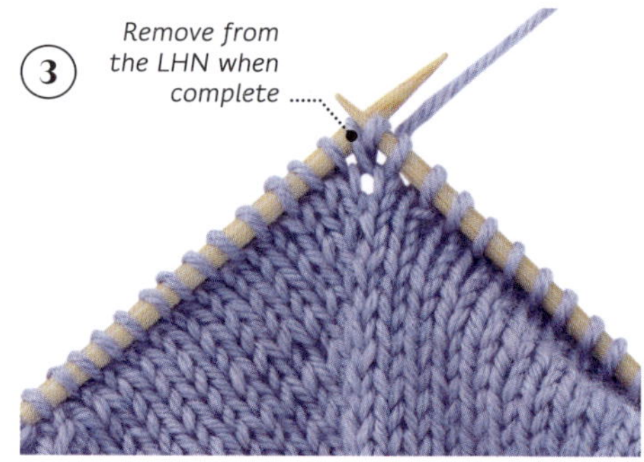

Make 1 Right

ABBREVIATION
m1r

SKILL LEVEL
Intermediate

STITCH RESULT
Lifted increase

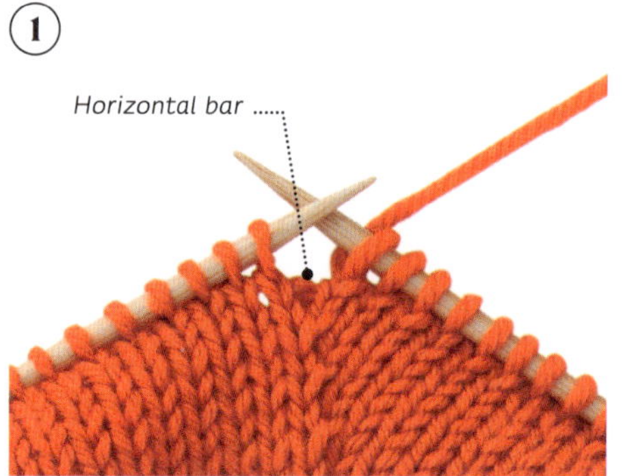

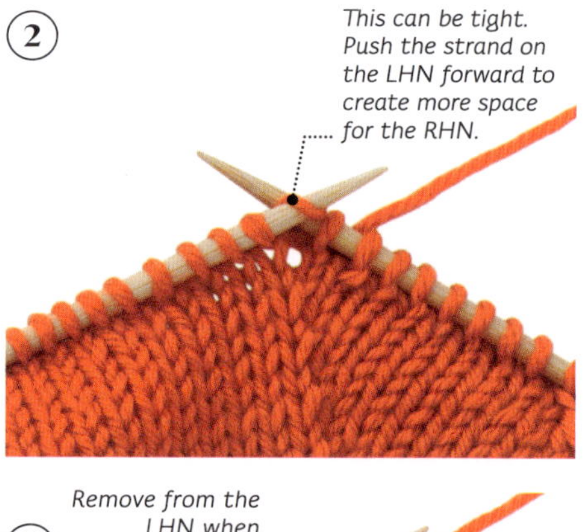

1 Insert the LHN from back to front into the horizontal bar between the stitches.

2 Insert the RHN from left to right into the front loop of this strand. Ensure that the RHN finishes behind the LHN. Wrap the working yarn anticlockwise around the RHN.

3 Keeping tension on the yarn, scoop the yarn back through the stitch to the left.

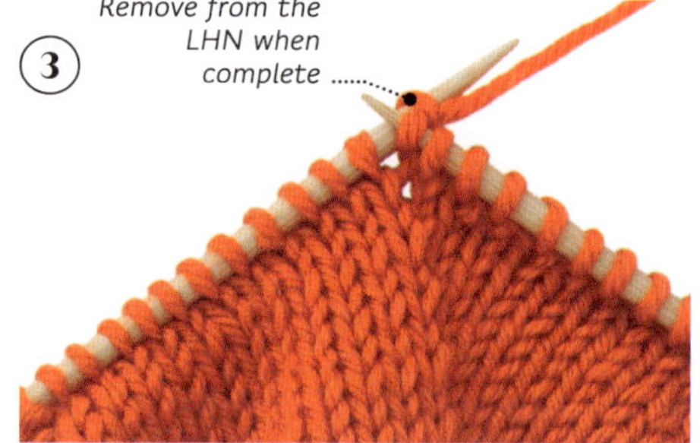

Knit Front and Back

ABBREVIATION
kfb

SKILL LEVEL
Intermediate

STITCH RESULT
Single increase

1 With the yarn at the back of the work, insert the RHN into the first stitch on the LHN from left to right. Wrap the working yarn anticlockwise around the RHN. Knit the stitch.

2 Insert the RHN into the back loop of the stitch on the LHN from right to left. Wrap the working yarn anticlockwise around the RHN. Keeping tension on the yarn, scoop the yarn back through the stitch to the right. Remove initial stitch from the LHN when complete.

Knit, Yarnover, Knit Into One Stitch

ABBREVIATION
kyok

SKILL LEVEL
Intermediate

STITCH RESULT
Double increase

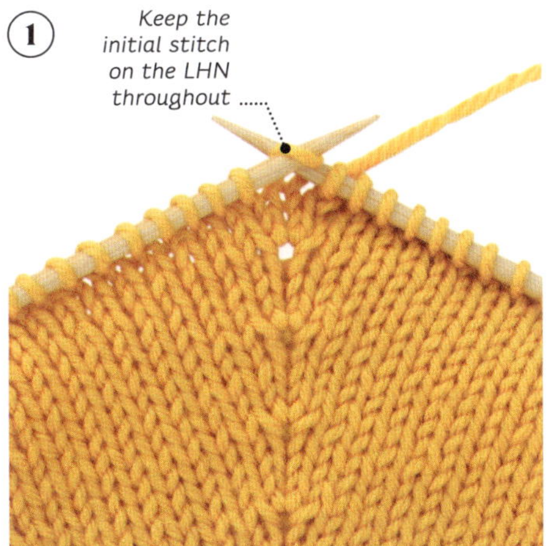

1 With the yarn at the back of the work, insert the RHN into the first stitch on the LHN from left to right. Wrap the working yarn anticlockwise around the RHN. Knit the stitch but do not remove it from the LHN.

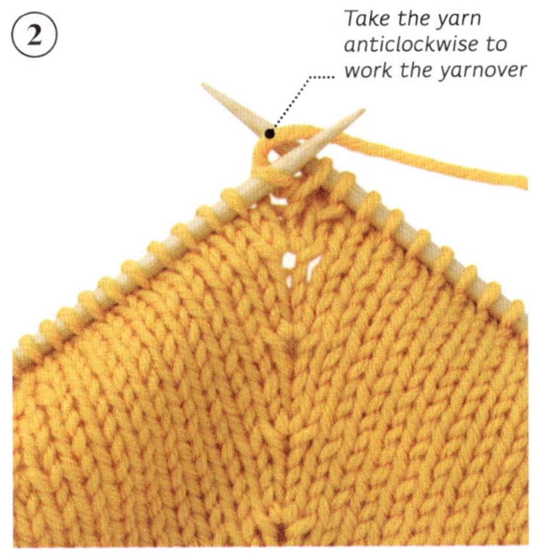

2 Bring the yarn to the front between the needles then insert the RHN from left to right into the same stitch. Take the yarn over the top of the RHN and knit the next stitch. Remove initial stitch from the LHN when complete.

Yarnovers

A yarnover is an increase that creates an open hole in the fabric. The following steps create the same stitch. However, they require different movements depending on the surrounding stitches. The working principle for creating a yarnover is to take the yarn anti-clockwise around the RHN until it wraps the needle once and the yarn ends in the position needed to work the next stitch.

Knit to Knit Yarnover

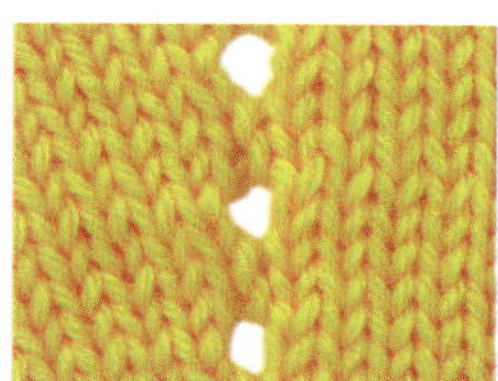

ABBREVIATION
yfwd, yo

SKILL LEVEL
Intermediate

STITCH RESULT
Single open increase

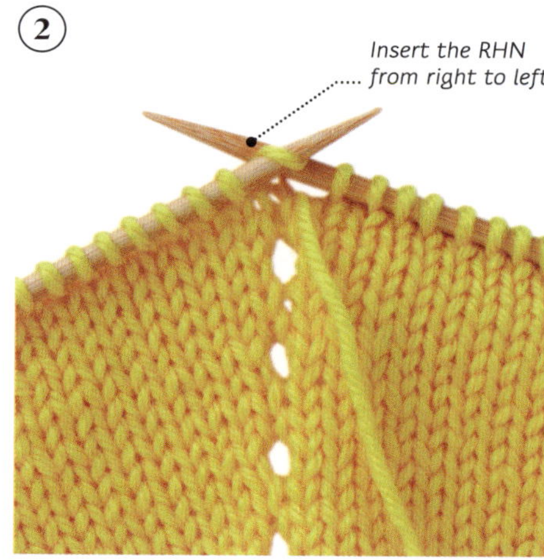

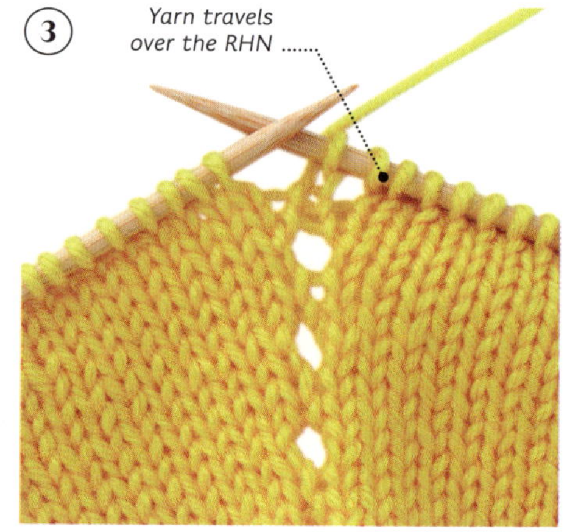

1 Knit one stitch, then bring the working yarn to the front of the work.

2 Insert the RHN from left to right into the next stitch.

3 Knit the next stitch as normal. The yarn travels over the RHN first, creating the yarnover.

Purl to Purl Yarnover

ABBREVIATION
yrn, yo

SKILL LEVEL
Intermediate

STITCH RESULT
Single open increase

Purl one stitch, leaving the yarn in front of the work. Take the yarn over the top of the RHN between the needles, then purl the next stitch.

Knit to Purl Yarnover

ABBREVIATION
yfrn, yo

SKILL LEVEL
Intermediate

STITCH RESULT
Single open increase

Knit one stitch, then bring the working yarn to the front of the work. Take the yarn over the top of the RHN and then back to the front of the work between the needles. The yarn will be in position ready to purl the next stitch.

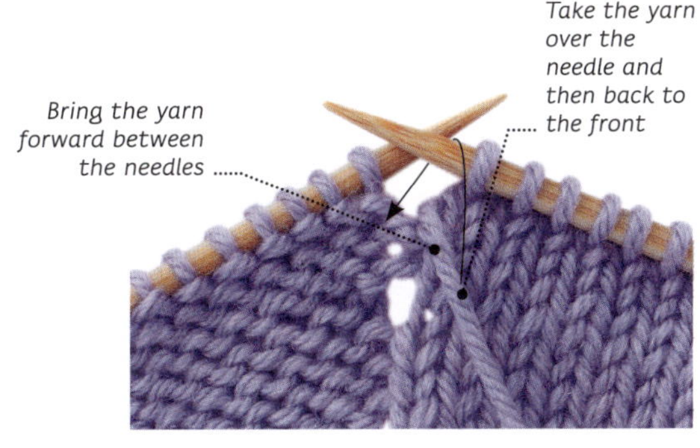

Purl to Knit Yarnover

ABBREVIATION
yon, yo

SKILL LEVEL
Intermediate

STITCH RESULT
Single open increase

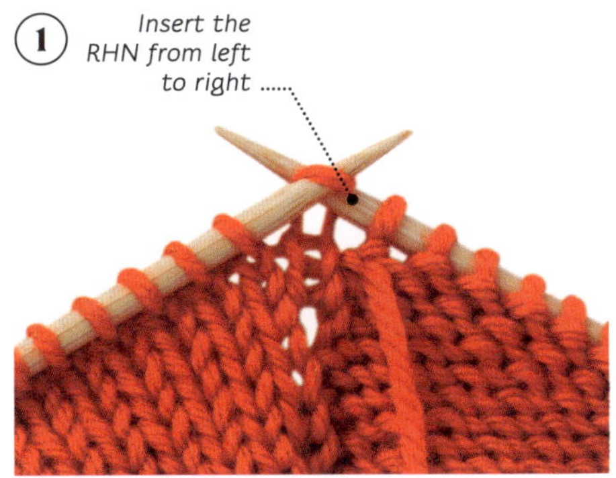

1 With the working yarn at the front of the work, insert the RHN needle from left to right into the next stitch.

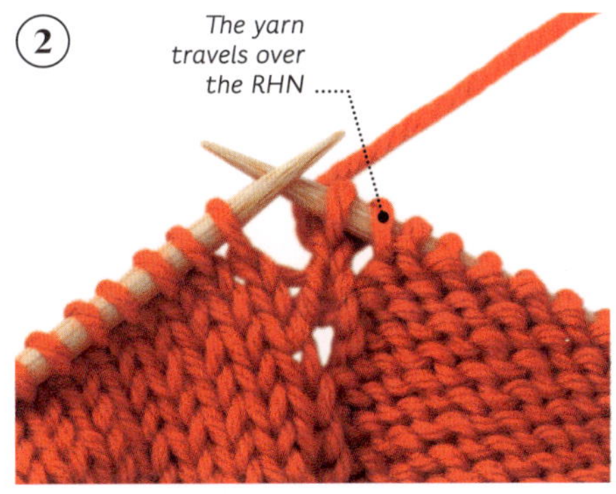

2 Knit the next stitch as normal; the yarn will need to travel over the RHN first, creating the yarnover.

Slip 1, Knit 2 Together, Pass Slipped Stitch Over

ABBREVIATION
sk2po, sl 1-k2tog-psso

SKILL LEVEL
Intermediate

STITCH RESULT
Double decrease

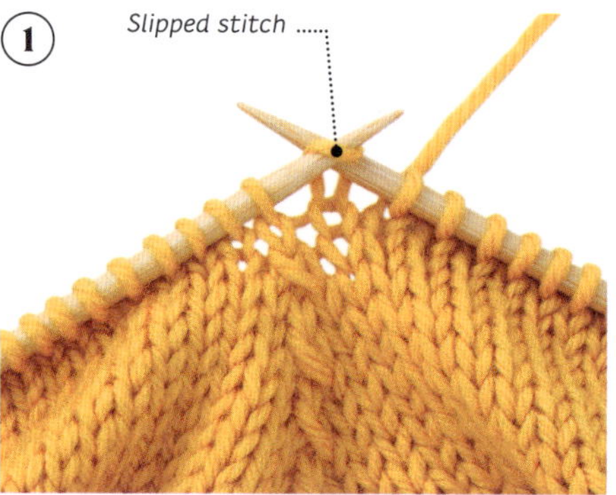

1 Slip the first stitch by inserting the RHN from left to right into the stitch, before removing the LHN.

2 Insert the RHN from left to right into the second stitch and then the first stitch (as if to k2tog, see p.38). Wrap the working yarn anticlockwise around the RHN. Scoop the yarn back through both stitches to the left and remove these from the LHN.

3 Insert the LHN into the slipped stitch (see step 1) from left to right. Lift this over the top of the first stitch and then drop from both needles.

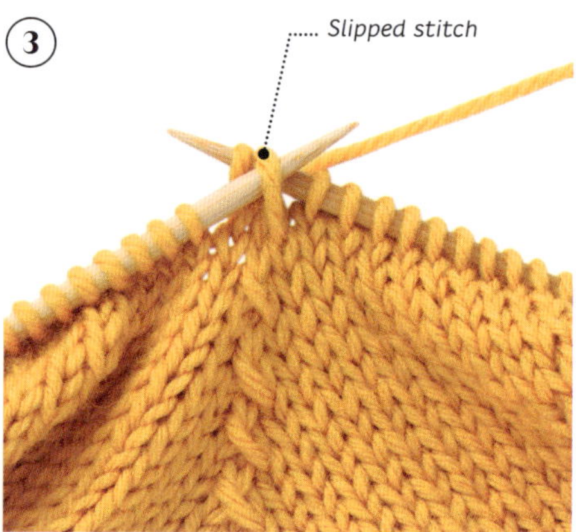

Slip 2 Stitches, Knit 1, Pass Slipped Stitches Over

ABBREVIATION
s2kpo, sl 2-k1-psso

SKILL LEVEL
Advanced

STITCH RESULT
Double decrease

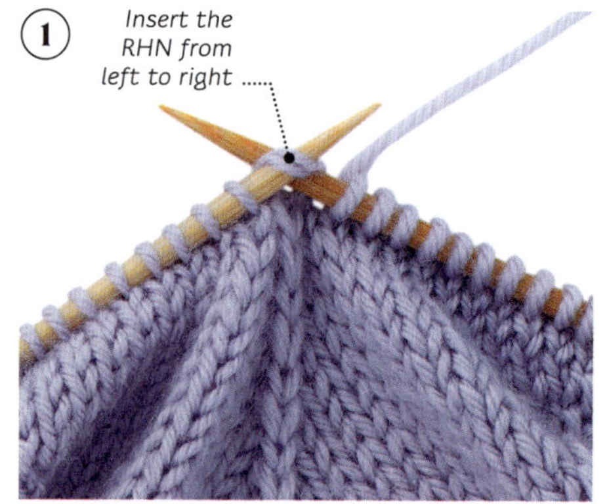

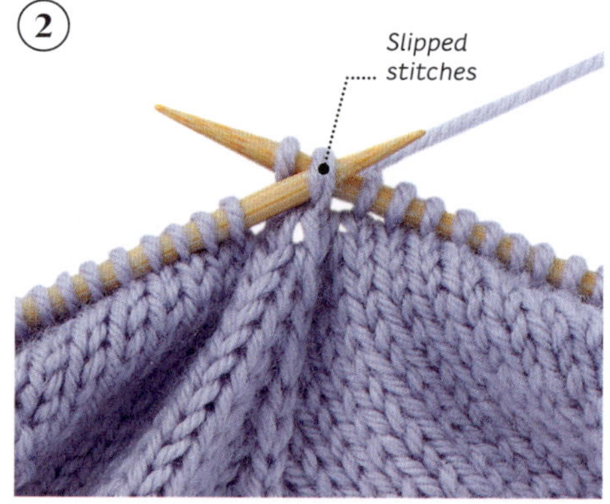

1 Slip two stitches by inserting the RHN from left to right into the second stitch and then the first stitch on the LHN (as if to k2tog, see p.38). Knit 1 stitch.

2 Insert the LHN from left to right into the 2 slipped stitches on the RHN. Lift these over the top of the first stitch and then drop them from both needles.

With Yarn in Front Slip 1

ABBREVIATION
wyif sl 1

SKILL LEVEL
Intermediate

STITCH RESULT
Slipped stitch

1 Bring the yarn to the front of the work between the needles.

2 Slip the next stitch onto the RHN. If the next stitch is a knit, take the yarn to the back of the work between the needles, then work as normal.

With Yarn in Back Slip 1

ABBREVIATION
wyib sl 1, sl 1

SKILL LEVEL
Easy

STITCH RESULT
Slipped stitch

With the yarn at the back of the work, slip the next stitch onto the RHN. Work the next stitch as normal.

Slipped Stitch Columns

This variation repeats Rows 1 and 2 of Eye of Partridge (see p.69) to create slipped stitch columns. These are commonly used in sock heels for reinforcement.

Knit and Purl Patterns

Simple textures

Knit and purl stitches (see p.36) are the foundation of all knitted fabrics. The simple textures in this section only use these two stitches, and as such are the easiest fabrics to create. The knit and purl stitches are opposite versions of each other, making the fabrics reversible. The "single-sided" stitches in this section will not show the same design on both sides, but the relief on the reverse side will often also look appealing. These simple textures can have a subtle finish, so accentuate the fabrics by using light to mid-tone colours that make the pattern clearly visible. Any novelty or highly textured yarn will hide the subtle texture of knit and purl patterns, so try to use smooth yarns.

Though textural, these fabrics have a low profile and can be used in all types of projects. One traditional use of these textures is in Ganseys, also known as guernseys. Jumpers traditionally worn by fishermen, they are worked at a dense gauge to keep the wind out.

Moss Stitch

OTHER NAME
Seed stitch

SKILL LEVEL
Easy

MULTIPLES
2 (+1) stitches; 2 rows

STITCHES INCLUDED
knit, purl

APPEARANCE
Reversible

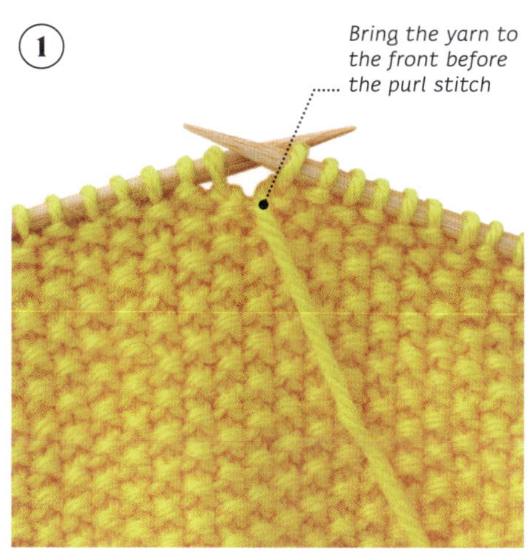

1 **Row 1:** With the yarn at the back, knit one stitch. *Bring the yarn to the front of the work between the needles. Purl 1 stitch.

2 Take the yarn to the back between the needles, knit one stitch. Repeat from * until the end of the row. **Row 2**: Repeat Row 1.

Double Moss Stitch

OTHER NAME
Irish Moss Stitch

SKILL LEVEL
Easy

MULTIPLES
2 stitches; 4 rows

STITCHES INCLUDED
knit, purl

APPEARANCE
Reversible

Row 1: k1, p1.
Row 2: Repeat Row 1.
Row 3: p1, k1.
Row 4: Repeat Row 1.

Row			Row
4		●	
		●	3
2	●		
	●		1

Garter Ridges

SKILL LEVEL
Easy

MULTIPLES
1 stitch; 4 rows

STITCHES INCLUDED
knit, purl

APPEARANCE
Single-sided

Row 1: knit.
Row 2: purl.
Row 3: knit.
Row 4: knit.

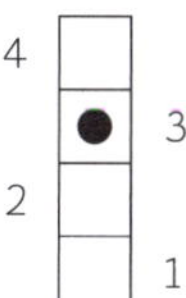

Foundations

SKILL LEVEL
Easy

MULTIPLES
4 stitches; 8 rows

STITCHES INCLUDED
knit, purl

APPEARANCE
Single-sided

Row 1: knit.
Row 2: p1, k3.
Row 3: knit.
Row 4: p1, k3.
Row 5: knit.
Row 6: k2, p1, k1.
Row 7: knit.
Row 8: k2, p1, k1.

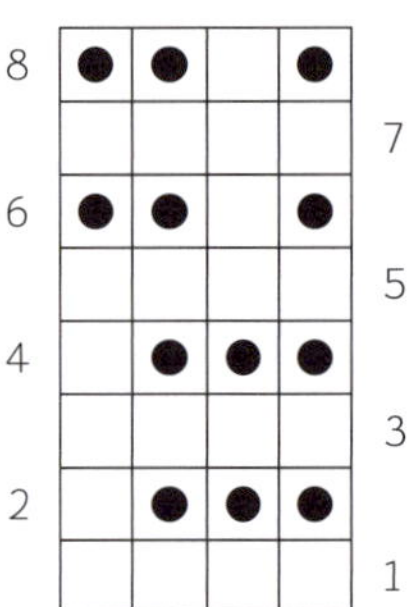

Horizontal Dash

SKILL LEVEL
Easy

MULTIPLES
7 (+2) stitches; 4 rows

STITCHES INCLUDED
knit, purl

APPEARANCE
Single-sided

Row 1: knit.
Row 2: purl.
Row 3: knit.
Row 4: p2, *k5, p2, rep from * until the end.

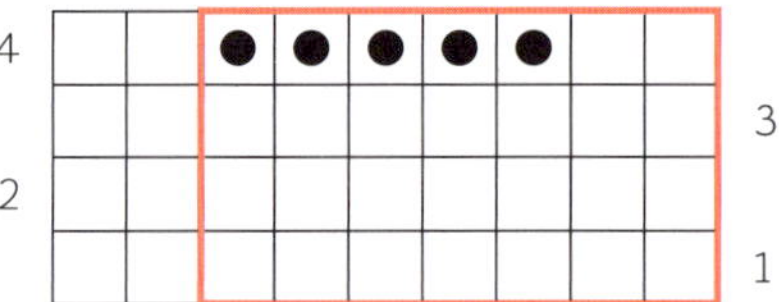

Mock Rib

OTHER NAMES
Seeded Rib, Mistake Rib

SKILL LEVEL
Easy

MULTIPLES
4 (+1) stitches; 2 rows

STITCHES INCLUDED
knit, purl

APPEARANCE
Reversible

Row 1: p1, *k3, p1, rep from * until the end.
Row 2: *k2, p1, k1, rep from * until the last stitch, k1.

Row						
2	●	●		●	●	
	●				●	1

Basketweave

SKILL LEVEL
Easy

MULTIPLES
6 stitches; 8 rows

STITCHES INCLUDED
knit, purl

APPEARANCE
Single-sided

Row 1: knit.
Row 2: k4, p2.
Row 3: k2, p4.
Row 4: k4, p2.
Row 5: knit.
Row 6: k1, p2, k3.
Row 7: p3, k2, p1.
Row 8: k1, p2, k3.

Row							
8	●			●	●	●	
	●			●	●	●	7
6	●			●	●	●	
							5
4	●	●	●	●			
	●	●	●	●			3
2	●	●	●	●			
							1

Textured Honeycomb

SKILL LEVEL
Easy

MULTIPLES
6 stitches; 12 rows

STITCHES INCLUDED
knit, purl

APPEARANCE
Both sides can be used as right side

Row 1: p1, k5.
Row 2: p5, k1.
Row 3: p1, k5.
Row 4: p5, k1.
Row 5: k1, p1, k3, p1.
Row 6: (p1, k1) twice, p2.
Row 7: k3, p1, k2.
Row 8: p2, k1, p3.
Row 9: k3, p1, k2.
Row 10: p2, k1, p3.
Row 11: k2, (p1, k1) twice.
Row 12: k1, p3, k1, p1.

12	●				●		
		●		●			11
10			●				
			●				9
8			●				
			●				7
6		●		●			
	●				●		5
4						●	
						●	3
2						●	
						●	1

Checkerboard Stitch

SKILL LEVEL
Easy

MULTIPLES
8 stitches; 12 rows

STITCHES INCLUDED
knit, purl

APPEARANCE
Single-sided

Row 1: p4, k4.
Row 2: p4, k1, p2, k1.
Row 3: p4, k4.
Row 4: p4, k1, p2, k1.
Row 5: p4, k4.
Row 6: p4, k1, p2, k1.
Row 7: k4, p4.
Row 8: k1, p2, k1, p4.
Row 9: k4, p4.
Row 10: k1, p2, k1, p4.
Row 11: k4, p4.
Row 12: k1, p2, k1, p4.

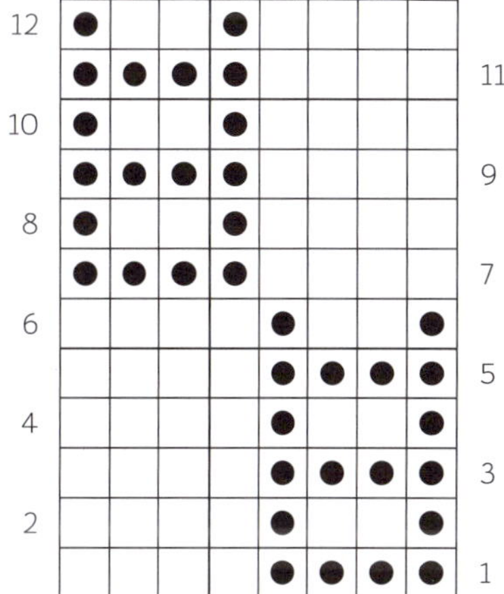

Stepping Stones

SKILL LEVEL
Easy

MULTIPLES
8 (+1) stitches; 12 rows

STITCHES INCLUDED
knit, purl

APPEARANCE
Single-sided

Row 1: *p1, k3, rep from * until the last st, p1.
Row 2: k1, *k4, p3, k1, rep from * until the end.
Row 3: Repeat Row 1.
Row 4: k1, *p3, k1, rep from * until the end.
Row 5: Repeat Row 1.
Row 6: k1, *p3, k5, rep from * until the end.
Row 7: Repeat Row 5.
Row 8: Repeat Row 6.
Row 9: Repeat Row 3.
Row 10: Repeat Row 4.
Row 11: Repeat Row 5.
Row 12: k1, *k4, p3, k1, rep from * until the end.

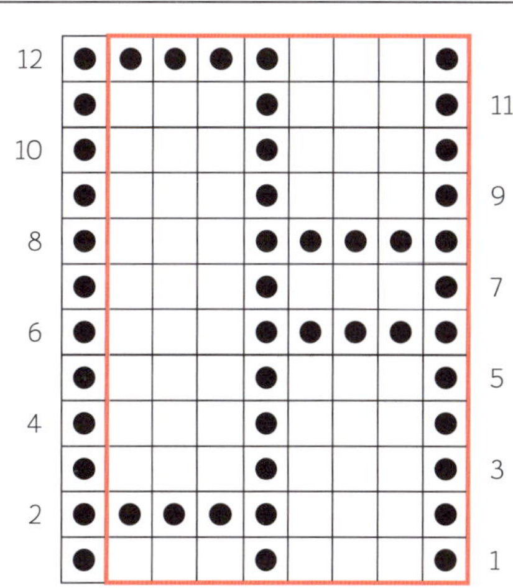

Ribbing

Ribbing stitches are a subset of knit and purl patterns, where the stitches are stacked in columns to create vertical lines. While many are created with just knit and purl stitches, the twisted versions of these stitches lend themselves well to ribbing, though they are less elastic and create a tighter line.

Most ribbings tend to be elastic and will pull in when in a relaxed state. The combination of knit and purl means that they won't curl from the edge either. This elasticity and flatness make them well-suited for use in welts and edges. They can be used to create natural shaping when paired with less elastic fabrics such as stocking stitch, as the section of ribbing will pull in. This is ideal for waistlines in fitted garments.

1 x 1 Ribbing

SKILL LEVEL
Easy

MULTIPLES
2 (+1) stitches; 2 rows

STITCHES INCLUDED
knit, purl

APPEARANCE
Reversible

1 **Row 1:** *With the yarn at the back, knit 1 stitch.

2 Bring the yarn to the front between the needles. Purl 1 stitch. Take the yarn to the back between the needles. Repeat from * until the last stitch. Knit 1 stitch. **Row 2:** Purl 1 stitch. *Take the yarn to the back between the needles. Knit 1 stitch. Bring the yarn to the front between the needles. Purl 1 stitch. Repeat from * until the end.

2 x 2 Ribbing

SKILL LEVEL
Easy

MULTIPLES
4 (+2) stitches; 2 rows

STITCHES INCLUDED
knit, purl

APPEARANCE
Reversible

1 **Row 1:** *Knit 2 stitches. Bring the yarn to the front between the needles. Purl 2 stitches. Take the yarn to the back between the needles. Repeat from * until the last 2 stitches. Knit 2 stitches.

2 **Row 2:** Purl 2 stitches. *Take the yarn to the back between the needles. Knit 2 stitches. Bring the yarn to the front between the needles. Purl 2 stitches. Repeat from * until the end.

Knit 3, Purl 2 Rib

The number of knit and purl stitches can vary to create a range of ribbing effects. Here you can see a 3 x 2 Rib made up of alternating rows of k3, p2 and p3, k2 rows.

Broken Rib

SKILL LEVEL
Easy

MULTIPLES
2 (+1) stitch; 2 rows

STITCHES INCLUDED
knit, purl

APPEARANCE
Single-sided

① *Take the yarn to the back after completing the purl stitch*

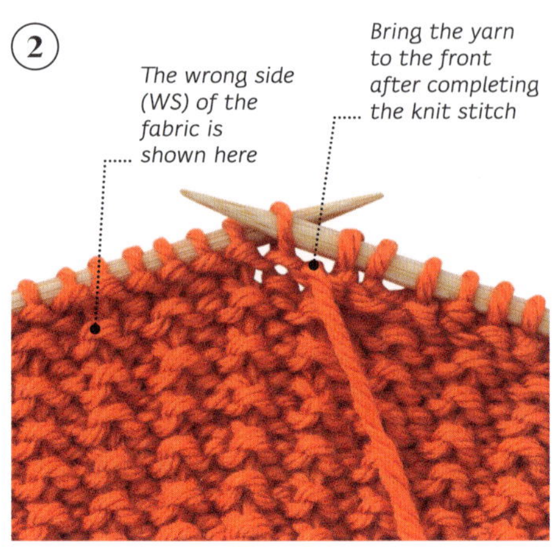

1 **Row 1:** Knit all the stitches.
Row 2: *Purl one stitch. Take the yarn to the back between the needles.

2 Knit one stitch. Bring the yarn to the front between the needles. Repeat from * until the last stitch. Purl one stitch.

Twisted Rib

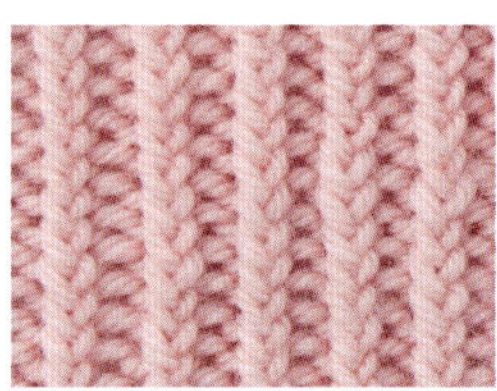

SKILL LEVEL
Easy

MULTIPLES
2 (+1) stitch; 2 rows

STITCHES INCLUDED
knit, purl, k1-tbl, p1-tbl

APPEARANCE
Single-sided (the WS will have the appearance of 1 x 1 ribbing)

1 **Row 1:** *Knit 1 through the back loop (k1-tbl) (see p.37). Knit this stitch. Bring the yarn to the front between the needles. Purl 1 stitch. Repeat from * until the last stitch. Knit 1 through the back loop.

2 **Row 2:** Purl 1 through the back loop: *with the RHN starting at the back, insert from left to right into the back loop of the purl stitch. Purl the stitch.* *Take the yarn to the back between the needles. Knit 1 stitch. Bring the yarn to the front. Purl 1 through the back loop. Repeat from * until the end.

Wider Twisted Ribbing

To alter the width of twisted ribbing, you can change the number of purl stitches and leave the k1-tbl as single columns. It is more common to only increase the number of purl stitches, rather than to have multiple twisted knit stitches next to each other. This sample has three purl stitches between the single twisted knit stitches, and is made up of alternating rows of p3, k1-tbl and p1-tbl, k3 rows.

Ropewalk Rib

SKILL LEVEL
Easy

MULTIPLES
5 (+2) stitches; 6 rows

STITCHES INCLUDED
knit, purl, k-tbl, p-tbl

APPEARANCE
Single-sided

1 **Row 1:** Purl 2 stitches. *Take the yarn to the back. Knit 1 through the back loop: *insert the RHN from right to left and towards the back into the first stitch on the LHN. Knit this stitch.* Bring the yarn to the front. Purl 1 stitch. Take the yarn to the back. Knit 1 through the back loop. Bring the yarn to the front. Purl 2 stitches. Repeat from * until the end.

2 **Row 2:** *Knit 2 stitches. Bring the yarn to the front. Purl 1 through the back loop: *with the RHN starting at the back, insert from left to right into the back loop of the purl stitch. Purl the stitch.* Take the yarn to the back. Knit 1 stitch. Bring the yarn to the front. Purl 1 through the back loop. Take the yarn to the back. Repeat from * until the last 2 stitches. Knit 2 stitches. **Row 3:** Repeat Row 1.

3 **Row 4:** Knit 2 stitches. Bring the yarn to the front.

4 Purl 3 stitches. Take the yarn to the back. Repeat from * until the last 2 stitches. Knit 2 stitches. **Row 5:** Purl 2 stitches. *Take the yarn to the back. Knit 3 stitches. Bring the yarn to the front. Purl 2 stitches. Repeat from * until the end. **Row 6:** Repeat Row 4.

Skyp Rib

SKILL LEVEL
Intermediate

MULTIPLES
8 stitches; 12 rows

STITCHES INCLUDED
knit, purl, skyp stitch

APPEARANCE
Single-sided

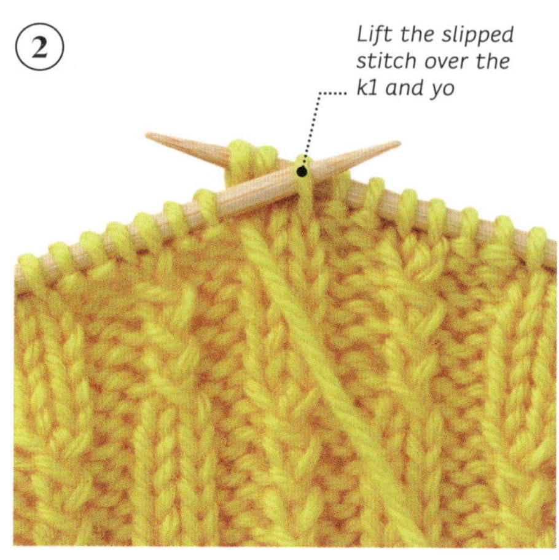

1 **Row 1:** Purl 1 stitch. Take the yarn to the back. Work a skyp stitch: *slip 1 stitch by inserting the RHN from right to left into the first stitch on the LHN. Knit 1 stitch. Bring the yarn to the front, then over the top of the needle and back to the front.*

2 *Insert the LHN from left to right into the slipped stitch. Lift over the k1 and yarnover and drop from the needle.* Purl 2 stitches. Take the yarn to the back. Knit 2 stitches. Bring the yarn to the front. Purl 1 stitch. **Row 2:** *Knit 1 stitch. Bring the yarn to the front. Purl 2 stitches. Take the yarn to the back. Knit 1 stitch. Repeat from * once more. **Rows 3–6:** Repeat Rows 1 and 2 twice more. **Row 7:** Purl 1 stitch. Take the yarn to the back. Knit 2 stitches. Bring the yarn to the front. Purl 2 stitches. Take the yarn to the back. Work a skyp stitch; the yarn will be at the front when complete. Purl 1 stitch. **Row 8:** Repeat Row 2. **Rows 9–12:** Repeat Rows 7 and 8 twice more.

The chart: Skyp Rib

The elongated leaf-like shape of the skyp symbol represents the slipped stitch that is passed over the next 2 stitches. The symbol covers 2 stitch squares, which represent the knit and yarnover that the slipped stitch is passed over.

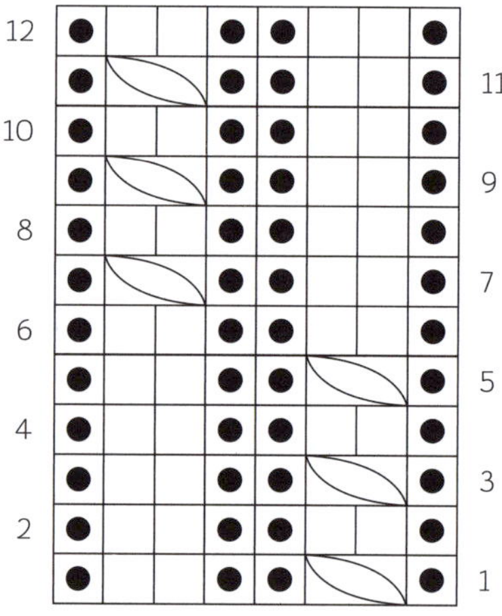

Twisted and Knit Rib

SKILL LEVEL
Easy

MULTIPLES
5 (+2) stitches; 2 rows

STITCHES INCLUDED
knit, purl, k-tbl, p-tbl

APPEARANCE
Single-sided

1 **Row 1:** *Knit 2 stitches. Bring the yarn to the front. Purl 1 stitch. Take the yarn to the back. Knit 1 through the back loop: *insert the RHN from right to left and towards the back into the first stitch. Knit this stitch.* Bring the yarn to the front. Purl 1 stitch. Take the yarn to the back. Repeat from * until the last 2 stitches. Knit 2 stitches.

2 **Row 2:** Purl 2 stitches. *Take the yarn to the back. Knit 1 stitch. Bring the yarn to the front. Purl 1 through the back loop: *with the RHN starting at the back, insert from left to right into the back loop of the purl stitch. Purl the stitch.* Take the yarn to the back. Knit 1 stitch. Bring the yarn to the front. Purl 2 stitches. Repeat from * until the end.

Beaded Rib

SKILL LEVEL
Easy

MULTIPLES
5 (+2) stitches; 2 rows

STITCHES INCLUDED
knit, purl

APPEARANCE
Different but both sides can be used as right side

Row 1: *p2, k3, rep from * until the last 2 sts, p2.
Row 2: k2, *p1, k1, p1, k2, rep from * until the end.

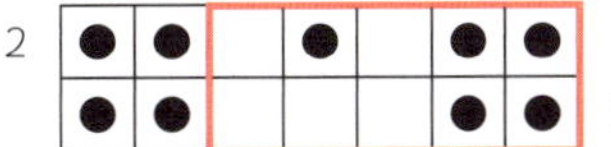

Garter Rib

SKILL LEVEL
Easy

MULTIPLES
4 stitches; 2 rows

STITCHES INCLUDED
knit, purl

APPEARANCE
Reversible

Row 1: k2, p2.
Row 2: p2, k2.

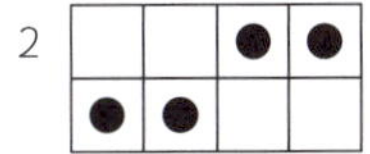

Increases, Decreases, and Slipped Stitches

Using Increases and Decreases

Increases and decreases on their own are used to create shapes in knitted fabric, such as shaping sleeves or armholes. Used in pairs, they can create interesting effects in the fabric such as a biasing, creating volume, or moving stitches across the fabric. An equal number of increases and decreases are used across the stitch pattern, meaning that the overall stitch count remains the same. The common use for increases and decreases in stitch patterns is for lace (see pp.114–21), which uses open yarnover increases. The increases in this section are mainly closed increases and are less obvious in the fabric – this allows for more subtle changes.

These increase and decrease patterns do not pair easily with other fabrics as they have changes in direction and/or gauge. They are more suited for decorative and non-fitted projects, such as scarves or shawls.

Garter Chevrons

SKILL LEVEL
Easy

MULTIPLES
9 (+2) stitches; 2 rows

STITCHES INCLUDED
knit, purl, kfb, s2kpo

APPEARANCE
Single-sided

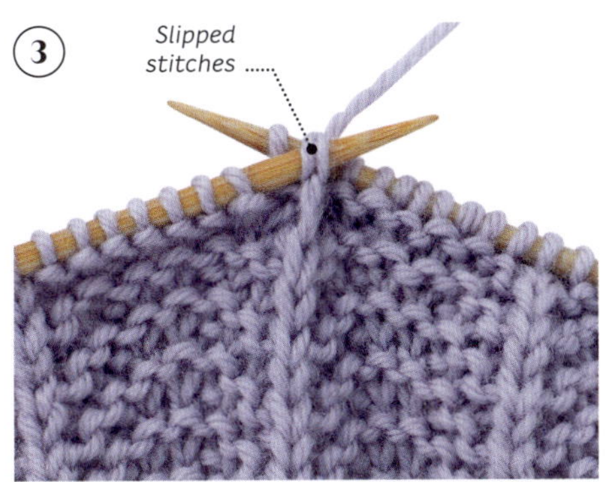

1 **Row 1:** Knit 1 stitch. * Knit 1 in the front and back: *knit 1 stitch without removing the initial stitch from the LHN. Insert the RHN from right to left and towards the back of the initial stitch. Knit 1 stitch then remove from the LHN.* Knit 2 stitches.

2 Work a s2kpo: *slip 2 stitches by inserting the RHN from left to right into the second stitch and then the first stitch on the LHN (as if to k2tog). Knit 1 stitch.*

3 *Insert the LHN from left to right into the 2 just slipped stitches on the RHN. Lift these over the top of the first stitch and then drop them from both needles.* Knit 1 stitch. Knit 1 in the front and back. Knit 1 stitch. Repeat from * until the last stitch. Knit 1 stitch.

4 **Row 2:** Knit 1 stitch. *Knit 4 stitches. Purl 1 stitch. Knit 4 stitches. Repeat from * until the last stitch. Knit 1 stitch.

The chart: Garter Chevrons

This stitch pattern has two increases and a double decrease, so the stitch count remains the same.

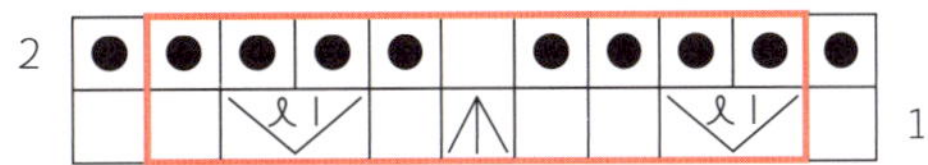

Stocking Stitch Chevrons

SKILL LEVEL
Intermediate

MULTIPLES
11 stitches; 2 rows

STITCHES INCLUDED
knit, purl, m1l, m1r, sk2po

APPEARANCE
Single-sided

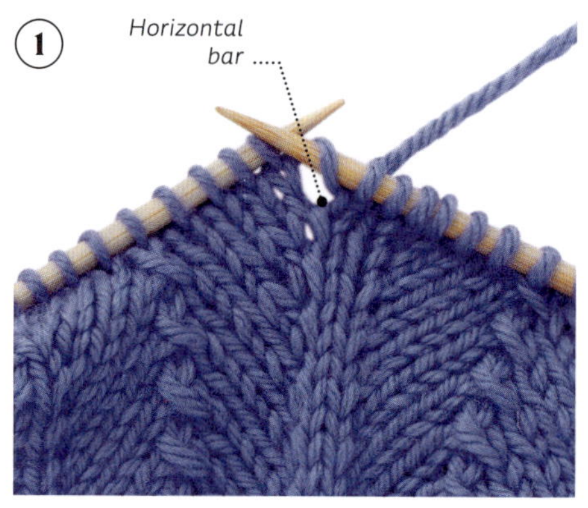

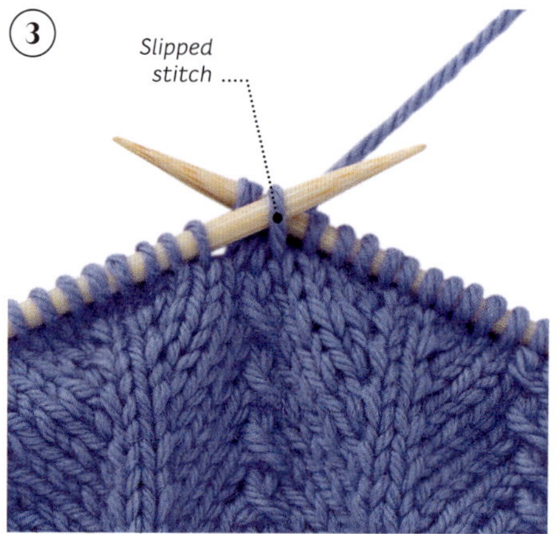

1 **Row 1:** Knit 1 stitch. Make 1 left: *insert the RHN from back to front into the horizontal bar between the stitches. Insert the LHN from left to right into the front loop of this strand. Ensure that the LHN finishes in front of the RHN. Knit the stitch.* Knit 3 stitches.

2 Work an sk2po: *slip the first stitch by inserting the RHN from left to right into the stitch. Insert the RHN from left to right into the second stitch and then the first stitch. Knit these stitches together.*

3 *Insert the LHN into the just slipped stitch from left to right. Lift this over the top of the first stitch and then drop from both needles.* Knit 3 stitches.

4 Make 1 right: *insert the LHN from back to front into the horizontal bar between the stitches. Insert the RHN from left to right into the front loop of this strand. Ensure that the RHN finishes behind the LHN. Knit the stitch.* Knit 1 stitch.
Row 2: Purl all stitches.

Herringbone Stitch

SKILL LEVEL
Intermediate

MULTIPLES
2 stitches; 2 rows

STITCHES INCLUDED
k1-tbl, purl, k2togtbl, p2tog

APPEARANCE
Different but both sides can be used as right side

OTHER MATERIALS
Larger needle (here, we've used an 8mm needle, around 4.25mm or 9 sizes larger than the 3.75mm needle used elsewhere)

1 **Row 1:** *Knit two stitches together through the back loop twice: *insert the RHN from right to left and towards the back into the first, then second stitch on the LHN. Knit these 2 stitches together but only drop the first stitch from the LHN.* Repeat from * until the end. For the final single twice knitted stitch, knit through the back loop: *insert the RHN from right to left and towards the back. Knit this stitch.*

2 **Row 2:** *Purl 2 stitches together twice: *insert the RHN from right to left into the first, then second stitch on the LHN. Purl these 2 stitches together but only drop the first stitch from the LHN.* Repeat from * until the end. For the final single twice purled stitch, purl this stitch.

Ridge Stitch

OTHER NAMES
Jute stitch, Granite stitch

SKILL LEVEL
Intermediate

MULTIPLES
2 stitches; 4 rows

STITCHES INCLUDED
knit, purl, k2tog, kfb

APPEARANCE
Single-sided

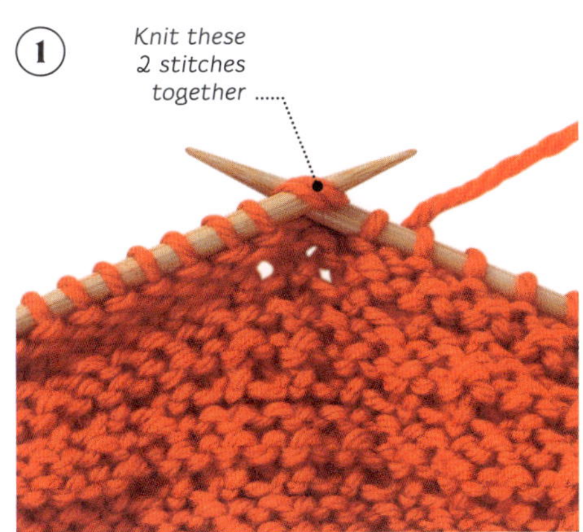

1 **Row 1:** Knit all stitches. **Row 2:** Knit 2 stitches together: *insert the RHN from left to right into the second then first stitch on the LHN. Knit these 2 stitches together.*

2 **Row 3:** Knit into the front and the back of the stitch: *knit 1 stitch but keep the initial stitch on the LHN. Insert the RHN into the back loop of the stitch on the LHN from right to left. Knit a stitch and remove from the LHN.* **Row 4:** Purl all stitches.

Faux Increase Cable

SKILL LEVEL
Intermediate

MULTIPLES
9 stitches; 20 rows

STITCHES INCLUDED
knit, purl, m1l, k2tog

APPEARANCE
Single-sided

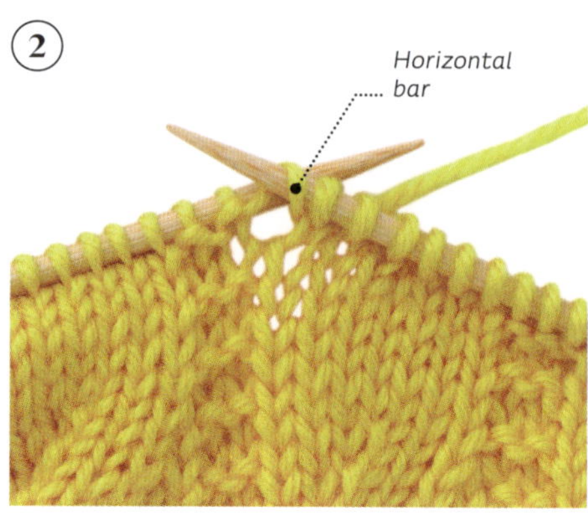

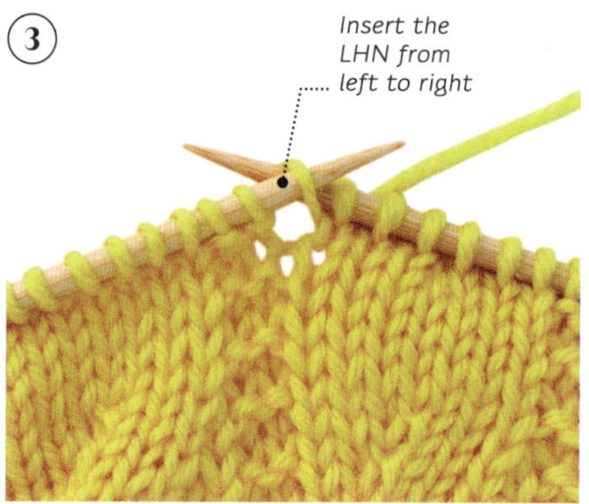

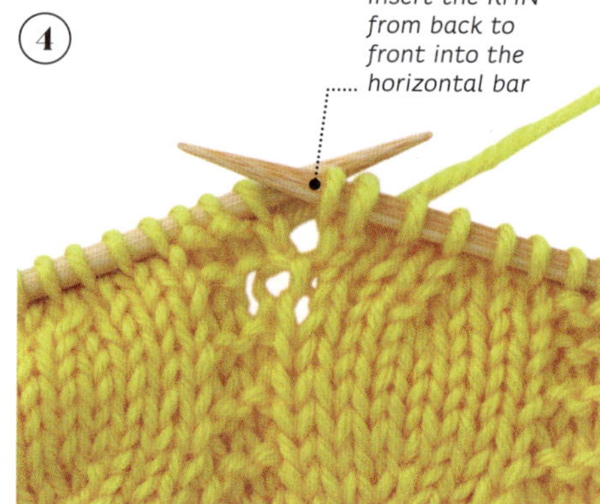

1 **Row 1:** Knit 4 stitches. Knit 2 stitches together: *insert the RHN from left to right into the second then first stitch on the LHN. Knit these 2 stitches together.* Knit 2 stitches.

2 Work a make one left: *insert the RHN from back to front into the horizontal bar between the stitches.*

3 *Insert the LHN from left to right into the front loop of this strand. Ensure that the LHN finishes in front of the RHN. Knit this stitch.* Knit 1 stitch. **Row 2 and all even rows including Row 20:** Knit 1 stitch. Purl 7 stitches. Knit 1 stitch.

4 **Row 3:** Knit 3 stitches. Knit 2 stitches together. Knit 2 stitches. Work a make one left. Knit 2 stitches. **Row 5:** Knit 2 stitches. Knit 2 stitches together. Knit 2 stitches. Work a make one left. Knit 3 stitches. **Row 7:** Knit 1 stitch. Knit 2 stitches together. Knit 2 stitches. Work a make one left. Knit 4 stitches. **Rows 9–16:** Repeat Rows 1–8 once. **Rows 17 and 19:** Knit all stitches.

Mock Cable

SKILL LEVEL
Intermediate

MULTIPLES
5 stitches; 4 rows

STITCHES INCLUDED
knit, purl, yo, sl 1-k2-psso

APPEARANCE
Single-sided

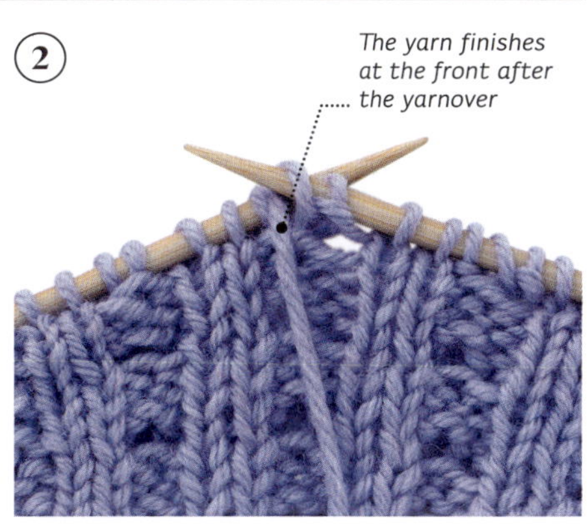

1 **Row 1:** Purl 1 stitch. Knit 3 stitches. Purl 1 stitch. **Row 2:** Knit 1 stitch. Purl 3 stitches. Knit 1 stitch. **Row 3:** Purl 1 stitch. Work a sl 1-k2-psso: *slip 1 stitch by inserting the RHN from right to left into the stitch on the LHN. Knit 2 stitches. Insert the LHN from left to right into the slipped stitch, then lift over the 2 knit stitches and drop.* Purl 1 stitch.

2 **Row 4:** Knit 1 stitch. Purl 1 stitch. Take the yarn over the RHN then back to the front between the needles. Purl 1 stitch. Knit 1 stitch.

Ruching

SKILL LEVEL
Intermediate

MULTIPLES
1 stitch; 16 rows

STITCHES INCLUDED
knit, purl, kfb, k2tog.

APPEARANCE
Single-sided

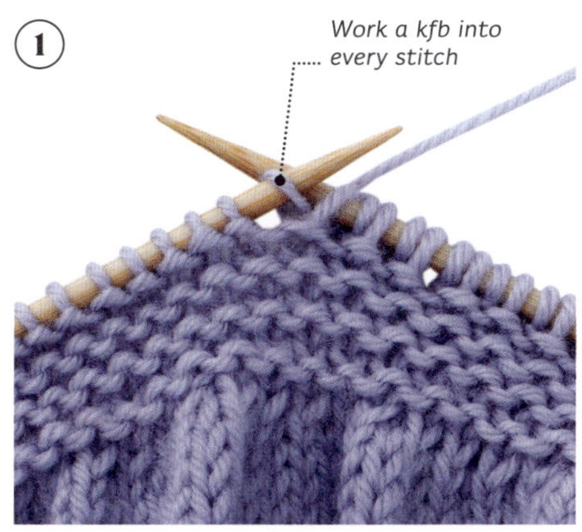

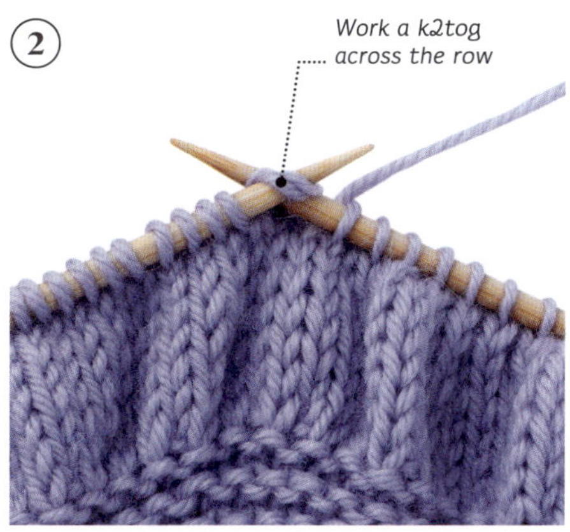

1 **Rows 1–4:** Work 4 rows of garter stitch: knit every row. **Row 5:** Knit into the front and the back of the stitch (see p.41) **Row 6–12:** Work 7 rows of stocking stitch: alternating 1 row of purl with 1 row of knit, starting with a purl row.

2 **Row 13:** Work a knit 2 stitches together: *insert the RHN from left to right into the second stitch and then the first stitch on the LHN. Knit these 2 stitches together.* **Rows 14–16:** Work 3 rows of garter stitch: knit every row.

Mini Leaf Rib

SKILL LEVEL
Advanced

MULTIPLES
4 (+1) stitches; 10 rows

STITCHES INCLUDED
knit, purl, k-tbl, p-tbl, twisted kyok, sk2po

APPEARANCE
Single-sided

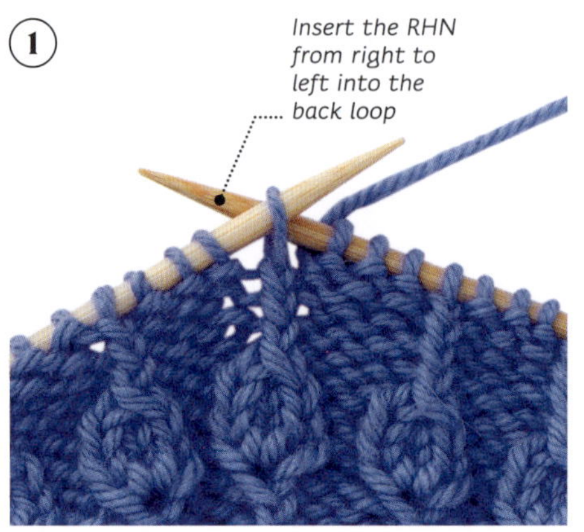

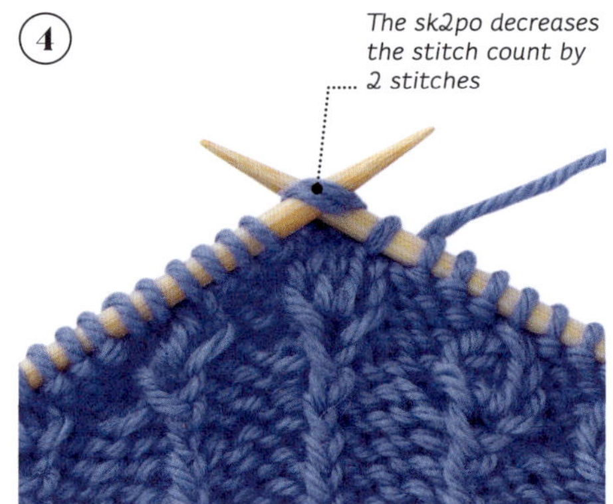

1 **Row 1:** Purl 1 stitch. *Purl 1 stitch. Knit 1 stitch through the back loop (see p.37). Purl 2 stitches.

2 **Row 2:** *Knit 2 stitches. Purl 1 stitch through the back loop (see p.37). Knit 1 stitch. Repeat from * until the last stitch. Knit 1 stitch.

3 **Row 3:** Purl 1 stitch. *Purl 1 stitch. Work a twisted kyok: *Knit 1 stitch through the back loop but keep the initial stitch on the LHN. Bring the yarn to the front between the needles, the yarn will travel over the RHN as the next stitch is worked. Knit 1 stitch through the back loop. Remove the initial stitch from the LHN.* Purl 2 stitches. **Row 4:** *Knit 2 stitches. Purl 3 stitches. Knit 1 stitch. Repeat from * until the last stitch. Knit 1 stitch. **Row 5:** Purl 1 stitch. *Purl 1 stitch. Knit 3 stitches. Purl 2 stitches. **Row 6:** Repeat Row 4.

4 **Row 7:** Purl 1 stitch. *Purl 1 stitch. Work a sk2po (see p.44). Purl 2 stitches. **Rows 8–10:** Repeat Row 2 then repeat Rows 1 and 2 again.

The chart: Mini Leaf Rib

The "no stitch" symbol of a grey box is used on this chart. Ignore this stitch and move to the next symbol. This is used when the stitch count changes, to keep the chart lined up.

Thorn Stitch

SKILL LEVEL
Advanced

MULTIPLES
4 (+5) stitches; 8 rows

STITCHES INCLUDED
knit, purl, kyok, wyib sl, wyif sl, k2tog, ssk

APPEARANCE
Single-sided

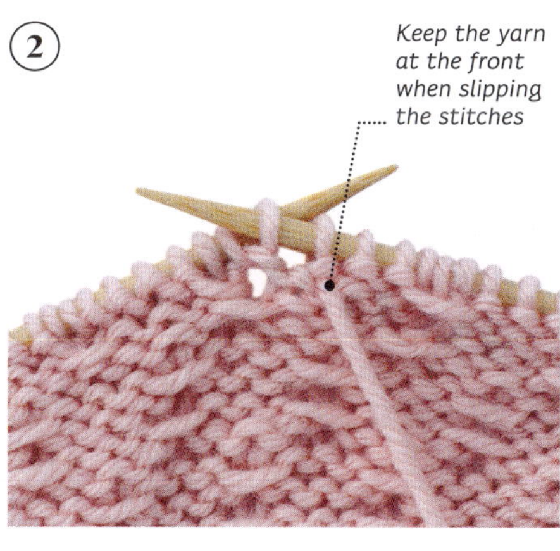

1 **Row 1:** Knit 2 stitches. *Work a kyok: *knit 1 stitch but keep the initial stitch on the LHN. Bring the yarn to the front between the needles. The yarn will travel over the RHN as the next stitch is worked. Knit 1 stitch. Remove the initial stitch from the LHN.* Knit 3 stitches. Repeat from * until the last 3 stitches. Work a kyok. Knit 2 stitches.

2 **Row 2:** Purl 2 stitches. Work a wyif sl 3: *keeping the yarn at the front, slip 3 stitches by inserting the RHN from right to left.* *Purl 3 stitches. Work a wyif sl 3. Repeat from * until the last 2 stitches. Purl 2 stitches.

3 **Row 3:** Knit 1 stitch. *Knit 2 stitches together (see p.38). Work a wyib sl 1: *keeping the yarn at the back, slip 1 stitch by inserting the RHN from right to left.*

4 Work an ssk (see p.38). Knit 1 stitch. Repeat from * until the end. **Row 4:** Purl 1 stitch. *Purl 3 stitches. Work a wyif sl 1. Repeat from * until the last 4 stitches. Purl 4 stitches. **Row 5:** Knit 4 stitches. *Work a kyok. Knit 3 stitches. Repeat from * until the last stitch. Knit 1 stitch. **Row 6:** Purl 1 stitch. *Purl 3 stitches. Work a wyif sl 3. Repeat from * until the last 4 stitches. Purl 4 stitches. **Row 7:** Knit 3 stitches. *Knit 2 stitches together. Work a wyib sl 1. Work an ssk. Knit 1 stitch. Repeat from * until the last 2 stitches. Knit 2 stitches. **Row 8:** Purl 2 stitches. *Work a wyif sl 1. Purl 3 stitches. Repeat from * until the last 3 stitches. Work a wyif sl 1. Purl 2 stitches.

Using Slipped Stitches

Using slipped stitches is a simple technique as the stitch is just moved from one needle to the other. There are two slipped-stitch variations: one with the yarn at the back and the other with the yarn at the front. Both stitches pull a stitch up from the row below, but the yarn in front version creates a visible bar on the right side. This means that slipped stitches can create both horizontal and vertical surface texture.

As a slipped stitch is not knitted on the row being worked, the gauge can be pulled in from both directions. The horizontal bars created make the fabric thicker, so these stitches can be used for heavy-wear areas, such as sock heels. Alternatively, the stitches can be decorative: the Little Tent stitch (see p.72) and Lattice stitch (see p.73) work under the horizontal bars on the front of the fabric to create diagonal surface texture.

Eye of Partridge

SKILL LEVEL
Easy

MULTIPLES
2 (+2) stitches; 4 rows

STITCHES INCLUDED
knit, purl, wyib sl

APPEARANCE
Single-sided

1 **Row 1:** Knit 1 stitch. *Work a wyib sl 1: *with the yarn at the back, slip 1 stitch by inserting the RHN from right to left into the first stitch on the LHN.* Knit 1 stitch. Repeat from * until the last stitch. Knit 1 stitch.

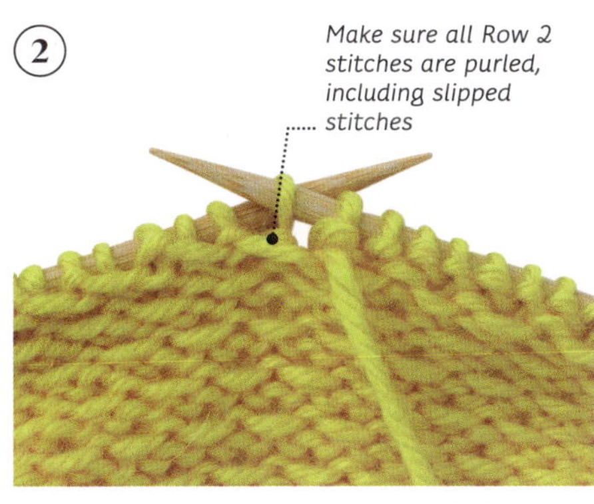

2 **Row 2:** Purl all stitches. **Row 3:** Knit 1 stitch. * Knit 1 stitch. Work a wyib sl 1. Repeat from * until the last stitch. Knit 1 stitch. **Row 4:** Purl all stitches.

The chart: Eye of Partridge

When working a slipped stitch, it is pulled up past its original row, which makes the stitch larger. The V-shaped symbol represents this enlarged stitch.

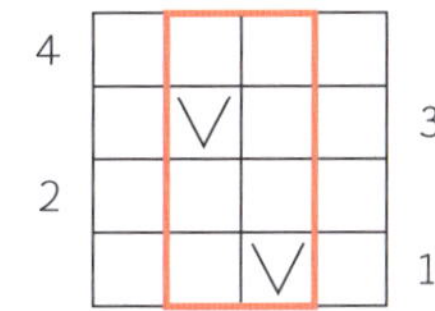

Linen Stitch

OTHER NAMES
Fabric stitch, Woven stitch

SKILL LEVEL
Easy

MULTIPLES
2 (+2) stitches; 2 rows

STITCHES INCLUDED
knit, purl, wyif sl, wyib sl

APPEARANCE
Single-sided (the WS will have the visual appearance of Moss Stitch)

1 **Row 1:** Knit 1 stitch. *Work a wyif sl 1: *bring the yarn to the front of the work. Slip 1 stitch by inserting the RHN from right to left into the first stitch on the LHN. Take the yarn to the back.* Knit 1 stitch. Repeat from * until the last stitch. Knit 1 stitch.

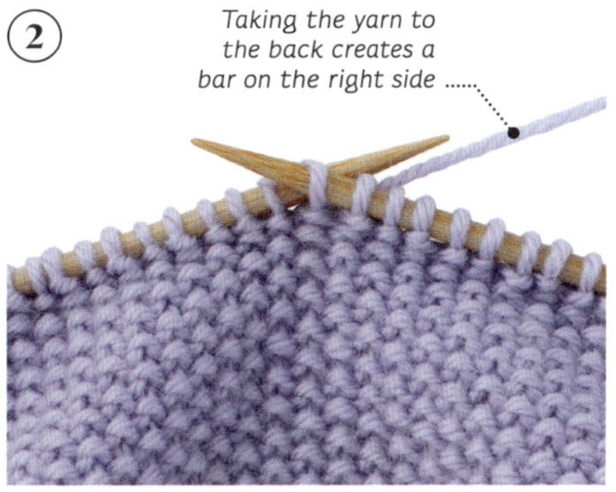

2 **Row 2:** Purl 1 stitch. *Work a wyib sl 1: *take the yarn back. Slip 1 stitch by inserting the RHN from right to left into the first stitch on the LHN. Bring the yarn to the front.* Purl 1 stitch. Repeat from * until the last stitch. Purl 1 stitch.

Slipped Stitch Ladder

SKILL LEVEL
Intermediate

MULTIPLES
3 (+3) stitches; 4 rows

STITCHES INCLUDED
knit, purl, wyib sl, wyif sl

APPEARANCE
Single-sided

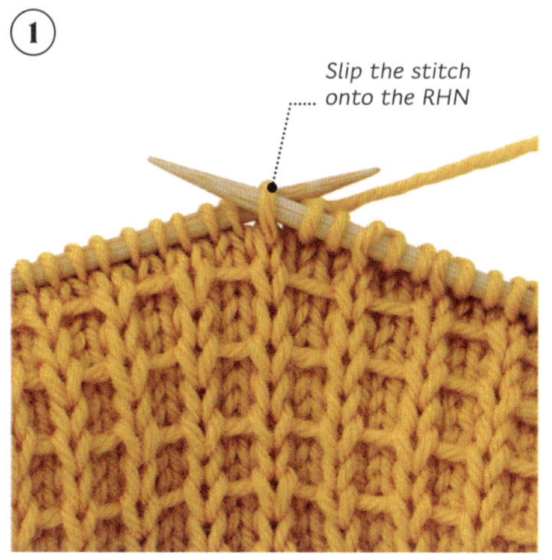

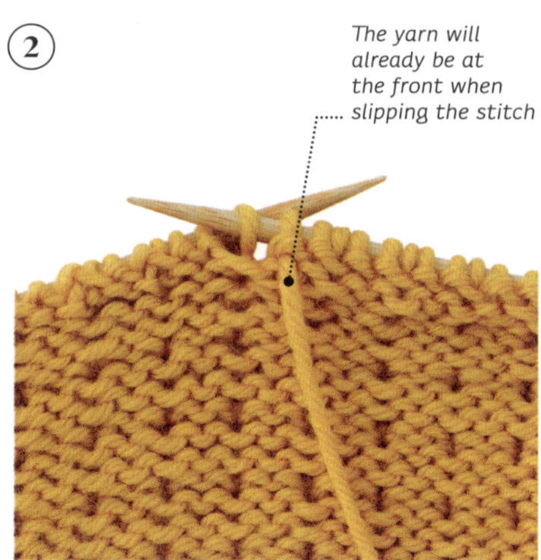

1 **Row 1:** Knit 1 stitch. *Work a wyib sl 1: *keeping the yarn at the back, slip 1 stitch by inserting the RHN from right to left.* Knit 2 stitches. Repeat from * until the last 2 stitches. Work a wyib sl 1. Knit 1 stitch.

2 **Row 2:** Purl 1 stitch. Work a wyif sl 1: *with the yarn at the front, slip 1 stitch by inserting the RHN from right to left into the first stitch on the LHN.* *Purl 2 stitches. Work a wyif sl 1. Repeat from * until the last stitch. Purl 1 stitch.

3 **Row 3:** Knit 1 stitch. *Knit 1 stitch. Work a wyif sl 2: *bring the yarn to the front. Slip 2 stitches by inserting the RHN from right to left into each stitch on the LHN. Take the yarn to the back.* Repeat from * until the last 2 stitches. Knit 2 stitches. **Row 4:** Purl all stitches.

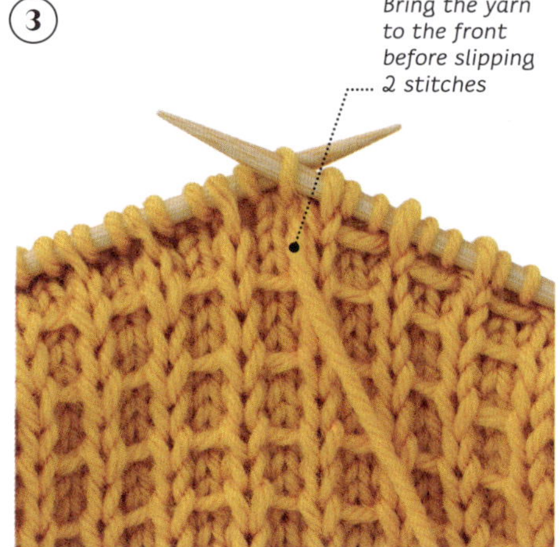

The chart: Slipped Stitch Ladder

There are 2 types of slipped stitch symbol shown in this chart. The wyif sl symbol has the horizontal bar across the front that is visible in the actual stitch.

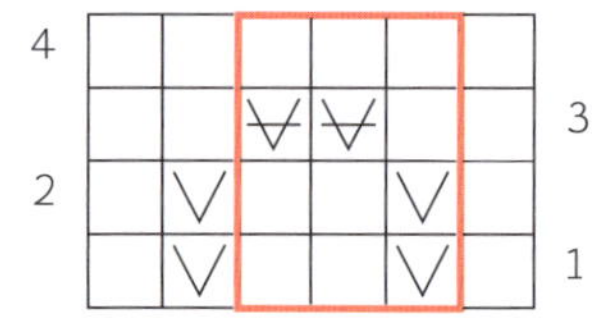

Woven Texture

SKILL LEVEL
Intermediate

MULTIPLES
5 (+2) stitches; 10 rows

STITCHES INCLUDED
knit, purl, wyif sl

APPEARANCE
Single-sided

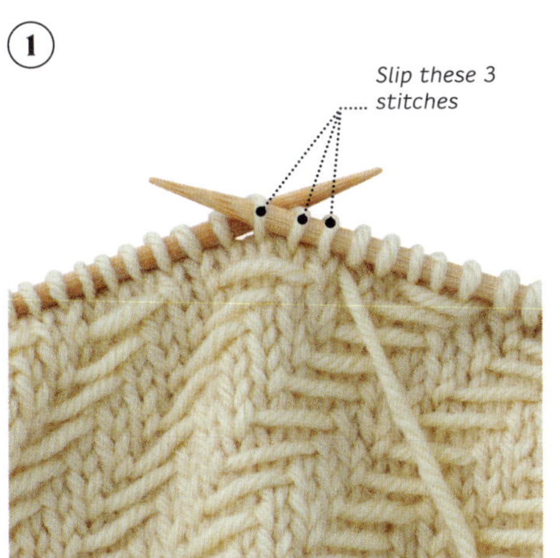

1 **Row 1:** Knit 1 stitch. *Work a wyif sl 3: *bring the yarn to the front. Slip 3 stitches by inserting the RHN from right to left into the stitch on the LHN. Take the yarn to the back.* Knit 2 stitches. Repeat from * until the last stitch. Knit 1 stitch. **Row 2 and all even rows including Row 10:** Purl all stitches.

2 **Row 3:** (Note: when working multiple repeats, do not take the yarn to the back if the following stitch is a slipped stitch.) Knit 1 stitch. Work a wyif sl 2: *bring the yarn to the front. Slip 2 stitches by inserting the RHN from right to left into the stitch on the LHN. Take the yarn to the back.* Knit 2 stitches. Work a wyif sl 1: *bring the yarn to the front. Slip 1 stitch by inserting the RHN from right to left into the stitch on the LHN. Take the yarn to the back.* Repeat from * until the last stitch. Knit 1 stitch. **Row 5:** Knit 1 stitch. *Work a wyif sl 1. Knit 2 stitches. Work a wyif sl 2. Repeat from * until the last stitch. Knit 1 stitch. **Row 7:** Knit 1 stitch. *Knit 2 stitches. Work a wyif sl 3. Repeat from * until the last stitch. Knit 1 stitch. **Row 9:** Knit 1 stitch. *Knit 1 stitch. Work a wyif sl 3. Knit 1 stitch. Repeat from * until the last stitch. Knit 1 stitch.

The chart: Woven Texture

A V-shaped symbol with a horizontal bar shows that the yarn crosses in front of the slipped stitch. If multiple stitches are worked, the yarn is only brought to the back again after the last wyif sl stitch.

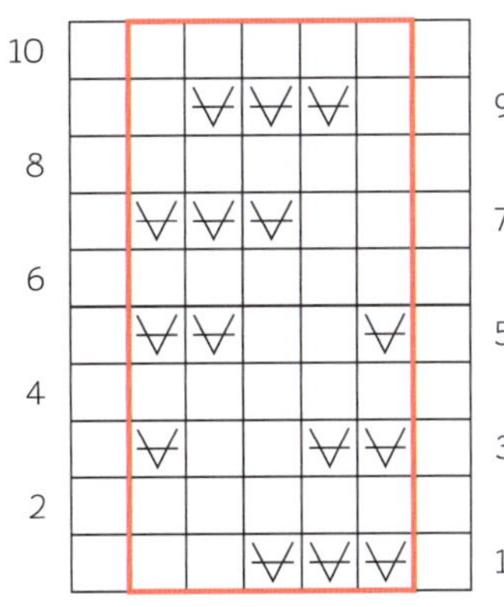

Little Tent Stitch

OTHER NAME
Garter and Gull

SKILL LEVEL
Advanced

MULTIPLES
8 (+1) stitches; 4 rows

STITCHES INCLUDED
knit, purl, wyif sl, knit under loop

APPEARANCE
Single-sided

1 **Row 1:** Knit 1 stitch. *Knit 1 stitch. Work a wyif sl 5: *bring the yarn to the front. Slip 5 stitches by inserting the RHN from right to left into each stitch on the LHN. Take the yarn to the back.* Knit 2 stitches. Repeat from * until the end. **Rows 2 and 4:** *Knit 2 stitches. Purl 5 stitches. Knit 1 stitch. Repeat from * until the last stitch. Knit 1 stitch.

2 **Row 3:** Knit 1 stitch. *Knit 3 stitches. Work a knit under loop: *Insert the RHN under the wyif sl 5 strand by inserting from below.*

3 *Insert the RHN from left to right into the first stitch on the LHN. Knit these two together.* Knit 4 stitches. Repeat from * until the end.

The chart: Little Tent Stitch

The U-shaped symbol is the knit under loop stitch. The horizontal band represented by the 5 consecutive slipped stitches on Row 1 is knitted together with the stitch on the LHN.

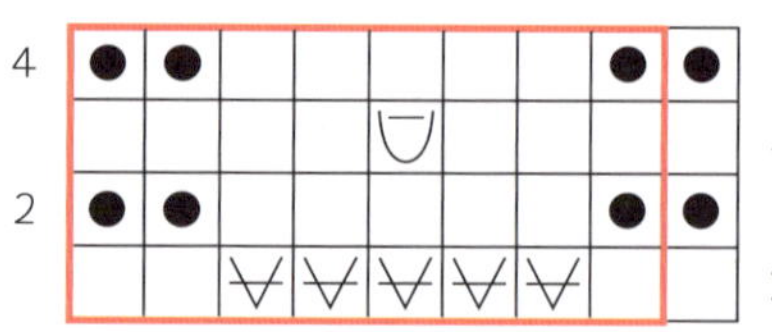

Lattice

OTHER NAME
Quilted Diamonds

SKILL LEVEL
Advanced

MULTIPLES
6 (+3) stitches; 8 rows

STITCHES INCLUDED
knit, purl, wyif sl, knit under loop

APPEARANCE
Single-sided

1 **Row 1:** Knit 1 stitch. *Knit 1 stitch. Work a wyif sl 5: *bring the yarn to the front. Slip 5 stitches by inserting the RHN from right to left into each stitch on the LHN. Take the yarn to the back.* Repeat from * until the last 2 stitches. Knit 2 stitches. **Row 2 and all even rows including Row 8:** Purl all the stitches.

2 **Row 3:** Knit 1 stitch. *Knit 3 stitches. Work a knit under loop: *insert the LHN under the wyif sl 5 strand from below.*

3 *Insert the RHN from left to right into the first stitch on the LHN. Knit these two together.* Knit 2 stitches. Repeat from * until the last 2 stitches. Knit 2 stitches.

4 **Row 5:** Knit 1 stitch. *Work a wyif sl 3 (see p.45). Knit 1 stitch. Work a wyif sl 2 (see p.45). Repeat until the last 2 stitches. Work a wyif sl 1 (see p.45). Knit 1 stitch. **Row 7:** Knit 1 stitch. *Work a knit under loop. Knit 5 stitches. Repeat until the last 2 stitches. Work a knit under loop. Knit 1 stitch.

Speckled Rib

Row 1: k1, *p1, wyib sl 1, rep from * until the end, k1.
Row 2: purl.
Row 3: k1, *wyib sl 1, p1, rep from * until the end, k1.
Row 4: purl.

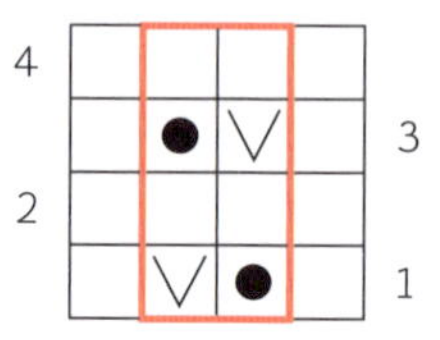

SKILL LEVEL
Intermediate

MULTIPLES
2 (+2) stitches; 4 rows

STITCHES INCLUDED
knit, purl, wyib sl

APPEARANCE
Single-sided

Alternating Ladders

Row 1: k1, *wyif sl 2, k2, rep from * until the last st, k1.
Row 2: p1, *p2, wyib sl 2, rep from * until the last st, p1.
Row 3: k1, *k2, wyif sl 2, rep from * until the last st, k1.
Row 4: p1, *wyib sl 2, p2, rep from * until the last st, p1.

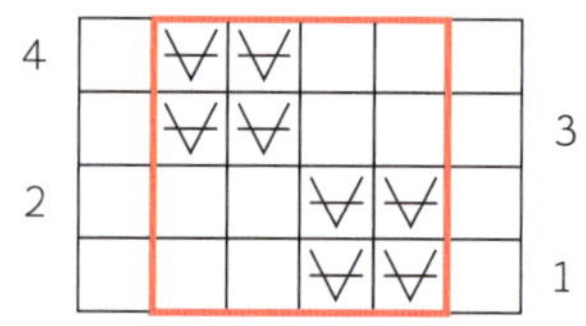

SKILL LEVEL
Intermediate

MULTIPLES
4 (+2) stitches; 4 rows

STITCHES INCLUDED
knit, purl, wyib sl, wyif sl

APPEARANCE
Single-sided

Honeycomb Slip Stitch

Row 1: knit.
Row 2: k1, *k1, wyib sl 1, rep from * until the last st, k1.
Row 3: knit.
Row 4: k1, *wyib sl 1, k1, rep from * until the last st, k1.

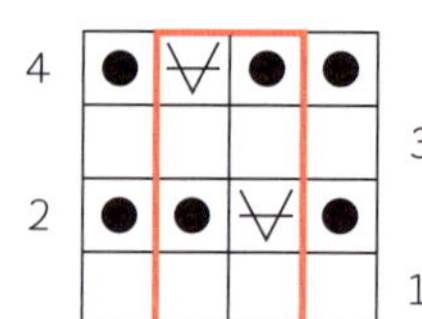

SKILL LEVEL
Easy

MULTIPLES
2 (+2) stitches; 4 rows

STITCHES INCLUDED
knit, purl, wyib sl 1

APPEARANCE
Single-sided

Half Linen Stitch

Row 1: k1, *wyif sl 1, k1, rep from * until the last st, k1.
Row 2: purl.
Row 3: k1, *k1, wyif sl 1, rep from * until the last st, k1.
Row 4: purl.

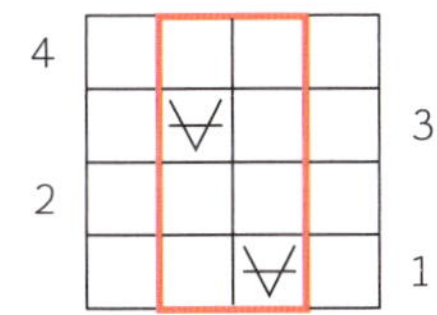

SKILL LEVEL
Easy

MULTIPLES
2 (+2) stitches; 4 rows

STITCHES INCLUDED
knit, purl, wyif sl

APPEARANCE
Single-sided

Reverse Brick Stitch

Row 1: knit.
Row 2: purl.
Row 3: p1, *wyib sl 1, p3, rep from * until the end.
Row 4: *k3, wyif sl 1, rep from * until the last st, k1.
Row 5: knit.
Row 6: purl.
Row 7: p1, *p2, wyib sl 1, p1, rep from * until the end.
Row 8: *k1, wyif sl 1, k2, rep from * until the last st, k1.

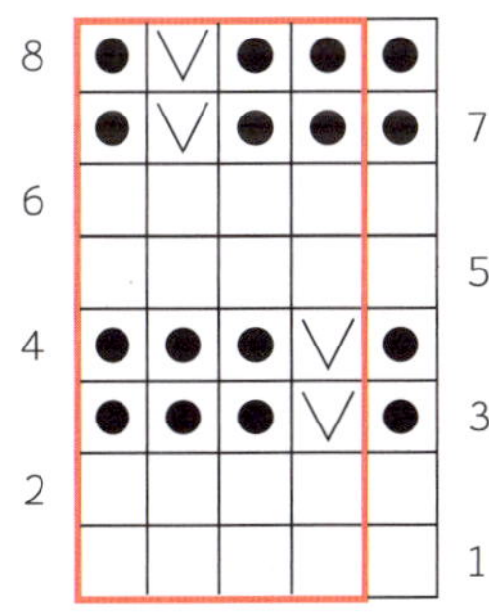

SKILL LEVEL
Intermediate

MULTIPLES
4 (+1) stitches; 8 rows

STITCHES INCLUDED
knit, purl, wyib sl, wyif sl

APPEARANCE
Single-sided

Colourwork

Simple Colourwork

Any stitch pattern can be worked using more than one colour of yarn. The patterns in this section introduce a contrasting colour in stripes or blocks to create new patterns and effects.

Almost all of the patterns in this section are made up of knit and purl stitches (String of Pearls on p.82 also uses increases and decreases), and use just one yarn per row. This makes them simple to work, as long as the yarn is left at the correct side to be reused later. Ideally, this means that even numbers of rows need to be worked in each colour. If working an odd number of rows in each colour, work the pattern flat on circular needles, sliding the stitches from one side to the other, where the next row's yarn has been left.

Intarsia (p.83), also known as picture knitting, uses bobbins to manage the yarn. Every section of colour on each row needs its own separate bobbin.

Garter Stripes

SKILL LEVEL
Easy

MULTIPLES
1 stitch; 10 rows

STITCHES INCLUDED
knit, purl

APPEARANCE
Single-sided

OTHER MATERIALS
Contrasting yarn

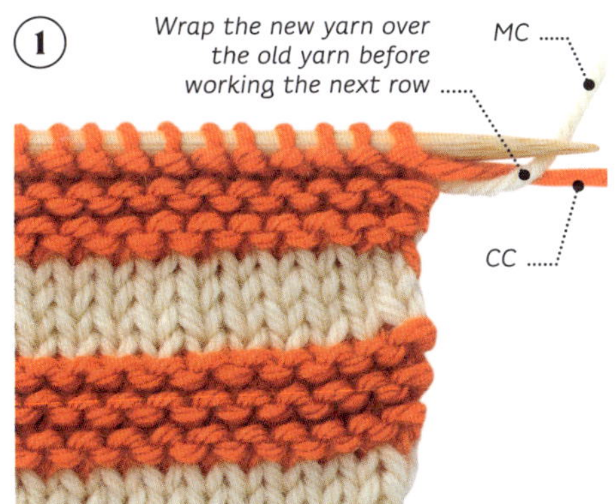

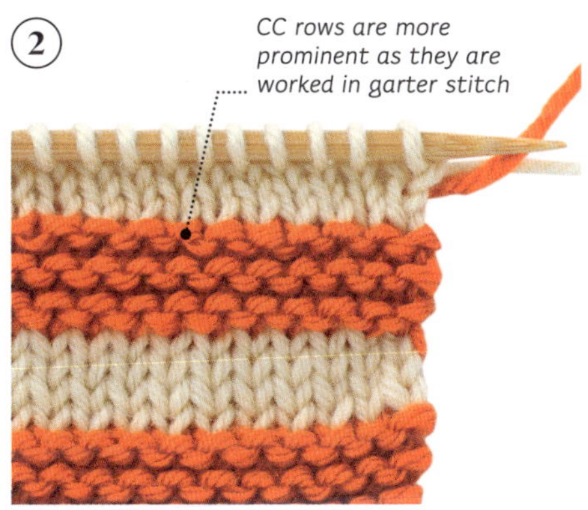

1 **Rows 1–4:** Using the main colour (MC), work 4 rows in stocking stitch: alternating a knit row with a purl row, starting with a knit row. Keep the MC attached.

2 **Rows 5–10:** Using the contrast colour (CC), work 6 rows of garter stitch: knit every row. Keep the CC attached.

Contrast Garter Ridges

SKILL LEVEL
Easy

MULTIPLES
1 stitch; 4 rows

STITCHES INCLUDED
knit, purl

APPEARANCE
Single-sided

OTHER MATERIALS
Contrasting yarn

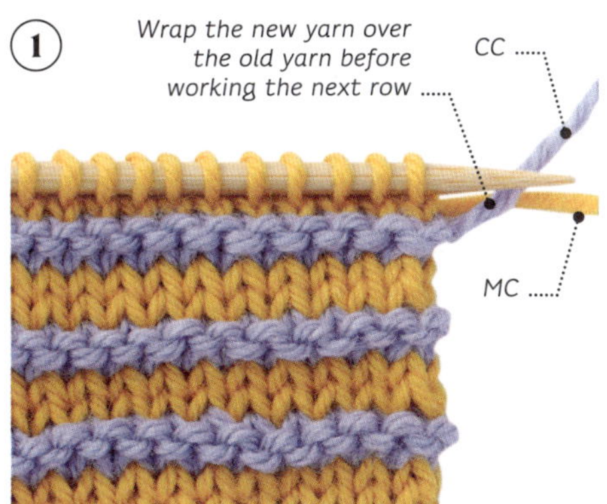

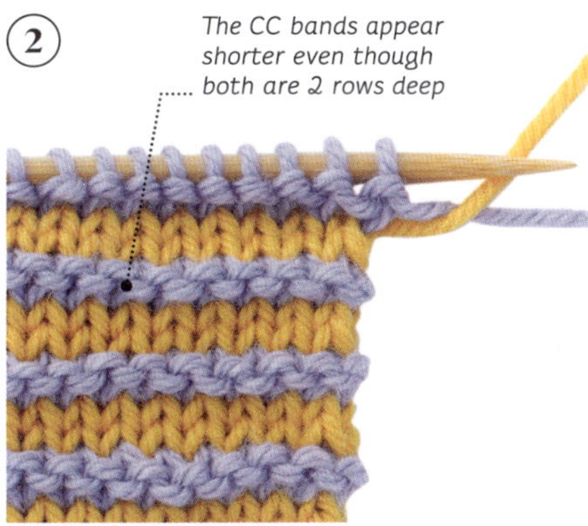

1 **Rows 1 and 2:** Using the main colour (MC), work 2 rows in stocking stitch: 1 row of knit followed by 1 row of purl. Keep the MC attached.

2 **Rows 3 and 4:** Using the contrast colour (CC), work 2 rows of garter stitch: knit every row. Keep the CC attached.

The chart: Contrast Garter Ridges

This chart shows the colour of the yarn changing every 2 rows. Only 1 stitch column is shown on the chart as the same stitch is worked across the entire row.

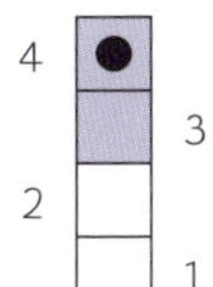

Two-row Garter Stitch

SKILL LEVEL
Easy

MULTIPLES
1 stitch; 4 rows

STITCHES INCLUDED
knit, purl

APPEARANCE
Reversible (different dominant colour)

OTHER MATERIALS
Contrasting yarn, circular needle

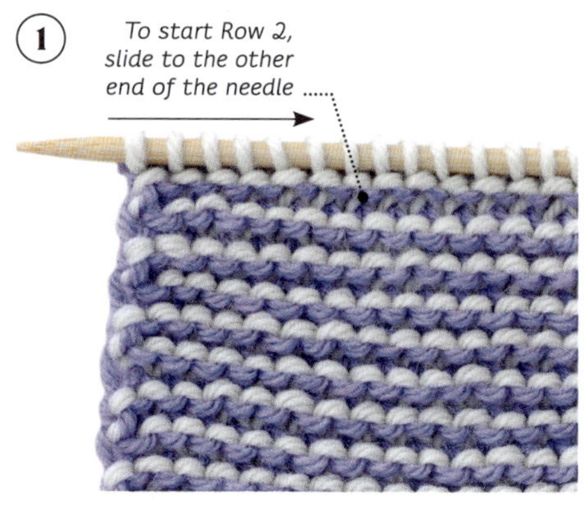

1 **Row 1:** Using the main colour (MC), knit all stitches. **Row 2:** Slide the stitches to the opposite end of the circular needle. Using the contrast colour (CC), purl all stitches. Turn work.

2 **Row 3:** Do not slide the stitches. Using the MC, purl all stitches. **Row 4:** Slide the stitches to the opposite end of the circular needle. Using the CC, knit all stitches. Turn work.

Two-colour Moss Stitch

SKILL LEVEL
Easy

MULTIPLES
2 stitches; 4 rows

STITCHES INCLUDED
knit, purl

APPEARANCE
Reversible

OTHER MATERIALS
Contrasting yarn

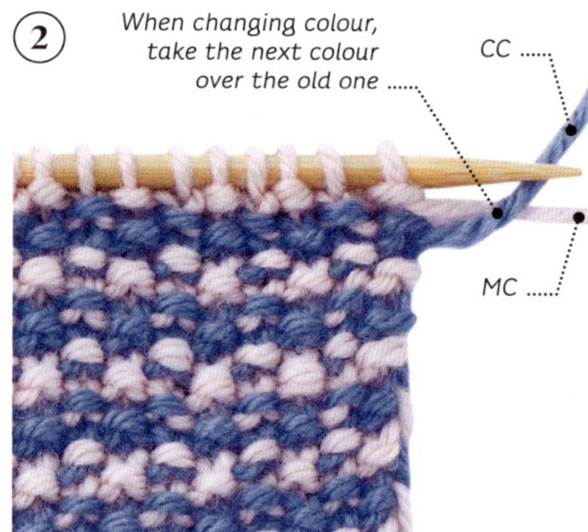

1 **Row 1:** Using the main colour (MC), knit 1 stitch. Bring the yarn to the front. Purl 1 stitch. Take the yarn to the back. **Row 2:** Purl 1 stitch. Take the yarn to the back. Knit 1 stitch. Bring the yarn to the front.

2 **Row 3:** Using the contrast colour (CC), knit 1 stitch. Bring the yarn to the front. Purl 1 stitch. Take the yarn to the back. **Row 4:** Purl 1 stitch. Take the yarn to the back. Knit 1 stitch. Bring the yarn to the front.

Tricolour Garter Rib

SKILL LEVEL
Easy

MULTIPLES
6 stitches; 6 rows

STITCHES INCLUDED
knit, purl

APPEARANCE
Reversible

OTHER MATERIALS
2 contrasting yarns

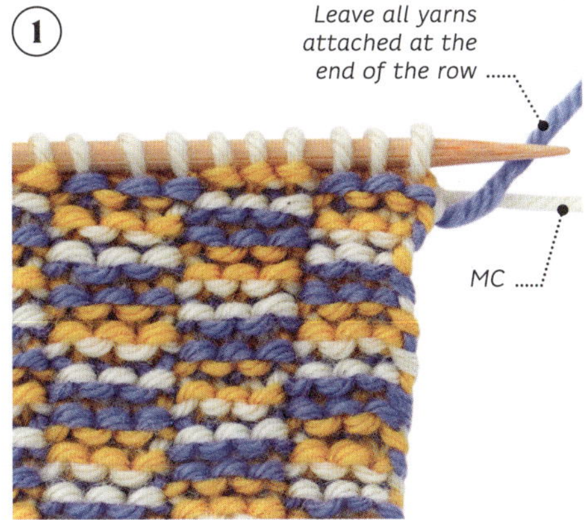

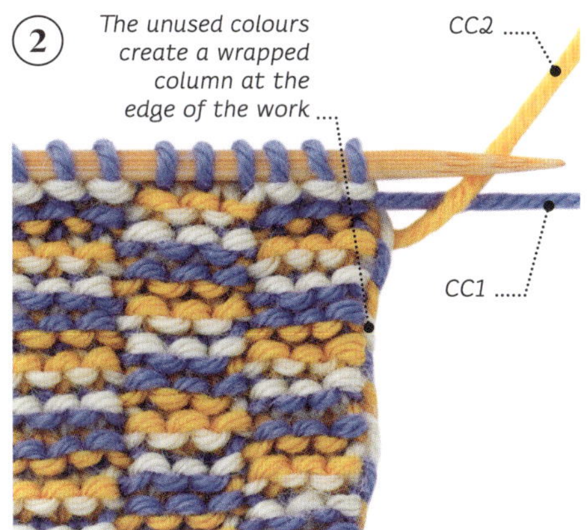

1 **Row 1:** Using the main colour (MC), knit 3 stitches. Bring the yarn to the front. Purl 3 stitches. Take the yarn to the back.

2 **Row 2:** Using the first contrast colour (CC), purl 3 stitches. Take the yarn to the back. Knit 3 stitches. Bring the yarn to the front.

3 **Row 3:** Using the second CC, knit 3 stitches. Bring the yarn to the front. Purl 3 stitches. Take the yarn to the back. **Row 4:** Using the MC, repeat Row 2. **Row 5:** Using the first CC, repeat Row 1. **Row 6:** Using the second CC, repeat Row 2.

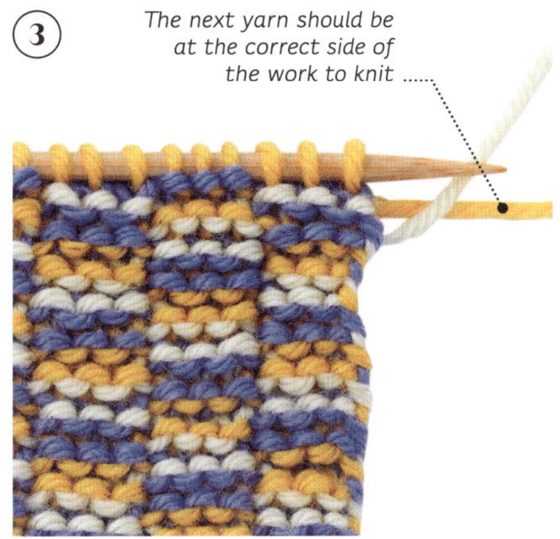

The chart: Tricolour Garter Rib

This stitch creates an optical illusion. The chart shows that each row is worked in a separate colour, but the resulting fabric looks like blocks. Because this stitch is worked in 3 colours, the correct colour is always left at the end of the row where it will be needed next.

Row							Row
6				●	●	●	
	●	●	●				5
4				●	●	●	
	●	●	●				3
2				●	●	●	
	●	●	●				1

Contrast Welts

SKILL LEVEL
Easy

MULTIPLES
1 stitch; 10 rows

STITCHES INCLUDED
knit, purl

APPEARANCE
Different but both sides can be used as right side

OTHER MATERIALS
Contrasting yarn

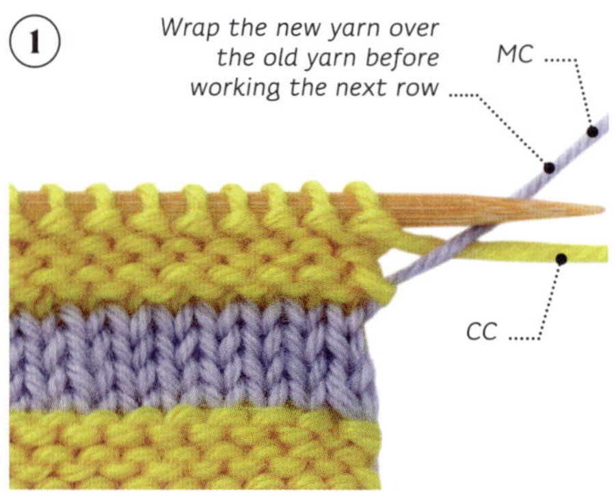

1 Row 1: Using the contrast colour (CC), knit all stitches. **Rows 2–6:** Work 5 rows in reverse stocking stitch: alternating 1 row of knit with 1 row of purl, starting with a knit row.

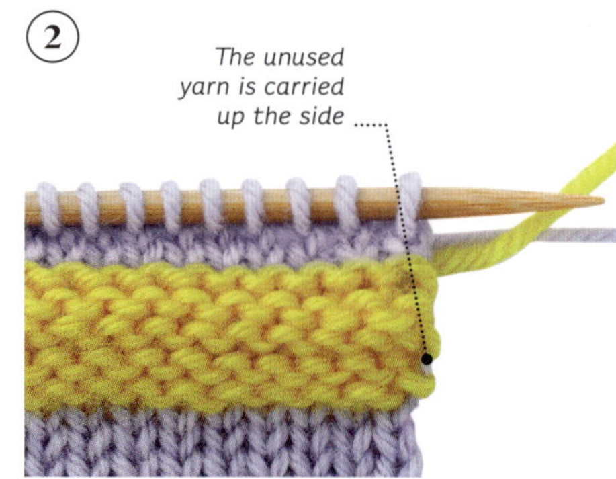

2 Rows 7–10: Using the main colour (MC), work 4 rows in stocking stitch: alternating 1 row of knit with 1 row of purl, starting with a knit row.

String of Pearls

SKILL LEVEL
Intermediate

MULTIPLES
2 (+2) stitches; 6 rows

STITCHES INCLUDED
knit, purl, kyok, wyib sl, k3togtbl

APPEARANCE
Single-sided

OTHER MATERIALS
Contrasting yarn

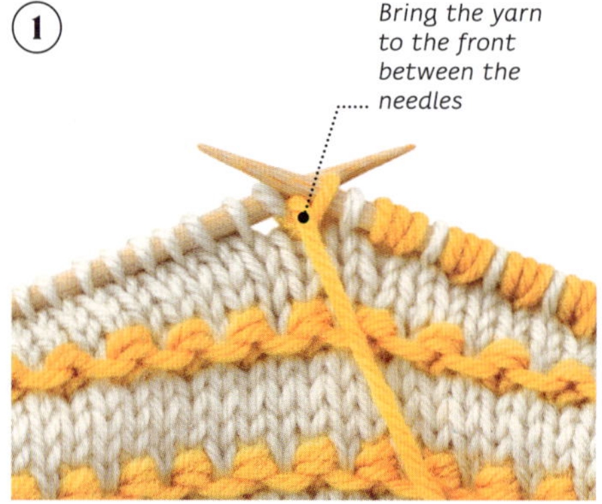

1 Rows 1 and 2: Using the main colour (MC), work 2 rows of stocking stitch: 1 row of knit followed by 1 row of purl. **Row 3:** Using the contrast colour (CC), knit 1 stitch. *Work a kyok: *knit 1 stitch but keep the initial stitch on the LHN. Bring the yarn to the front between the needles; the yarn will travel over the RHN as the next stitch is worked. Knit 1 stitch. Remove the initial stitch from the LHN.* Work a wyib sl 1: *with the yarn at the back, slip 1 stitch by inserting the RHN from right to left.* Repeat from * until the last stitch. Knit 1 stitch.

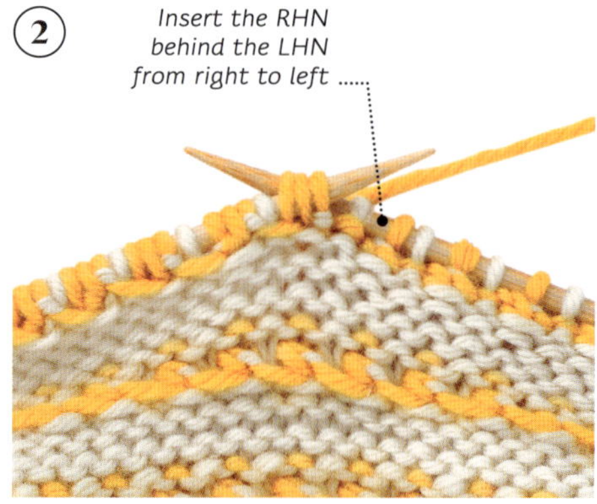

2 Row 4: Purl 1 stitch. *Work a wyib sl 1. Work a k3togtbl: *insert the RHN from right to left and towards the back into the first, second, then third stitch on the LHN. Knit these 3 stitches together.* Repeat from * until the last stitch. Purl 1 stitch. **Rows 5 and 6:** Using the MC, work 2 rows of stocking stitch, starting with a knit row.

Intarsia Diamond

SKILL LEVEL
Intermediate

MULTIPLES
13 stitches; 16 rows

STITCHES INCLUDED
knit, purl

APPEARANCE
Single-sided

OTHER MATERIALS
Contrasting yarn, yarn bobbins x 3

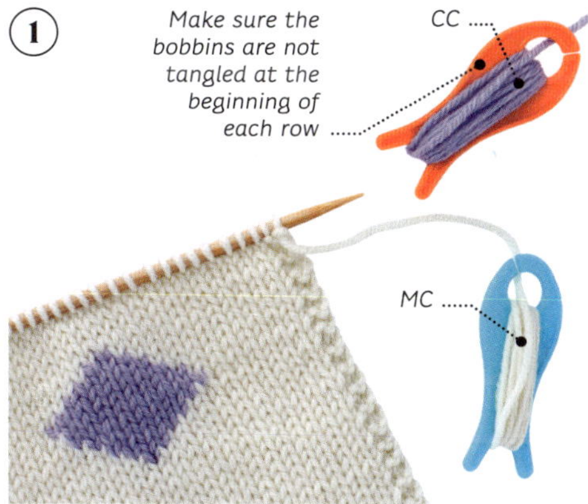

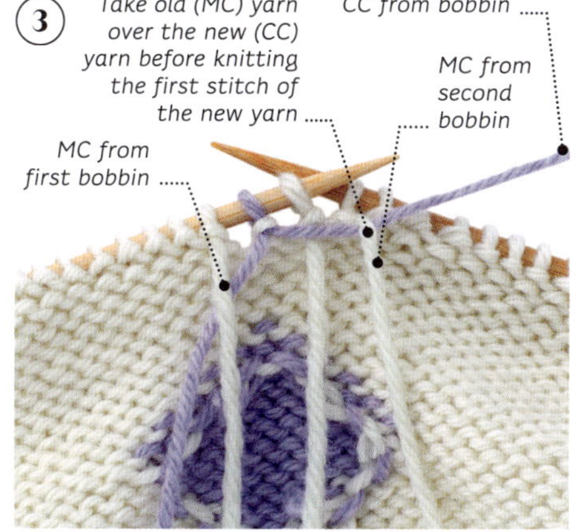

1 Wind plenty of yarn onto the bobbins: 2 of the main colour (MC) and 1 of the contrast colour (CC).

2 **Rows 1–2:** Using the MC, work 2 rows of stocking stitch: 1 row of knit followed by 1 row of purl. **Row 3:** Using a bobbin of the MC, knit 6 stitches. Using a bobbin of the CC, knit 1 stitch. Using a bobbin of the MC, knit 6 stitches.

3 **Row 4:** Using the attached bobbin of the MC, purl 5 stitches. Work an intarsia twist: take the MC yarn just used over the top and to the left of the new CC yarn. Pick up the new yarn from the right; this will create a twist between the two. Purl 3 stitches in the CC bobbin. Work an intarsia twist. Purl 5 stitches in the MC bobbin that is attached at this point.

4 **Row 5:** Using the MC, knit 4 stitches. Work an intarsia twist. (Note: For every colour change, work an intarsia twist.) Using the CC, knit 5 stitches. Using MC, knit 4 stitches **Row 6:** Using the MC, purl 3 stitches. Using the CC, purl 7 stitches. Using the MC, purl 3 stitches. **Row 7:** Using the MC, knit 2 stitches. Using the CC, knit 9 stitches. Using the MC, knit 2 stitches. **Row 8:** Using the MC, purl 1 stitch. Using the CC, purl 11 stitches. Using the MC, purl 1 stitch. **Rows 9–13:** Repeat Row 7, then Row 6, then Row 5, then Row 4, then Row 3. **Rows 14–16:** Work 2 rows of stocking stitch, starting with a purl row.

Slip-stitch Colourwork

Using colour with slipped stitches creates some creative patterns, as the horizontal and vertical movement of stitches means that different colours can travel in those directions too. Only one colour at a time is used in slip-stitch knitting, so it is a simpler technique to use than stranded colourwork (see pp.94–103). As with single-colour slipped stitches, there can be a reduction in length and width in the gauge. It is ideal for adding interesting colour to a project in a relatively simple manner and is suitable for most projects.

There is a subset of slip-stitch colourwork called mosaic knitting, when the slip stitches always have the yarn on the wrong side of the work and two consecutive and visually identical rows are worked per colour. Corner Square (see p.91) is an example of mosaic knitting.

Basic Mosaic Dots

SKILL LEVEL
Easy

MULTIPLES
4 (+2) stitches; 8 rows

STITCHES INCLUDED
knit, purl, wyib sl, wyif sl

APPEARANCE
Single-sided

OTHER MATERIALS
Contrasting yarn

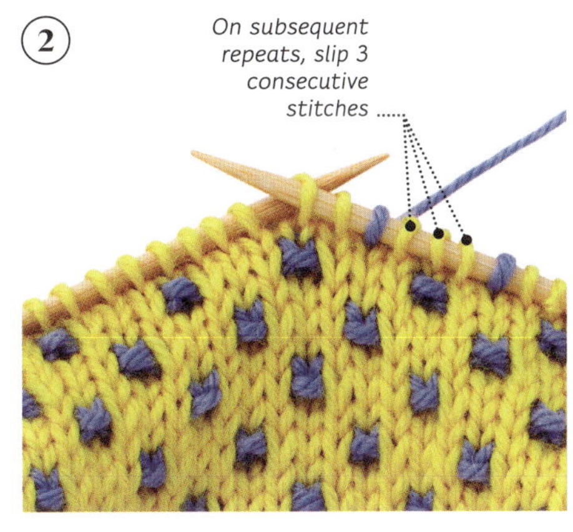

1 **Rows 1 and 2:** Using the main colour (MC), work two rows of stocking stitch: 1 row of knit followed by 1 row of purl. **Row 3:** Using the contrast colour (CC), knit 1 stitch. *Work a wyib sl 1: *slip 1 stitch from the LHN by inserting the RHN from right to left.* Knit 1 stitch.

2 Work a wyib sl 2: *slip 2 stitches from the LHN by inserting the RHN from right to left.* Repeat from * until the last stitch. Knit 1 stitch.

3 **Row 4:** Knit 1 stitch. *Work a wyif sl 2: *bring the yarn to the front, then slip 2 stitches from the LHN by inserting the RHN from right to left into each stitch. Take the yarn to the back.* Knit 1 stitch. Work a wyif sl 1: *bring the yarn to the front. Slip 1 stitch from the LHN by inserting the RHN from right to left. Take the yarn to the back.* Repeat from * until the last stitch. Knit 1 stitch. **Rows 5 and 6:** Repeat Rows 1 and 2. **Row 7:** Using the CC, knit 1 stitch. *Work a wyib sl 3: *slip 3 stitches from the LHN by inserting the RHN from right to left.* Knit 1 stitch. Repeat from * until the last stitch. Knit 1 stitch.

4 **Row 8:** Knit 1 stitch. *Knit 1 stitch. Work a wyif sl 3: *bring the yarn to the front. Slip 3 stitches from the LHN by inserting the RHN from right to left into each stitch. Take the yarn to the back.* Repeat from * until the last stitch. Knit 1 stitch.

Slip Garter Columns

SKILL LEVEL
Intermediate

MULTIPLES
5 stitches; 4 rows

STITCHES INCLUDED
knit, purl, wyib sl, wyif sl

APPEARANCE
Single-sided

OTHER MATERIALS
Contrasting yarn

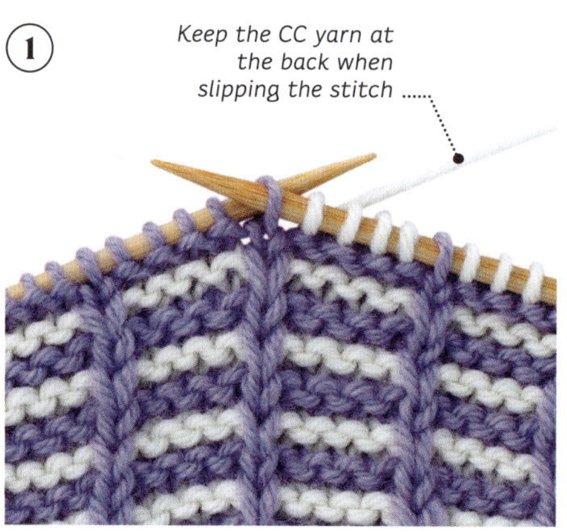

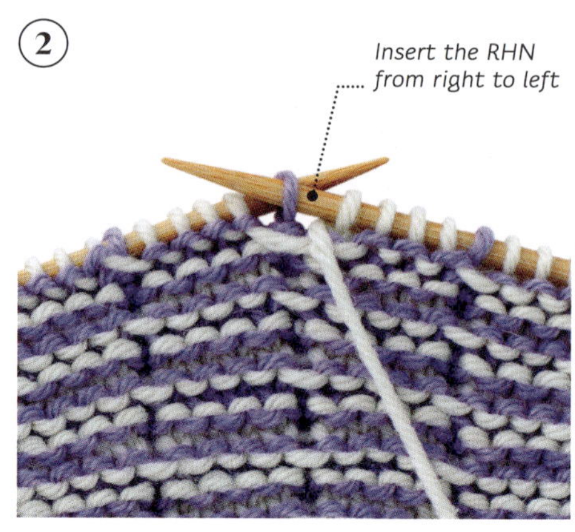

1 **Row 1:** Using the main colour (MC), knit all stitches. **Row 2:** Knit 2 stitches. Purl 1 stitch. Knit 2 stitches. **Row 3:** Using the contrast colour (CC), knit 2 stitches. Work a wyib sl 1: *slip 1 stitch from the LHN by inserting the RHN from right to left*. Knit 2 stitches.

2 **Row 4:** Knit 2 stitches. Work a wyif sl 1: *bring the yarn to the front. Slip 1 stitch from the LHN by inserting the RHN from right to left. Take the yarn to the back.* Knit 2 stitches.

Ridge Check

SKILL LEVEL
Easy

MULTIPLES
4 (+1) stitches; 8 (+2) rows

STITCHES INCLUDED
knit, purl, wyib sl, wyif sl

APPEARANCE
Single-sided

OTHER MATERIALS
Contrasting yarn

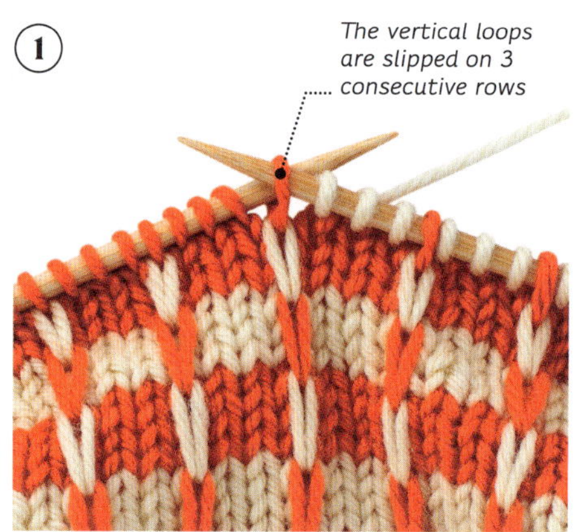

1 **Setup Rows 1 and 2:** Using the contrast colour (CC), work 2 rows of stocking: 1 row of knit followed by 1 row of purl. **Row 3:** Using the main colour (MC), knit 1 stitch. *Knit 1 stitch. Work a wyib sl 1: *keeping the yarn at the back, slip 1 stitch from the LHN by inserting the RHN from right to left*. Knit 2 stitches. Repeat from * until the end.

2 **Row 4:** *Purl 2 stitches. Work a wyif sl 1: *keeping the yarn at the front, slip 1 stitch from the LHN by inserting the RHN from right to left*. Repeat from * until the last stitch. Purl 1 stitch. **Row 5:** Repeat Row 3. **Row 6:** Purl all the stitches. **Rows 7–10:** Using the CC, repeat Rows 3–6.

Triple Tweed

SKILL LEVEL
Intermediate

MULTIPLES
4 (+1) stitches;
12 (+2) rows

STITCHES INCLUDED
knit, purl, wyib sl, wyif sl

APPEARANCE
Single-sided

OTHER MATERIALS
2 contrasting yarns

1

Slipped stitch

MC

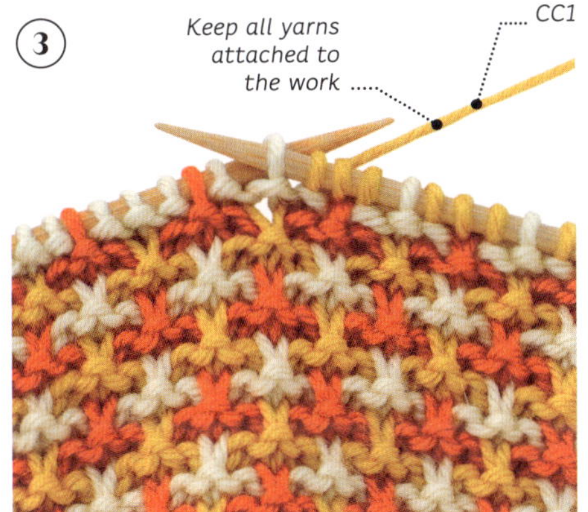

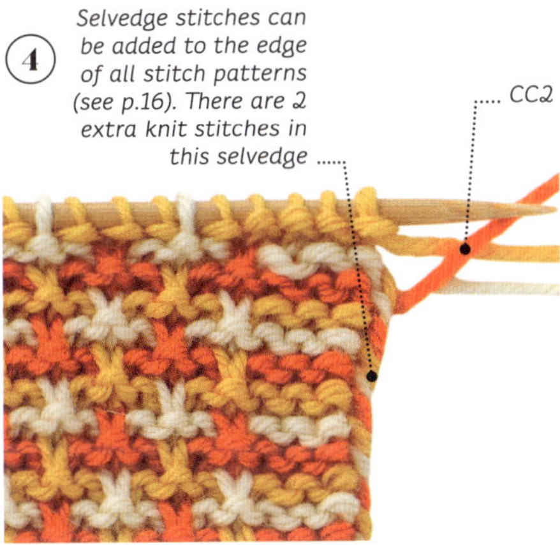

1 **Setup Rows 1 and 2:** Using the second contrast colour (CC2), work 2 rows in garter stitch: knit both rows. **Row 3:** Using the main colour (MC), knit 1 stitch. *Work a wyib sl 1: *keeping the yarn at the back, slip 1 stitch from the LHN by inserting the RHN from right to left*. Knit 3 stitches. Repeat from * until the end.

2 **Row 4:** *Knit 3 stitches. Work a wyif sl 1: *bring the yarn to the front between the needles. Slip 1 stitch from the LHN by inserting the RHN from right to left. Take the yarn to the back*. Repeat from * until the last stitch. Knit 1 stitch.

3 **Row 5:** Using the first contrast colour (CC1), knit 1 stitch. *Knit 2 stitches. Work a wyib sl 1. Knit 1 stitch. Repeat from * until the end. **Row 6:** Knit 1 stitch. Work a wyif sl 1. Knit 2 stitches. Repeat from * until the last stitch. Knit 1 stitch.

4 **Rows 7 and 8:** Using the CC2, repeat Rows 3 and 4 once. **Rows 9 and 10:** Using the MC, repeat Rows 5 and 6 once. **Rows 11 and 12:** Using the CC1, repeat Rows 3 and 4 once. **Rows 13 and 14:** Using the CC2, Repeat Rows 5 and 6 once.

Fish Scale

SKILL LEVEL
Advanced

MULTIPLES
6 (+2) stitches;
8 (+4) rows

STITCHES INCLUDED
knit, purl, wyib sl, wyif sl, knit under 2 loops

APPEARANCE
Single-sided

OTHER MATERIALS
Contrasting yarn

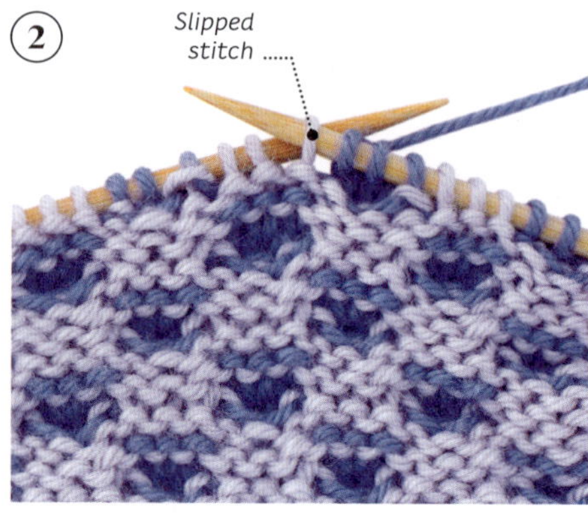

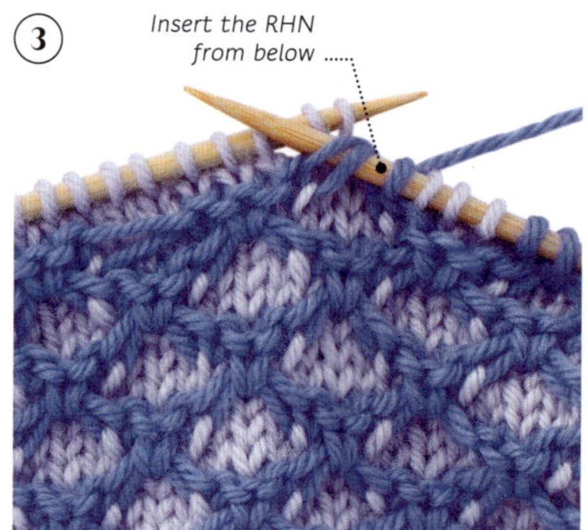

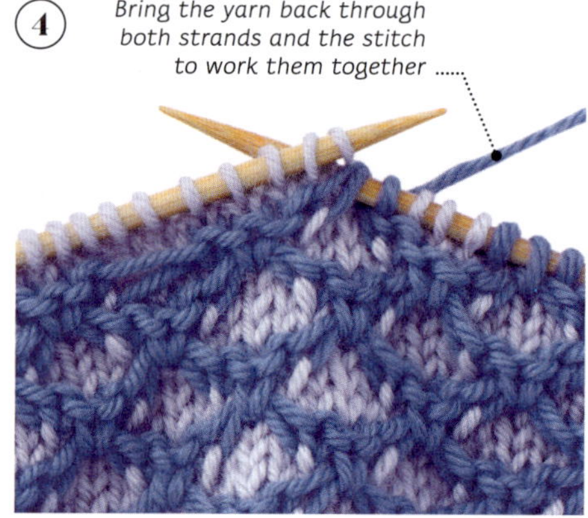

1 **Setup Rows 1 and 2:** Using the main colour (MC), work 2 rows of stocking stitch: 1 row of knit followed by 1 row of purl. **Setup Row 3:** Using the contrast colour (CC), knit 1 stitch. *Knit 3 stitches. Work a wyif sl 3: *bring yarn to the front. Slip 3 stitches from LHN by inserting RHN from right to left into each stitch. Take the yarn to the back.* Repeat from * until the last stitch. Knit 1 stitch.

2 **Setup Row 4:** Knit 1 stitch. *Work a wyib sl 3: *with the yarn to the back. Slip 3 stitches from the LHN by inserting the RHN from right to left.* Knit 3 stitches. Repeat from * until the last stitch. Knit 1 stitch. **Rows 5 and 6:** Using the MC, work 2 rows of stocking stitch, starting with a knit row. **Row 7:** Using the CC, knit 1 stitch. *Work a wyif sl 3. Knit 1 stitch.

3 Work a knit under 2 loops: *insert the RHN under both slip strands from bottom to top then from left to right into the stitch on the LHN.*

4 *Knit these 2 strands and the stitch together.* Knit 1 stitch. Repeat from * until the last stitch. Knit 1 stitch. **Row 8:** Knit 1 stitch. *Knit 3 stitches. Work a wyib sl 3. Repeat from * until the last stitch. Knit 1 stitch. **Rows 9 and 10:** Repeat Rows 5 and 6. **Row 11:** (Note: On the final repeat, work the sl 3 on Rows 11 and 12 as knit stitches instead.) Using the CC, knit 1 stitch. *Knit 1 stitch. Knit under the 2 loops. Knit 1 stitch. Work a wyif sl 3. Repeat from * until the last stitch. Knit 1 stitch. **Row 12:** Knit 1 stitch. *Work a wyib sl 3. Knit 3 stitches. Repeat from * until the last stitch. Knit 1 stitch.

Contrast Bow Tie Stitch

SKILL LEVEL
Advanced

MULTIPLES
6 (+1) stitches; 8 (+2) rows

STITCHES INCLUDED
knit, purl, wyif sl, knit under 3 loops

APPEARANCE
Single-sided

OTHER MATERIALS
2 contrasting yarns

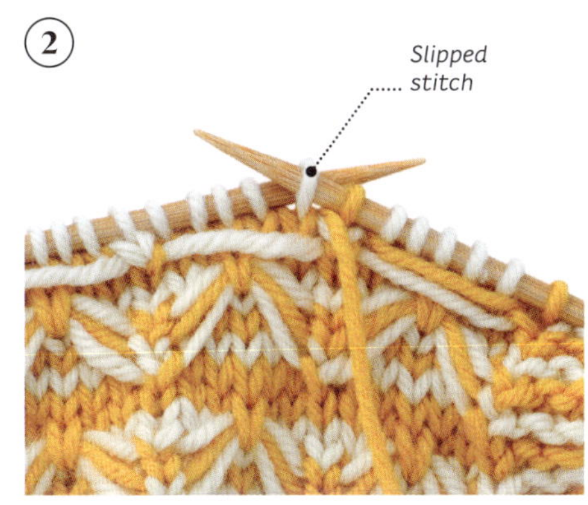

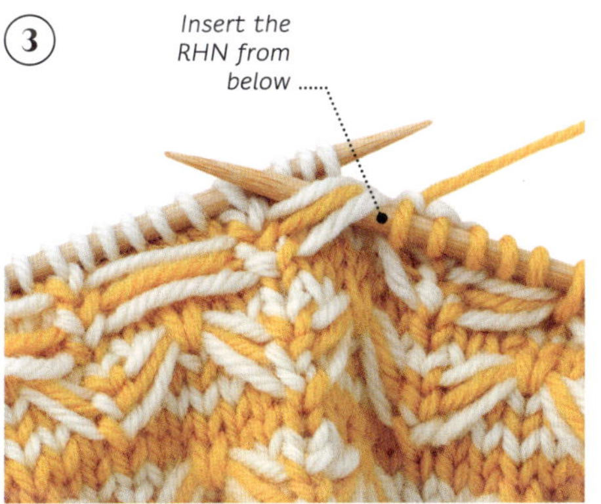

1 **Setup Rows 1 and 2:** Using the main colour (MC), work 2 rows of stocking: 1 row of knit followed by 1 row of purl. **Row 3:** *Using the contrast colour (CC), knit 1 stitch. Work a wyif sl 5: *bring the yarn to the front. Slip 5 stitches from the LHN by inserting the RHN from right to left into each stitch. Take the yarn to the back.* Repeat from * until the last stitch. Knit 1 stitch. **Row 4:** Purl all stitches.

2 **Row 5 and 6:** Using the MC, repeat Rows 3 and 4. **Rows 7 and 8:** Using the CC, repeat Rows 3 and 4.

3 **Row 9:** *Knit 3 stitches. Knit under 3 loops: *Insert the RHN into the 3 slip strands at the front by inserting from bottom to top.*

4 *Insert from left to right into the first stitch on the LHN.* Knit all 3 strands and the stitch together. Knit 2 stitches. Repeat from * until the last stitch. Knit 1 stitch. **Row 10:** Purl all the stitches.

The chart: Contrast Bow Tie Stitch

The setup row pattern repeat is shown with a blue line, and is only repeated across the row and not on any other repeats. Only repeat Rows 3–10.

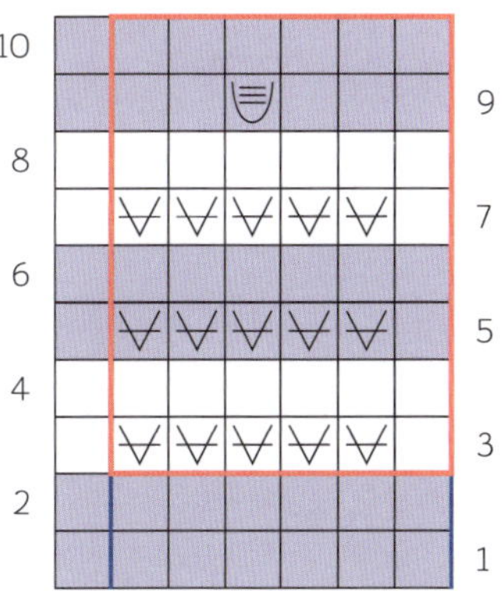

Stepped

SKILL LEVEL
Easy

MULTIPLES
4 (+2) stitches;
8 (+2) rows

STITCHES INCLUDED
knit, purl, wyib sl, wyif sl

APPEARANCE
Single-sided

OTHER MATERIALS
Contrasting yarn

Setup Row 1: Using MC, knit.
Setup Row 2: purl.
Row 3: Using CC, k1, *k3, wyib sl 1, rep from * until the last st, k1.
Row 4: p1, *wyif sl 1, p3, rep from * until the last st, p1.
Row 5: Using MC, k1, *wyib sl 1, k3, rep from * until the last st, k1.
Row 6: p1, *p3, wyif sl 1, rep from * until the last st, p1.
Row 7: Using CC, k1, *k1, wyib sl 1, k2, rep from * until the last st, k1.
Row 8: p1, *p2, wyif sl 1, p1, rep from * until the last st, p1.
Row 9: Using MC, k1, *k2, wyib sl 1, k1, rep from * until the last st, k1.
Row 10: p1, *p1, wyif sl 1, p2, rep from * until the last st, p1.

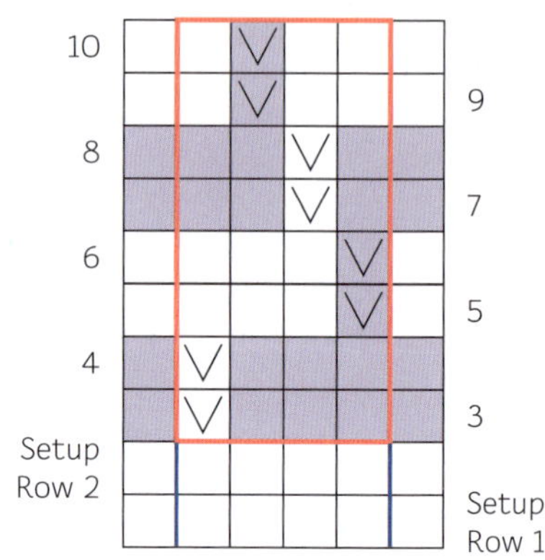

Working the slipped stitches

In Stepped, the yarn remains on the wrong side of the work at all times. This means that when working the wrong side rows, the yarn remains at the side facing you when slipping the stitches. The abbreviation "wyif" means with yarn in front. The "front" is the side that is facing you as you work that row, not the right side of the work.

Keep the yarn at the front when slipping the stitch

Corner Square

SKILL LEVEL
Intermediate

MULTIPLES
6 (+3) stitches; 16 rows

STITCHES INCLUDED
knit, wyib sl, wyif sl

APPEARANCE
Single-sided

OTHER MATERIALS
Contrasting yarn

Row 1: Using MC, knit.
Row 2: knit.
Row 3: Using CC, k1, wyib sl 1, *(wyib sl 1, k1) twice, wyib sl 2, rep from * until the last st, k1.
Row 4: k1, *wyif sl 2, (k1, wyif sl 1) twice, rep from * until the last 2 sts, wyif sl 1, k1.
Row 5: Repeat Row 1.
Row 6: Repeat Row 2.
Row 7: Repeat Row 3.
Row 8: Repeat Row 4.
Row 9: Repeat Row 1.
Row 10: Repeat Row 2.
Row 11: Using CC, k1, wyib sl 1, *k1, wyib sl 3, k1, wyib sl 1, rep from * until the last st, k1.
Row 12: k1, *wyif sl 1, k1, wyif sl 3, k1, rep from * until last 2 sts, wyif sl 1, k1.
Row 13: Repeat Row 1.
Row 14: Repeat Row 2.
Row 15: Repeat Row 11.
Row 16: Repeat Row 12.

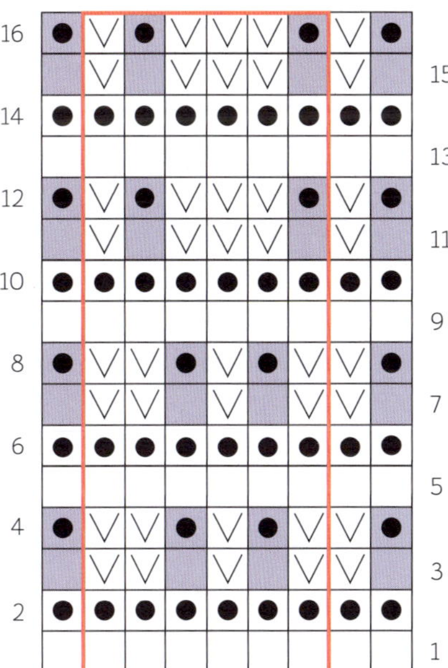

Mosaic knitting

Corner Square is an example of mosaic knitting. This is a subset of slip-stitch knitting that uses multiple colours. In mosaic knitting, the yarns are always kept at the wrong side of the work and two consecutive rows are worked in the same colour and identical pattern. It can be worked on a base of garter stitch, as used here, or in stocking stitch as in Stepped (see p.90).

Chain Link

SKILL LEVEL
Easy

MULTIPLES
8 (+1) stitches; 8 (+2) rows

STITCHES INCLUDED
knit, purl, wyib sl, wyif sl

APPEARANCE
Single-sided

OTHER MATERIALS
Contrasting yarn

Setup Row 1: Using CC, knit.
Setup Row 2: purl.
Row 3: Using MC, k1, *k3, wyib sl 1, k4, rep from * until the end.
Row 4: *p4, wyif sl 1, p3, rep from * until the last st, p1.
Row 5: Using CC, k1, *wyib sl 1, k5, wyib sl 1, k1, rep from * until the end.
Row 6: *p1, wyif sl 1, p5, wyif sl 1, rep from * until the last st, p1.
Row 7: Using MC, k1, *k1, wyib sl 1, k3, wyib sl 1, k2, rep from * until the end.
Row 8: *p2, wyif sl 1, p3, wyif sl 1, p1, rep from * until the last st, p1.
Row 9: Using CC, k1, *wyib sl 1, k5, wyib sl 1, k1, rep from * until the end.
Row 10: *p1, wyif sl 1, p5, wyif sl 1, rep from * until the last st, p1.

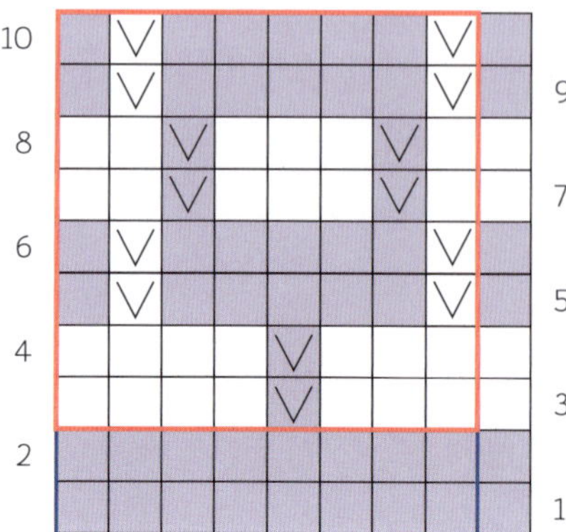

Tartan

SKILL LEVEL
Easy

MULTIPLES
10 stitches; 14 rows

STITCHES INCLUDED
knit, purl, wyib sl, wyif sl

APPEARANCE
Single-sided

OTHER MATERIALS
Contrasting yarn

Row 1: Using MC, knit.
Row 2: purl.
Row 3: Repeat Row 1.
Row 4: Repeat Row 2.
Row 5: Using CC, k2, wyib sl 1, k1, (wyib sl 1, k2) twice.
Row 6: (p2, wyif sl 1) twice, p1, wyif sl 1, p2.
Row 7: Repeat Row 3.
Row 8: Repeat Row 4.
Row 9: Repeat Row 5.
Row 10: Repeat Row 6.
Row 11: Repeat Row 3.
Row 12: Repeat Row 4.
Row 13: Repeat Row 5.
Row 14: Repeat Row 6.

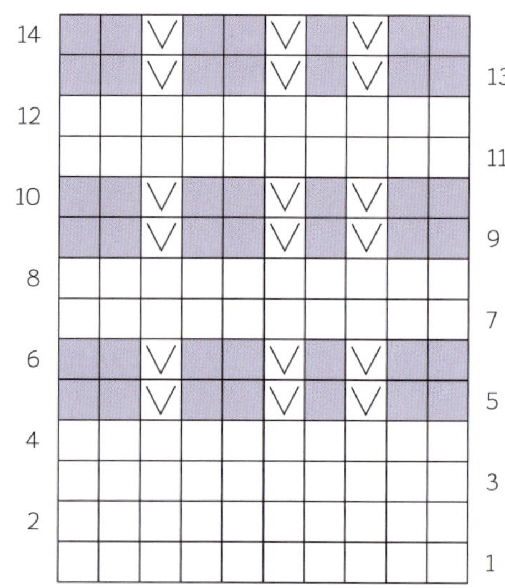

Brick Stitch

SKILL LEVEL
Easy

MULTIPLES
6 (+2) stitches; 8 rows

STITCHES INCLUDED
knit, purl, wyib sl, wyif sl

APPEARANCE
Single-sided

OTHER MATERIALS
Contrasting yarn

Row 1: Using MC, knit.
Row 2: knit.
Row 3: Using CC, k1, *wyib sl 2, k4, rep from * until the last st, k1.
Row 4: p1, *p4, wyif sl 2, rep from * until the last st, p1.
Row 5: Repeat Row 1.
Row 6: Repeat Row 2.
Row 7: k1, *k3, wyib sl 2, k1, rep from * until the last st, k1.
Row 8: p1, *p1, wyif sl 2, p3, rep from * until the last st, p1.

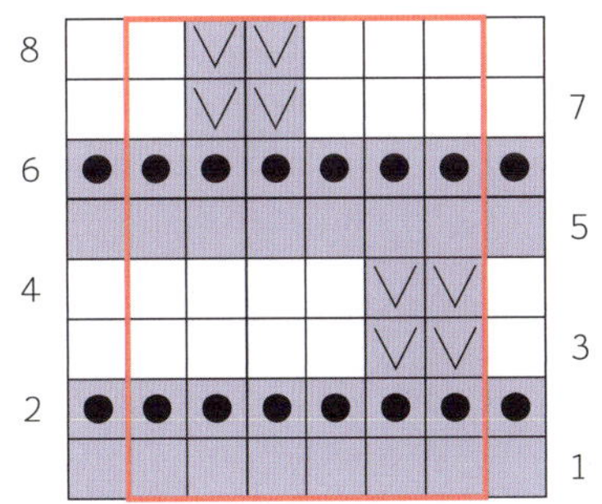

Peaks

SKILL LEVEL
Intermediate

MULTIPLES
6 (+1) stitches; 12 rows

STITCHES INCLUDED
knit, purl, wyib sl, wyif sl

APPEARANCE
Single-sided

OTHER MATERIALS
Contrasting yarn

Row 1: Using CC, knit.
Row 2: knit.
Row 3: Using MC, k1, *wyib sl 1, k3, wyib sl 1, k1, rep from * until the end.
Row 4: *p1, wyif sl 1, p3, wyif sl 1, rep from * until the last st, p1.
Row 5: Repeat Row 1.
Row 6: Repeat Row 2.
Row 7: k1, *(k1, wyib sl 1) twice, k2, rep from * until the end.
Row 8: *p2, (wyif sl 1, p1) twice, rep from * until the last st, p1.
Row 9: Repeat Row 1.
Row 10: Repeat Row 2.
Row 11: k1, *k2, wyib sl 1, k3, rep from * until the end.
Row 12: *p3, wyif sl 1, p2, rep from * until the last st, p1.

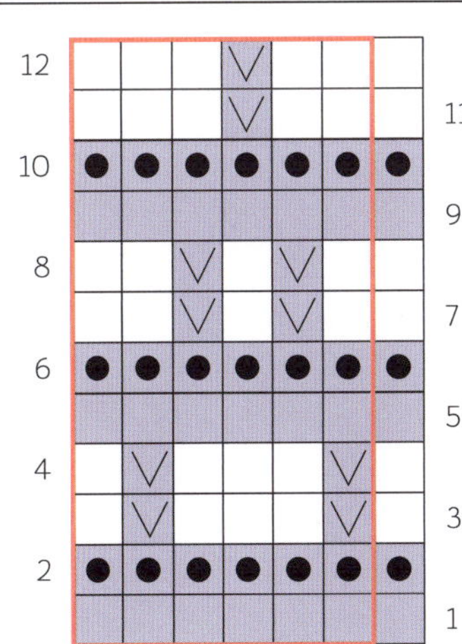

Stranded Colourwork

Stranded knitting uses two or more colours on the same row. Each stitch is a different colour, and the work alternates between the colours. When the yarn is not in use it is "stranded" across the back of the work, creating "floats". The stitch patterns in this section all create relatively short floats, with none of them being longer than 2.5cm (1in) in length. If working a stranded knitting stitch pattern with long floats, the yarns can be twisted or woven in on the back.

These floats in stranded knitting prevent the fabric from having the same stretch as other knitted fabrics; this means that the width is reduced, too. On the other hand, they help to create a denser, warmer piece of fabric such as the Fair Isle garments of the Shetland Isles and the vast array of Scandinavian sweaters, such as the Norwegian Marius® and Icelandic Lopapeysa.

The instructions guide you on how to work stranded knitting by using just one yarn at a time. However, if you are comfortable working continental (left-handed) and throwing (right-handed), a colour can be held in each hand.

Lice Stitch

SKILL LEVEL
Intermediate

MULTIPLES
4 (+1) stitches; 6 rows

STITCHES INCLUDED
knit, purl

APPEARANCE
Single-sided

OTHER MATERIALS
Contrasting yarn

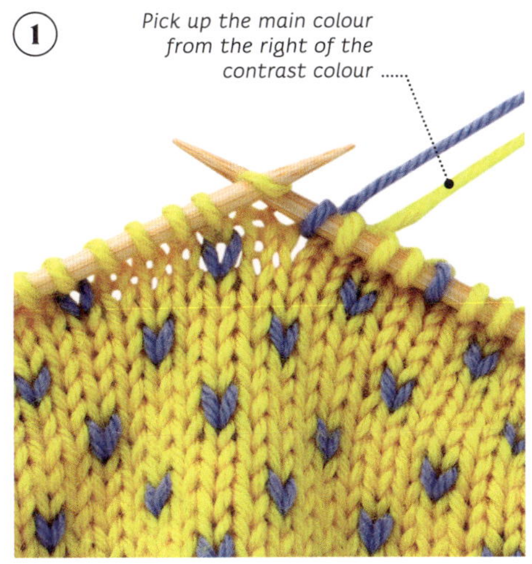

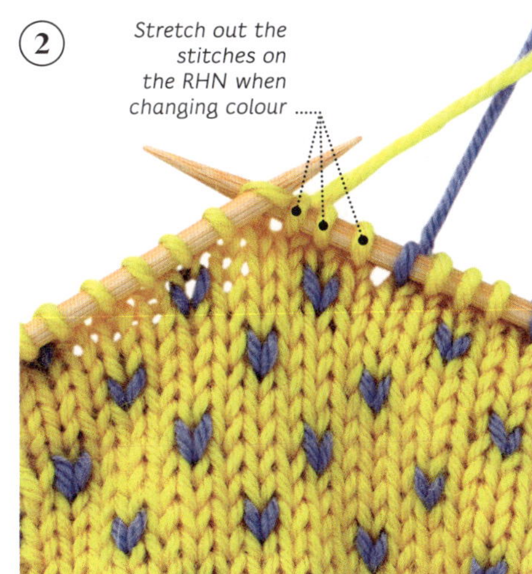

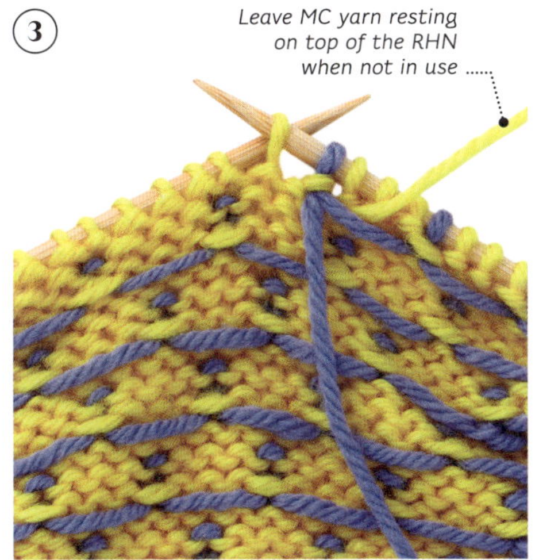

1 **Row 1:** Using the main colour (MC), knit 1 stitch. Using the contrast colour (CC), knit 1 stitch, leaving a tail at least 6cm (15in) long; this can be sewn in later. *Using the MC, knit 3 stitches.

2 Using the CC, knit 1 stitch. Repeat from * in Step 1 until the last 3 stitches. Knit 3 stitches in MC. **Rows 2 and 3:** Using the MC, work 2 rows of stocking stitch: 1 row of purl followed by 1 row of knit.

3 **Row 4:** Using the MC, purl 1 stitch.

4 *Using the CC, purl 1 stitch. Using the MC, purl 3 stitches. Repeat from * until the end. Using the MC, purl 2 stitches. **Rows 5 and 6:** Using the MC, work 2 rows of stocking stitch, starting with a knit row.

The chart: Lice Stitch

Each coloured square indicates a different colour of yarn to be used. The white boxes represent the MC (main colour) and the coloured boxes are the CC (contrast colour).

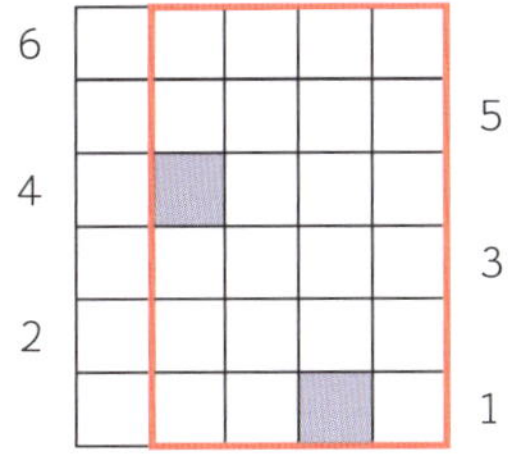

1 x 1 Stranding

SKILL LEVEL
Intermediate

MULTIPLES
2 stitches; 2 rows

STITCHES INCLUDED
knit, purl

APPEARANCE
Single-sided

OTHER MATERIALS
Contrasting yarn

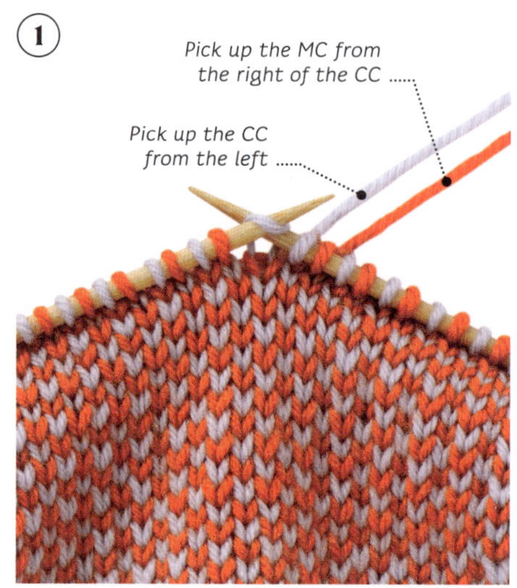

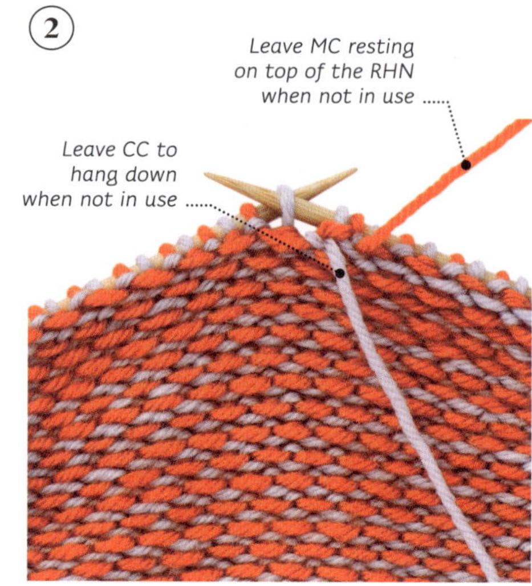

1 **Row 1:** Using the main colour (MC), knit 1 stitch. Using the contrast colour (CC), knit one stitch, leaving a tail. *Using the MC, knit 1 stitch. Using the CC, knit 1 stitch. Repeat from * until the end.

2 **Row 2:** Using the MC, purl 1 stitch. Using the CC, purl 1 stitch.

The chart: 1 x 1 Stranding

This is a very simple chart. The stitches create a stocking stitch fabric. Theblank squares are knit on the right side rows and purl on the wrong side. However, the colour of the yarn is alternated every stitch.

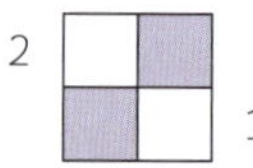

2 x 2 Stranding

SKILL LEVEL
Intermediate

MULTIPLES
4 stitches; 4 rows

STITCHES INCLUDED
knit, purl

APPEARANCE
Single-sided

OTHER MATERIALS
Contrasting yarn

1 **Row 1:** Using the main colour (MC), knit 2 stitches. Using the contrast colour (CC), knit 2 stitches, leaving a tail. *Using the MC, knit 2 stitches. Using the CC, knit 2 stitches. Repeat from * until the end.

2 **Row 2:** Using the CC, purl 2 stitches. Using the MC, purl 2 stitches.

3 **Row 3:** Using the CC, knit 2 stitches. Using the MC, knit 2 stitches. Repeat until the end. Row 4: Using the MC, purl 2 stitches. Using the CC, purl 2 stitches.

The chart: 2 x 2 Stranding

The chart shows that the wrong side rows are identical to the previous right side row. This means that you can read your knitting and purl each stitch in the same colour as the one on the needle without having to refer to the chart.

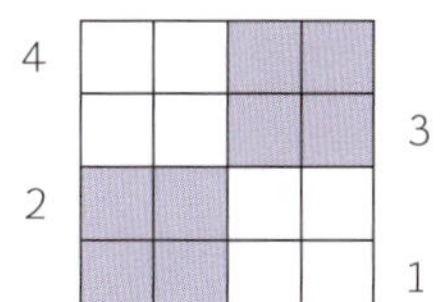

Corrugated Check

SKILL LEVEL
Intermediate

MULTIPLES
2 stitches; 4 rows

STITCHES INCLUDED
knit, purl

APPEARANCE
Single-sided

OTHER MATERIALS
Contrasting yarn

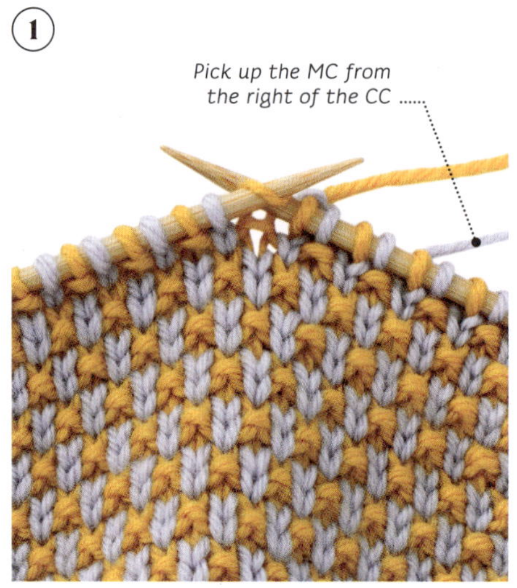

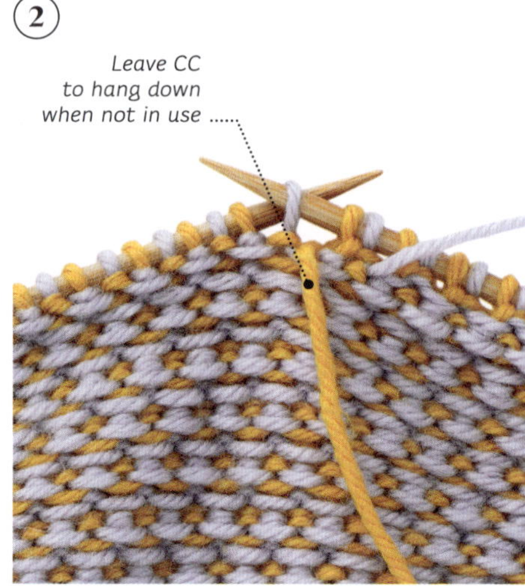

1 **Row 1:** Using the main colour (MC), knit 1 stitch. Using the contrast colour (CC), knit one stitch, leaving a tail. *Using the MC, knit 1 stitch. Using the CC, knit 1 stitch. Repeat from * until the end.

2 **Row 2:** Using the CC, take the yarn to the back of the work. Knit 1 stitch then bring the yarn to the front. Using the MC, purl 1 stitch.

3 **Row 3:** Using the CC, knit 1 stitch. Using the MC, knit 1 stitch. **Row 4:** Using the MC, purl 1 stitch. Take the CC to the back of the work. Using the CC, knit 1 stitch then bring to the front of the work.

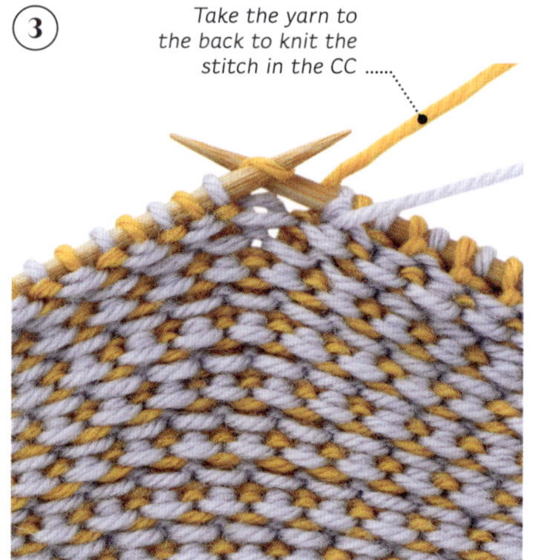

The chart: Corrugated Check

As in this chart, some patterns can use a different colour yarn paired with a different stitch. The contrast colour has a purl dot on the even rows, which indicates that the CC is used to knit the stitch on the wrong side.

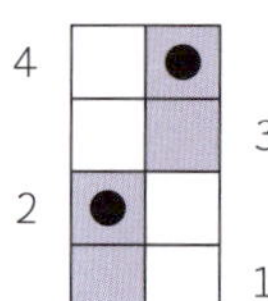

2 x 2 Corrugated Ribbing

SKILL LEVEL
Intermediate

MULTIPLES
4 (+2) stitches; 2 rows

STITCHES INCLUDED
knit, purl

APPEARANCE
Single-sided

OTHER MATERIALS
Contrasting yarn

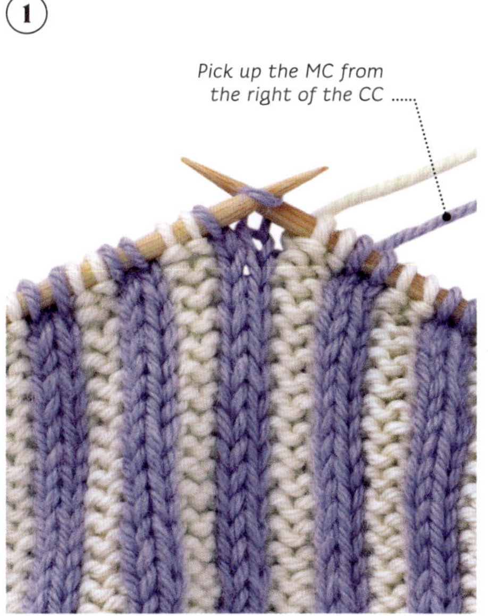

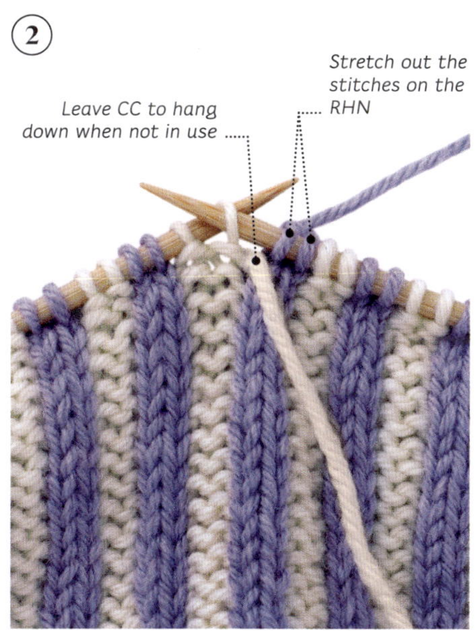

1 **Row 1:** Using the main colour (MC), knit 2 stitches. Using the contrast colour (CC), leave a tail at the back and bring the yarn to the front. Purl 2 stitches, then take the yarn to the back. Using the MC, knit 2 stitches.

2 *Using the CC, bring the yarn to the front. Purl 2 stitches, then take the yarn to the back. Using the MC, knit 2 stitches. Repeat from * until the end.

3 **Row 2:** *Using the MC, purl 2 stitches. Using the CC, take the yarn to the back of the work. Knit 2 stitches then bring the yarn to the front. Repeat from * until the last 2 stitches. Using the MC, purl 2 stitches.

The chart: Corrugated Ribbing

The red outline shows the pattern repeat. The first two stitches are worked before the pattern repeat stitches are repeated across the row, to create an extra MC stripe.

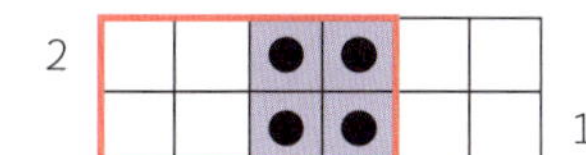

Tessellated Flowers

SKILL LEVEL
Intermediate

MULTIPLES
6 stitches; 8 rows

STITCHES INCLUDED
knit, purl

APPEARANCE
Single-sided

OTHER MATERIALS
2 contrasting yarns

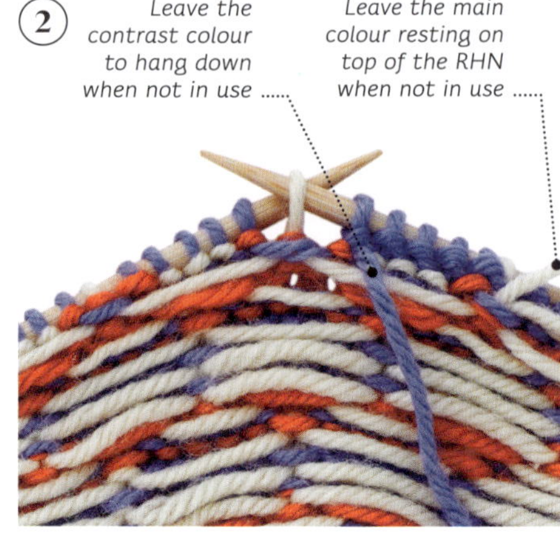

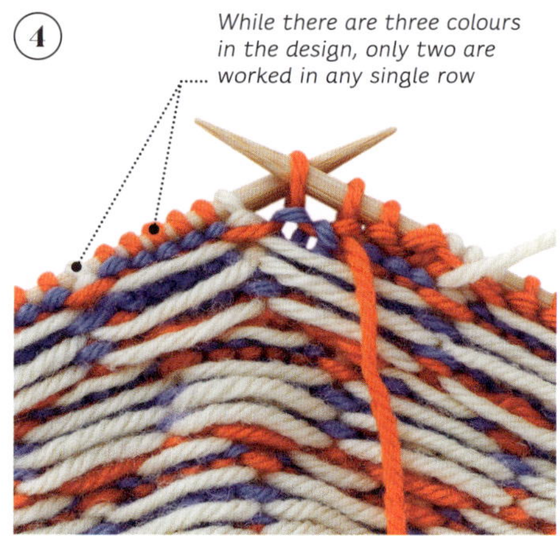

1 **Row 1:** Using the contrast colour 1 (CC1), knit 2 stitches. Using the main colour (MC), leave a tail and knit 1 stitch. Using the CC1, knit 3 stitches.

2 **Row 2:** Using the CC1, purl 3 stitches. Using the MC, purl 1 stitch. Using the CC1, purl 2 stitches.

3 **Row 3:** Leave CC1 to hang. Using the contrast colour 2 (CC2), knit 2 stitches. Using the MC, knit 1 stitch. Using the CC2, knit 3 stitches.

4 **Row 4:** Using the CC2, purl 2 stitches. Using the MC, purl 3 stitches. Using the CC2, purl 1 stitch. **Row 5:** Leave CC2 to hang. Using CC1, knit five stitches. Using the MC, knit 1 stitch. **Row 6:** Using the MC, purl 1 stitch. Using the CC1, purl five stitches. **Row 7:** Leave CC1 to hang. Using the CC2, knit five stitches. Using the MC, knit 1 stitch. **Row 8:** Using the MC, purl 2 stitches. Using the CC2, purl 3 stitches. Using the MC, purl 1 stitch.

Wave

SKILL LEVEL
Intermediate

MULTIPLES
4 (+1) stitches; 6 rows

STITCHES INCLUDED
knit, purl

APPEARANCE
Single-sided

OTHER MATERIALS
Contrasting yarn

Row 1: k1 in CC, *k1 in CC, k1 in MC, k2 in CC, rep from * until the end.
Row 2: *(p1 in MC, p1 in CC) twice, rep from * until the last st, p1 in MC.
Row 3: k1 in MC, *(k1 in CC, k1 in MC) twice, rep from * until the end.
Row 4: *p1 in MC, p3 in CC, rep from * until the last st, p1 in MC.
Row 5: Using MC, knit.
Row 6: purl.

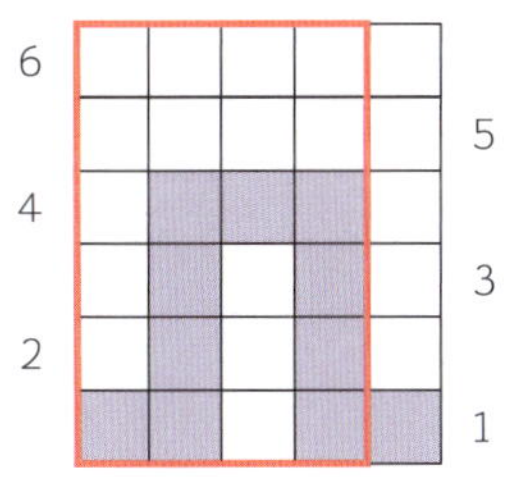

Dots and Dashes

SKILL LEVEL
Intermediate

MULTIPLES
6 (+1) stitches; 10 rows

STITCHES INCLUDED
knit, purl

APPEARANCE
Single-sided

OTHER MATERIALS
Contrasting yarn

Row 1: k1 in CC, *k2 in MC, k4 in CC, rep from * until the end.
Row 2: *p1 in CC, p2 in MC, p3 in CC, rep from * until the last st, p1 in CC.
Row 3: k1 in CC, *(k2 in MC, k1 in CC) twice, rep from * until the end.
Row 4: *p4 in CC, p2 in MC, rep from * until the last st, p1 in CC.
Row 5: k1 in CC, *k3 in CC, k2 in MC, k1 in CC, rep from * until the end.
Row 6: Repeat Row 4.
Row 7: Repeat Row 5.
Row 8: *(p1 in CC, p2 in MC) twice, rep from * until the last st, p1 in CC.
Row 9: Repeat Row 1.
Row 10: Repeat Row 2.

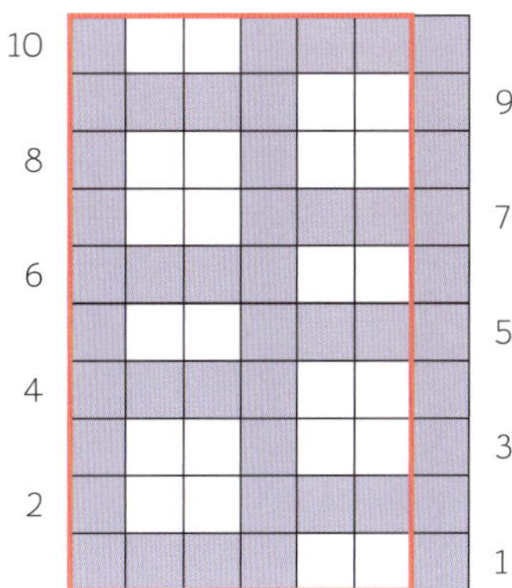

Butterfly

SKILL LEVEL
Intermediate

MULTIPLES
8 stitches; 6 rows

STITCHES INCLUDED
knit, purl

APPEARANCE
Single-sided

OTHER MATERIALS
Contrasting yarn

Row 1: k2 in MC, k2 in CC, k1 in MC, k3 in CC.
Row 2: p2 in CC, p2 in MC, p3 in CC, p1 in MC.
Row 3: k3 in CC, k4 in MC, k1 in CC.
Row 4: p4 in CC, p3 in MC, p1 in CC.
Row 5: k2 in CC, k2 in MC, k3 in CC, k1 in MC.
Row 6: p2 in MC, p2 in CC, p1 in MC, p3 in CC.

Animal Print

SKILL LEVEL
Intermediate

MULTIPLES
9 stitches; 10 rows

STITCHES INCLUDED
knit, purl

APPEARANCE
Single-sided

OTHER MATERIALS
Contrasting yarn

Row 1: k2 in MC, k1 in CC, k4 in MC, k2 in CC.
Row 2: p2 in CC, p4 in MC, p2 in CC, p1 in MC.
Row 3: k1 in MC, k1 in CC, k2 in MC, k2 in CC, k2 in MC, k1 in CC.
Row 4: p2 in MC, p3 in CC, p4 in MC.
Row 5: k3 in CC, k1 in MC, k1 in CC, k4 in MC.
Row 6: p1 in MC, p1 in CC, p4 in MC, p3 in CC.
Row 7: k1 in MC, k1 in CC, k3 in MC, k3 in CC, k1 in MC.
Row 8: p1 in MC, p2 in CC, p2 in MC, p1 in CC, p3 in MC.
Row 9: k1 in CC, k2 in MC, k2 in CC, k4 in MC.
Row 10: p1 in CC, p2 in MC, p2 in CC, p3 in MC, p1 in CC.

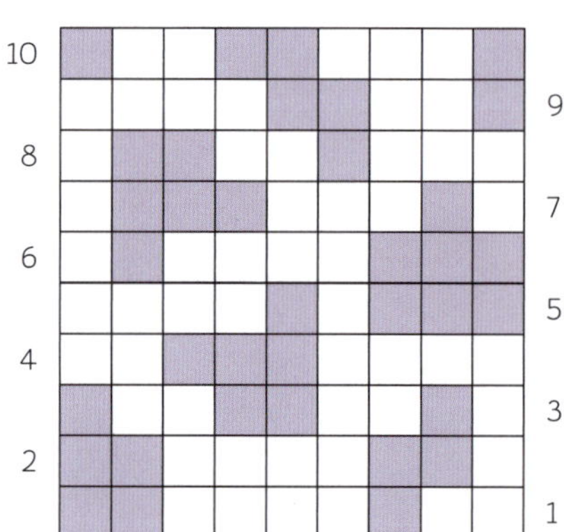

Unbalanced Checkerboard

SKILL LEVEL
Intermediate

MULTIPLES
3 (+1) stitches; 8 rows

STITCHES INCLUDED
knit, purl

APPEARANCE
Single-sided

OTHER MATERIALS
Contrasting yarn

Row 1: k1 in MC, *k2 in CC, k1 in MC, rep from * until the end.
Row 2: *p1 in MC, p2 in CC, rep from * until last st, p1 in MC.
Row 3: k1 in CC, *k2 in MC, k1 in CC, rep from * until the end.
Row 4: *p1 in CC, p2 in MC, rep from * until last st, p1 in CC.
Row 5: Repeat Row 1.
Row 6: Repeat Row 4.
Row 7: Repeat Row 3.
Row 8: Repeat Row 4.

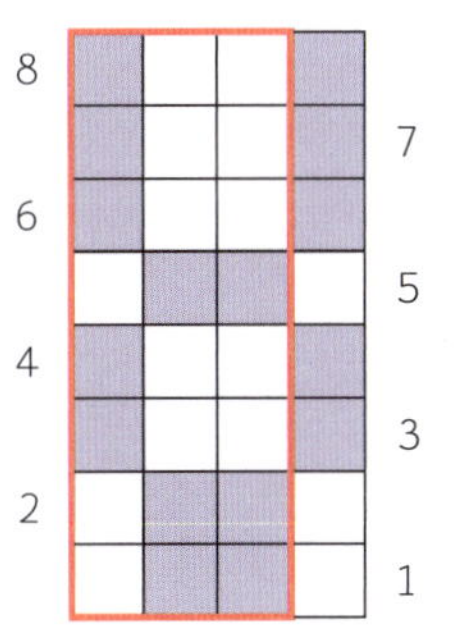

Ellipses

SKILL LEVEL
Intermediate

MULTIPLES
12 stitches; 22 rows

STITCHES INCLUDED
knit, purl

APPEARANCE
Single-sided

OTHER MATERIALS
Contrasting yarn

Row 1: k2 in CC, k1 in MC, (k1 in CC, k2 in MC) twice, k1 in CC, k1 in MC, k1 in CC.
Row 2: *p2 in MC, p1 in CC, rep from * until the end.
Row 3: *k1 in CC, k2 in MC, rep from * until the end.
Row 4: p2 in MC, p2 in CC, p1 in MC, p1 in CC, p1 in MC, p2 in CC, p2 in MC, p1 in CC.
Row 5: k2 in CC, k2 in MC, k5 in CC, k2 in MC, k1 in CC.
Row 6: p2 in CC, (p2 in MC, p3 in CC) twice.
Row 7: k1 in CC, k1 in MC, k2 in CC, k2 in MC, k1 in CC, k2 in MC, k2 in CC, k1 in MC.
Row 8: Repeat Row 2.
Row 9: Repeat Row 3.
Row 10: p2 in MC, p1 in CC, p1 in MC, p3 in CC, p1 in MC, p1 in CC, p2 in MC, p1 in CC.
Row 11: k1 in CC, k2 in MC, k1 in CC, k1 in MC, k3 in CC, k1 in MC, k1 in CC, k2 in MC.
Row 12: Repeat Row 10.
Row 13: Repeat Row 3.
Row 14: Repeat Row 2.
Row 15: Repeat Row 7.
Row 16: Repeat Row 6.
Row 17: Repeat Row 1.
Row 18: Repeat Row 4.
Row 19: Repeat Row 3.
Row 20: Repeat Row 2.
Row 21: Repeat Row 1.
Row 22: p1 in CC, p1 in MC, (p1 in CC, p2 in MC) twice, p1 in CC, p1 in MC, p2 in CC.

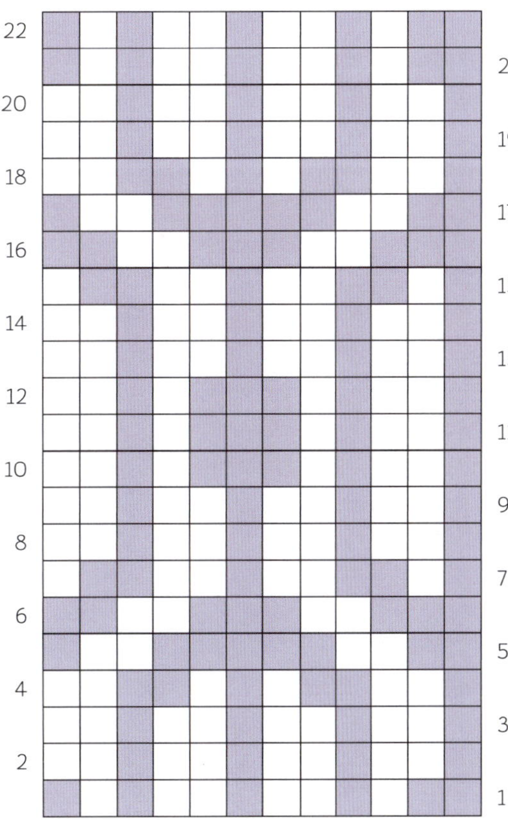

Openwork and Lace

Eyelets

Eyelets are a basic form of lace knitting. They are used with knit and purl fabrics, with the proportion of solid fabric tending to be higher than the yarnover "holes". They are easier to work than other types of lace knitting because of the high number of basic knit and purl stitches. Eyelets are created with single yarnovers (see p.42) and decrease pairs (see p.44). This creates an open hole in the fabric but doesn't change the stitch count.

These open holes create a delicate fabric, which tends to be used for decorative items such as shawls and baby clothes, though eyelets on a cardigan works well too.

Basic Eyelet

SKILL LEVEL
Intermediate

MULTIPLES
4 stitches; 8 rows

STITCHES INCLUDED
knit, purl, k2tog, ssk, yo

APPEARANCE
Single-sided

1 Insert from left to right into both stitches

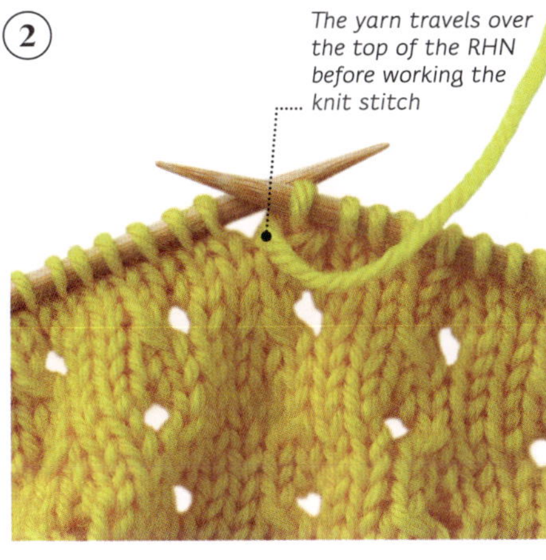

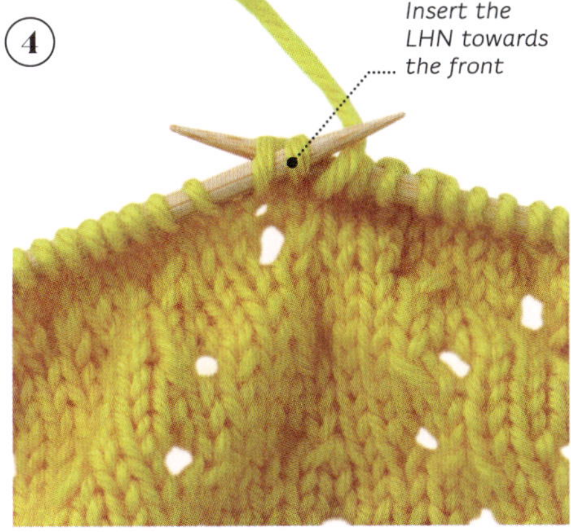

1 **Row 1:** Knit 1 stitch. Knit 2 stitches together: *insert the RHN from left to right into the second stitch and then the first stitch on the LHN. Knit these 2 stitches together.*

2 Bring the yarn to the front between the needles. Knit one stitch; the yarn will travel over the RHN as part of this stitch, creating a yarnover. **Rows 2–4:** Work 3 rows of stocking stitch, alternating 1 row of purl with 1 row of knit, starting with a purl row.

3 **Row 5:** Knit 1 stitch. Work a yarnover. Work an ssk: *insert the RHN into the first stitch from left to right and slip from the LHN to the RHN. Repeat for the second stitch.*

4 *Insert the LHN from left to right and towards the front into both stitches just slipped. Knit these stitches together.* Knit 1 stitch. **Rows 6–8:** Work 3 rows of stocking stitch, starting with a purl row.

The chart: Basic Eyelet

This chart includes both increases and decreases. However, the number of boxes remains the same and there are no greyed "no stitch" squares, which shows that the stitch count remains the same throughout.

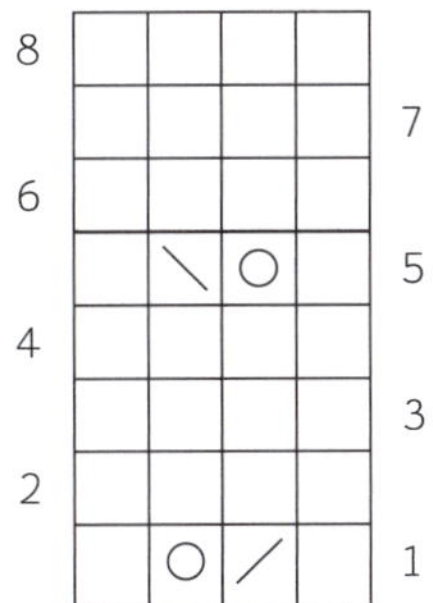

V Eyelets

SKILL LEVEL
Intermediate

MULTIPLES
8 (+1) stitches; 6 rows

STITCHES INCLUDED
knit, purl, k2tog, ssk, yo

APPEARANCE
Single-sided

1 **Row 1:** * Knit 2 stitches. Work a k2tog (see p.38). Work a yarnover (see p.42). Knit the next stitch. Work a yarnover.

2 Work an ssk (see p.38). Knit 1 stitch. Repeat from * until the last stitch. Knit 1 stitch. **Row 2:** Purl all stitches. **Row 3:** ** Knit 1 stitch. Knit 2 stitches together. Work a yarnover. Knit 3 stitches. Work a yarnover. Work an ssk. Repeat from ** until the last stitch. Knit 1 stitch. **Rows 4–6:** Work 3 rows of stocking stitch, alternating 1 row of purl with 1 row of knit, starting with a purl row.

Punchwork

SKILL LEVEL
Intermediate

MULTIPLES
3 (+1) stitches; 4 rows

STITCHES INCLUDED
knit, purl, yo, k2tog

APPEARANCE
Single-sided

1 **Row 1:** Knit 1 stitch. *Bring the yarn to the front between the needles.

2 Knit 2 stitches together (see p.38). Knit 1 stitch. Repeat from * until the end. **Row 2:** Purl all the stitches. **Row 3:** Knit 1 stitch. *Knit 2 stitches together. Work a yarnover. Knit 1 stitch. **Row 4:** Purl all the stitches. The yarn will travel over the RHN as part of this stitch, creating a yarnover.

Contrast Eyelet Band

SKILL LEVEL
Intermediate

MULTIPLES
2 (+2) stitches; 10 rows

STITCHES INCLUDED
knit, purl, yo, p2tog

APPEARANCE
Single-sided

OTHER MATERIALS
Contrasting yarn

1 **Rows 1–4:** Using the main colour, work 4 rows in stocking stitch: alternating one row of knit with one row of purl, starting with a knit row. **Rows 5 and 6:** Using the contrast colour, knit two rows. **Row 7:** Purl 1 stitch. *Purl 2 stitches together (see p.39).

2 Work a purl to purl yarnover (see p.43) Repeat from * until the last stitch. Purl 1 stitch. **Row 8:** Knit all stitches. **Rows 9 and 10:** Using the main colour, work 2 rows in stocking stitch, starting with a knit row.

The chart: Contrast Eyelet Band

Much of the contrast band is worked in purl stitches to create a textured band on the stocking stitch surface. The chart represents that texture with the purl dots.

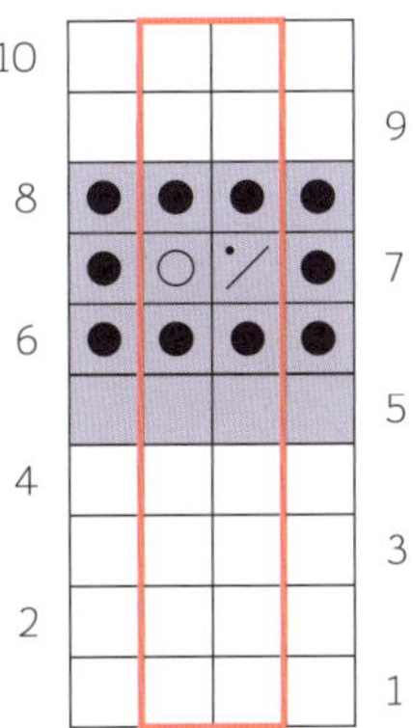

Clover Lace

SKILL LEVEL
Intermediate

MULTIPLES
10 stitches; 8 rows

STITCHES INCLUDED
knit, purl, yo, k2tog, ssk

APPEARANCE
Single-sided

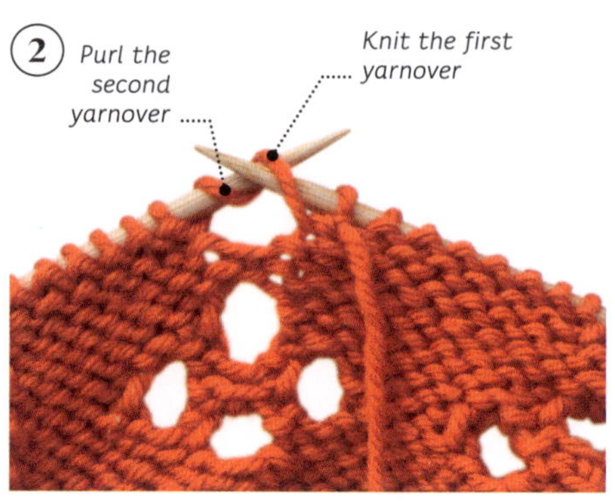

1 **Row 1:** Knit 3 stitches. Work an ssk (see p.38). Work a double yarnover: *bring the yarn to the front between the needles, then take the yarn over the top of the RHN before bringing it back to the front between the needles. The yarn will travel over the RHN as the next stitch is worked, creating a second yarnover.* Knit 2 stitches together (see p.38). Knit 3 stitches.

2 **Row 2:** Purl 4 stitches. Purl the first yarnover and drop just the first loop from the LHN. Take the yarn to the back. Knit the second yarnover and drop from the LHN. Bring the yarn to the front. Purl 4 stitches. **Row 3:** Knit 1 stitch. *Work an ssk. Work a double yarnover. Knit 2 stitches together. Repeat from * once more. Knit 1 stitch. **Row 4:** *Purl 3 stitches. Knit 1 stitch. Repeat from * once more. Purl 2 stitches. **Row 5:** Repeat Row 1. **Row 6:** Repeat Row 2. **Rows 7 and 8:** Work 2 rows of stocking stitch: 1 row of knit followed by 1 row purl.

Purl Eyelet Rib

SKILL LEVEL
Intermediate

MULTIPLES
4 (+3) stitches; 4 rows

STITCHES INCLUDED
knit, purl, yo, k2tog

APPEARANCE
Different, but both sides can be used as right side

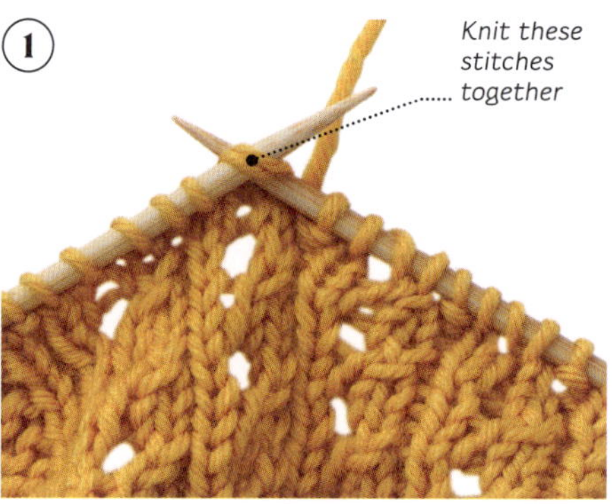

1 **Row 1:** Purl 1 stitch. *Knit 1 stitch. Purl 3 stitches. Repeat from * until the last 2 stitches. Knit 1 stitch. Purl 1 stitch. **Row 2:** Knit 1 stitch. Purl 1 stitch. *Knit 2 stitches together: *insert the RHN from left to right into the second then first stitch on the LHN. Knit these 2 stitches together.*

2 Work a yarnover (see p.42). Knit the next stitch. Purl 1 stitch. Repeat from * until the last stitch. Knit 1 stitch. **Row 3:** Repeat Row 1. **Row 4:** Knit 1 stitch. Purl 1 stitch. *Knit 3 stitches. Purl 1 stitch. Repeat from * until the last stitch. Knit 1 stitch.

Elongated Lace Rib

SKILL LEVEL
Intermediate

MULTIPLES
4 stitches; 8 rows

STITCHES INCLUDED
knit, purl, yo, k2tog, ssk

APPEARANCE
Single-sided

Row 1: p1, k2tog, yo, p1.
Row 2: k1, p2, k1.
Row 3: p1, k2, p1.
Row 4: k1, p2, k1.
Row 5: p1, yo, ssk, p1.
Row 6: k1, p2, k1.
Row 7: p1, k2, p1.
Row 8: k1, p2, k1.

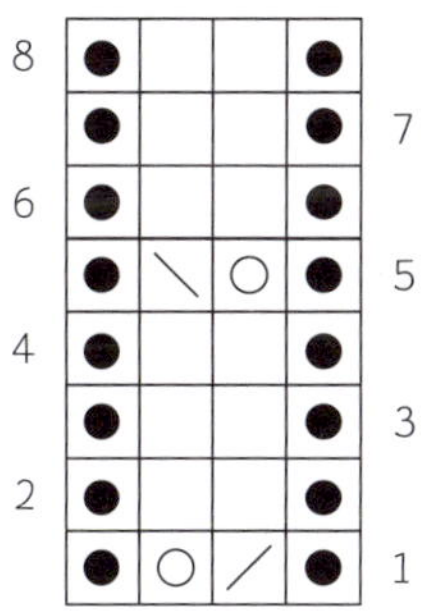

Working the yarnovers

This stitch involves yarnovers that have knit and purl stitches surrounding them (see pp.42–43). Make sure that the yarn travels anticlockwise and wraps over the RHN once, and ends at the correct side of the work for the next stitch.

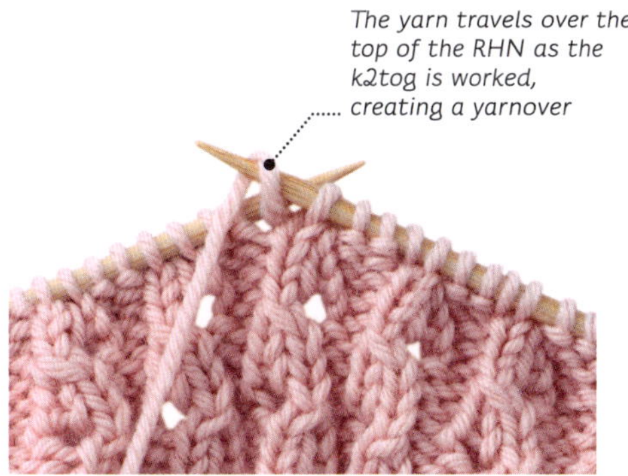

The yarn travels over the top of the RHN as the k2tog is worked, creating a yarnover

Eyelet Meander

SKILL LEVEL
Easy

MULTIPLES
5 (+1) stitches; 8 rows

STITCHES INCLUDED
knit, purl, yo, k2tog, ssk

APPEARANCE
Single-sided

Row 1: k1, *k1, k2tog, yo, k2, rep from * until the end.
Row 2: purl.
Row 3: k1, *k2tog, yo, k3, rep from * until the end.
Row 4: purl.
Row 5: k1, *k1, yo, ssk, k2, rep from * until the end.
Row 6: purl.
Row 7: k1, *k2, yo, ssk, k1, rep from * until the end.
Row 8: purl.

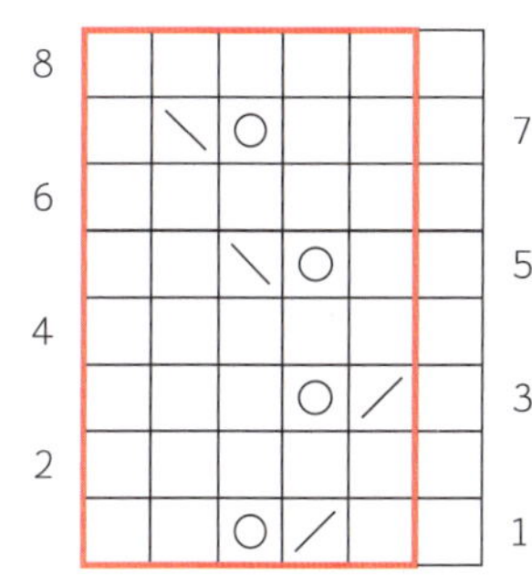

Openwork Hourglass

SKILL LEVEL
Intermediate

MULTIPLES
6 (+3) stitches; 8 rows

STITCHES INCLUDED
knit, purl, yo, k2tog, ssk

APPEARANCE
Single-sided

Row 1: k1, *yo, ssk, k2tog, yo, k2, rep from * until the last 2 sts, yo, ssk.
Row 2: purl.
Row 3: k1, *k2tog, yo twice, ssk, k2, rep from * until the last 2 sts, k2.
Row 4: p2, *p4, k1, p1, rep from * until the last st, p1.
Row 5: k2tog, yo, *k2, yo, ssk, k2tog, yo, rep from * until the last st, k1.
Row 6: purl.
Row 7: k2, *k2, k2tog, yo twice, ssk, rep from * until the last st, k1.
Row 8: p1, *p2, k1, p3, rep from until the last 2 sts, p2.

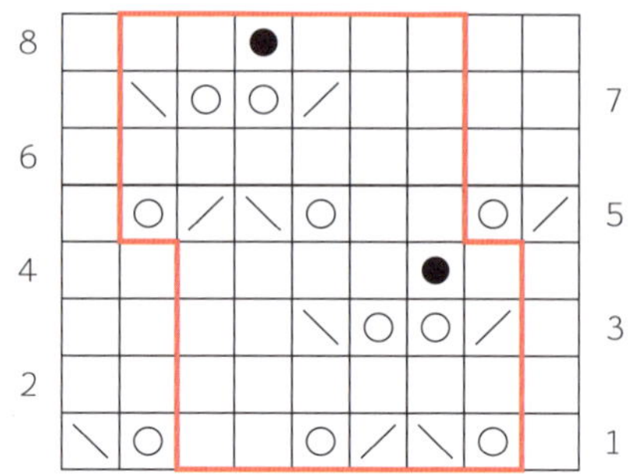

Working the double yarnovers

The double yarnover creates a larger hole in the fabric. When returning to this stitch on the wrong side, the first yarnover is purled and only the first loop is dropped. The second yarnover wrap is then knitted.

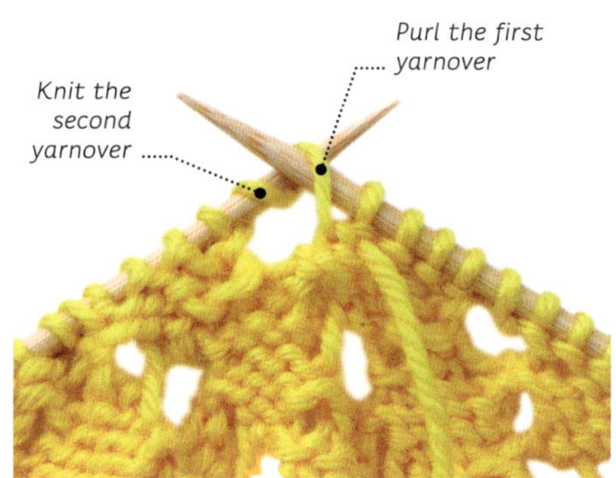

Woven Lace

SKILL LEVEL
Intermediate

MULTIPLES
8 (+1) stitches; 12 rows

STITCHES INCLUDED
knit, purl, yo, k2tog, ssk

APPEARANCE
Single-sided

Row 1: k1, *k1, p5, k2, rep from * until the end.
Row 2: *p2, k5, p1, rep from * until the last st, p1.
Row 3: Repeat Row 1.
Row 4: Repeat Row 2.
Row 5: k1, *ssk, yo, k3, yo, k2tog, k1, rep from * until the end.
Row 6: purl.
Row 7: p1, *p2, k3, p3, rep from * until the end.
Row 8: *k3, p3, k2, rep from * until the last st, k1.
Row 9: Repeat Row 7.
Row 10: Repeat Row 8.
Row 11: k1, *k1, yo, k2tog, k1, ssk, yo, k2, rep from * until the end.
Row 12: purl.

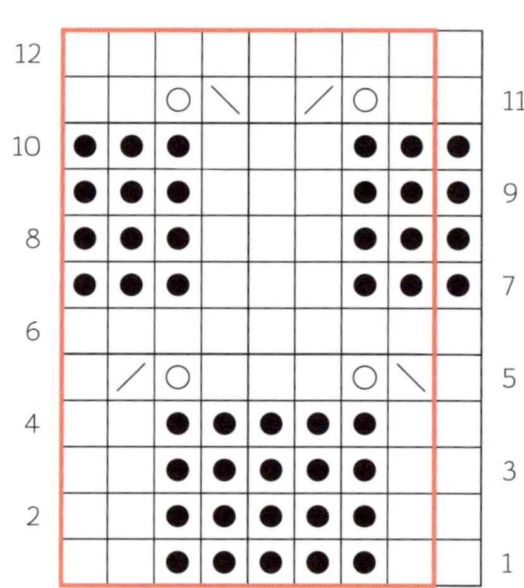

Ladder Stitch

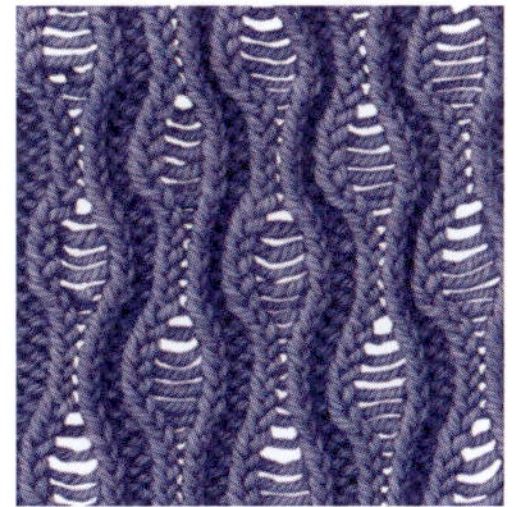

SKILL LEVEL
Intermediate

MULTIPLES
8 stitches; 14 (+4) rows

STITCHES INCLUDED
knit, purl, k1-tbl, p1-tbl, yo, drop stitch

APPEARANCE
Single-sided

Setup Row 1: *p1, k2-tbl, p1, rep from * until the end.
Setup Row 2: *k1, p2-tbl, k1, rep from * until the end.
Setup Row 3: p1, k1-tbl, yo, k1-tbl, p2, k2-tbl, p1.
Setup Row 4: k1, p2-tbl, k2, p1-tbl, p1, p1-tbl, k1.
Row 5: p1, k1-tbl, k1, k1-tbl, p2, k2-tbl, p1.
Row 6: k1, p2-tbl, k2, p1-tbl, p1, p1-tbl, k1.
Row 7: Repeat Row 5.
Row 8: Repeat Row 6.
Row 9: p1, k1-tbl, drop stitch, k1-tbl, p2, k1-tbl, yo, k1-tbl, p1.
Row 10: k1, p1-tbl, p1, p1-tbl, k2, p2-tbl, k1.
Row 11: p1, k2-tbl, p2, k1-tbl, k1, k1-tbl, p1.
Row 12: k1, p1-tbl, p1, p1-tbl, k2, p2-tbl, k1.
Row 13: Repeat Row 11.
Row 14: Repeat Row 12.
Row 15: (Note: on final repeat, omit the yarnover) p1, k1-tbl, yo, k1-tbl, p2, k1-tbl, drop stitch, k1-tbl, p1.
Row 16: Repeat Row 5.

Row											Row
16	●	ℓ	■	ℓ	●	●	ℓ		ℓ	●	
	●	ℓ	∪	ℓ	●	●	ℓ	○	ℓ	●	15
14	●	ℓ		ℓ	●	●	ℓ	■	ℓ	●	
	●	ℓ		ℓ	●	●	ℓ	■	ℓ	●	13
12	●	ℓ		ℓ	●	●	ℓ	■	ℓ	●	
	●	ℓ		ℓ	●	●	ℓ	■	ℓ	●	11
10	●	ℓ		ℓ	●	●	ℓ	■	ℓ	●	
	●	ℓ	○	ℓ	●	●	ℓ	∪	ℓ	●	9
8	●	ℓ	■	ℓ	●	●	ℓ		ℓ	●	
	●	ℓ	■	ℓ	●	●	ℓ		ℓ	●	7
6	●	ℓ	■	ℓ	●	●	ℓ		ℓ	●	
	●	ℓ	■	ℓ	●	●	ℓ		ℓ	●	5
Setup Row 4	●	ℓ	■	ℓ	●	●	ℓ		ℓ	●	
	●	ℓ	■	ℓ	●	●	ℓ	○	ℓ	●	Setup Row 3
Setup Row 2	●	ℓ	■	ℓ	●	●	ℓ	■	ℓ	●	
	●	ℓ	■	ℓ	●	●	ℓ	■	ℓ	●	Setup Row 1

Working the drop stitch

To create the ladder stitch, the yarnovers from a previous row are dropped from the needle. Help the stitch to unravel down to the yarnover to create the horizontal bars.

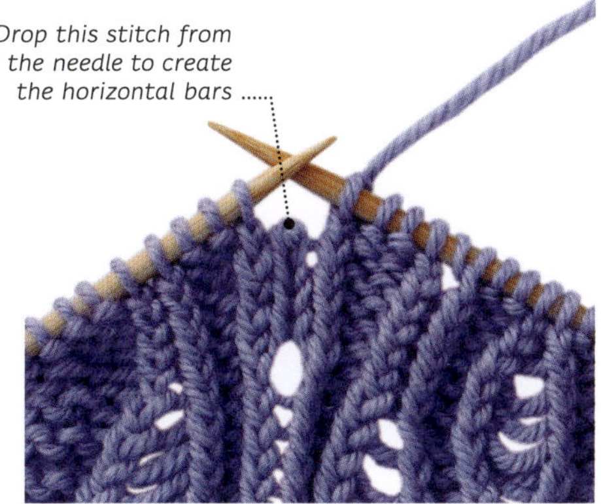

Drop this stitch from the needle to create the horizontal bars

Lace

Lace knitting uses eyelets, but often in conjunction with other types of decreases, such as the double decrease. The yarnover and decrease can be spaced further apart on the fabric too, which causes the fabric to change direction (bias) creating new shapes. As with eyelets, lace fabrics are used for decorative items such as shawls. Since it has an open fabric, it isn't the first choice for warm clothing, but works well for decorative garments.

Lace knitting can be more complex than other types as it is more difficult to identify and fix any errors, since the stitches move across columns of stitches, plus there is a larger variety of stitches involved. Because of this intricacy, lacework is a highly respected skill, and heirloom lacework items should be treasured. There are many lace knitting traditions from different parts of the world that use lace in shawls to create beautiful and special pieces, such as the Shetland Islands, Estonia, and Orenburg in Russia.

Contrast Garter Column

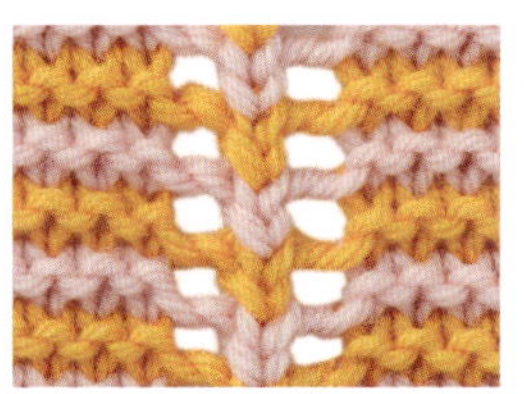

SKILL LEVEL
Intermediate

MULTIPLES
7 stitches; 4 rows

STITCHES INCLUDED
knit, yo, s2kpo

APPEARANCE
Reversible

OTHER MATERIALS
Contrasting yarn

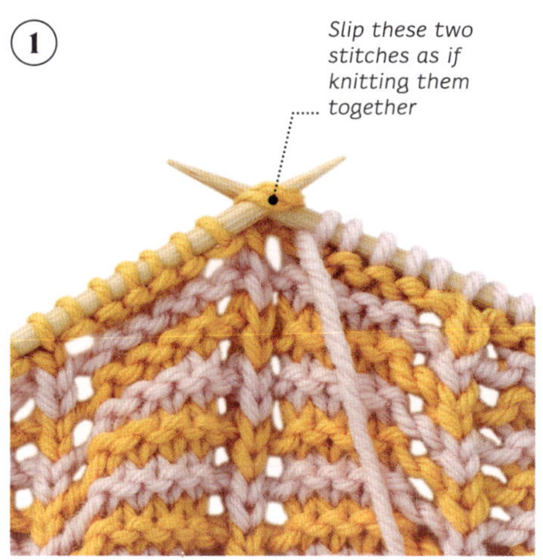

1 **Row 1:** Using the main colour, knit 2 stitches. Work a yarnover (see p.42). Work a s2kpo: *insert the RHN from left to right into the second then first stitch on the LHN. Slip from the LHN. Knit one stitch.*

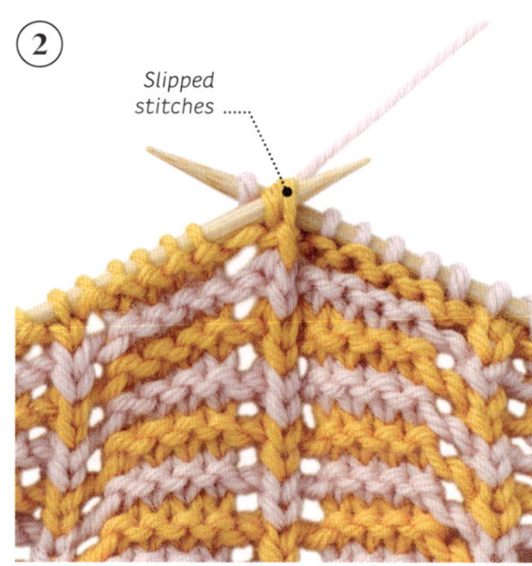

2 *Insert the LHN from left to right into the slipped stitches. Lift them up and over the knit stitch. Drop the slipped stitches.* Work a yarnover. Knit 2 stitches. **Row 2:** Knit 3 stitches. Purl 1 stitch. Knit 3 stitches. **Rows 3 and 4:** Using the contrast colour, repeat Rows 1 and 2 once.

The chart: Contrast Garter Column

This chart shows that the colour of yarn is changed every 2 rows, but the actual stitch pattern remains the same.

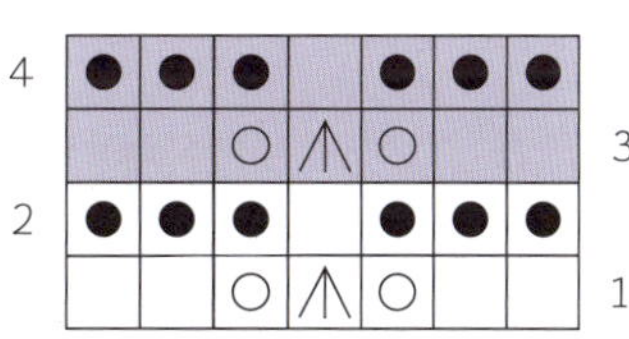

Lapwing Lace

SKILL LEVEL
Intermediate

MULTIPLES
4 (+2) stitches; 2 rows

STITCHES INCLUDED
knit, yo, k2tog

APPEARANCE
Reversible

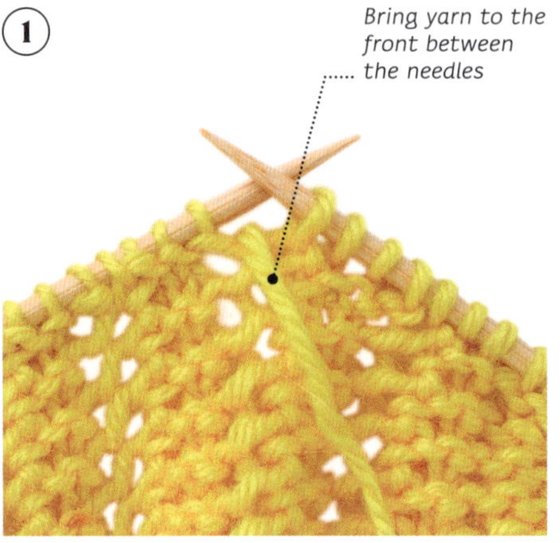

1 **Row 1:** Knit 1 stitch. *Work a yarnover: *bring the yarn to the front between the needles, the yarn travels over the RHN as the next stitch is worked.*

2 Work a knit 2 stitches together (see p.38). Knit 2 stitches. Repeat from * until the last stitch. Knit 1 stitch. **Row 2:** Repeat Row 1.

Mesh Lace

SKILL LEVEL
Intermediate

MULTIPLES
2 (+2) stitches; 2 rows

STITCHES INCLUDED
purl, yo, p2tog

APPEARANCE
Single-sided

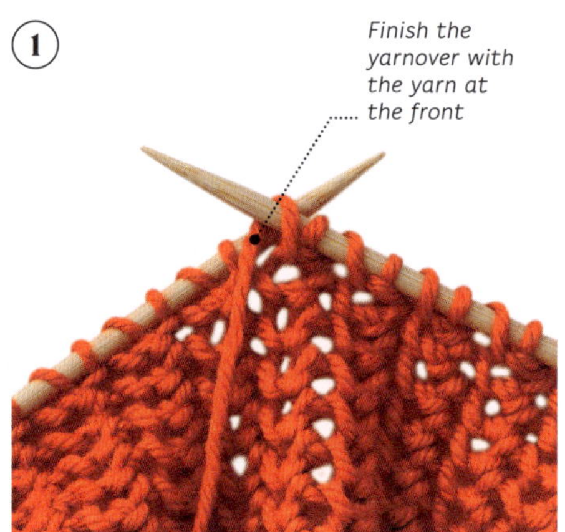

1 **Row 1:** Purl 1 stitch. *Work a purl to purl yarnover: *take the yarn over the top of the RHN, then back to the front between the needles.*

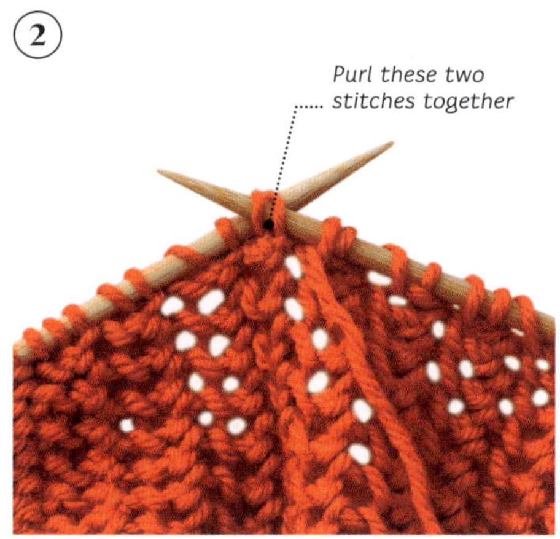

2 Purl 2 stitches together (see p.39). Repeat until the last stitch. Purl 1 stitch. **Row 2:** Repeat Row 1.

Mariposa

SKILL LEVEL
Advanced

MULTIPLES
8 (+1) stitches; 6 rows

STITCHES INCLUDED
knit, purl, yo, k2tog, ssk, p2tog, ssp

APPEARANCE
Single-sided

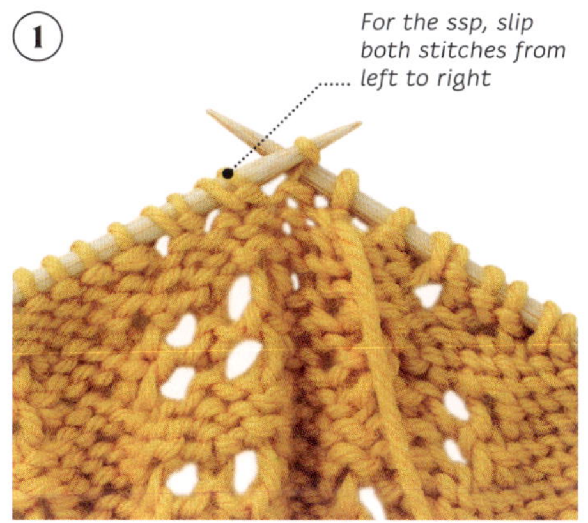

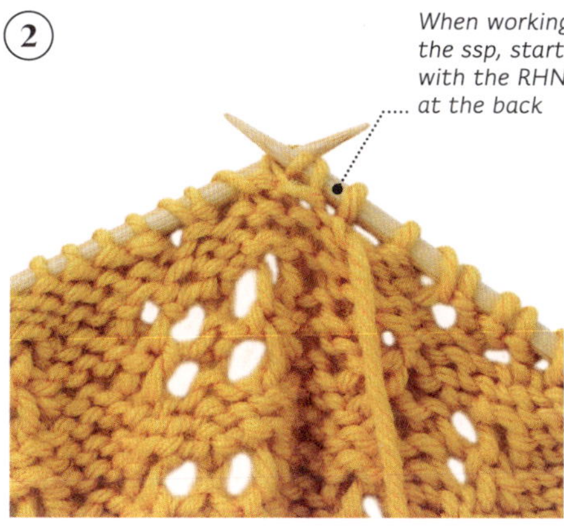

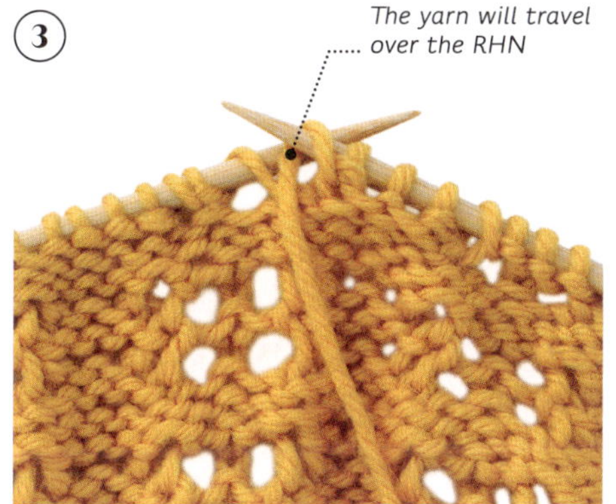

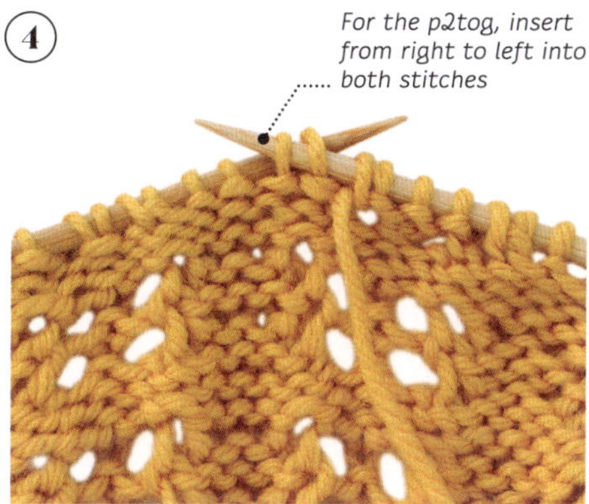

1 **Row 1:** Knit 1 stitch. *Knit 1 stitch. Knit 2 stitches together (see p.38). Work a yarnover (see p.42). Knit 1 stitch. Work a yarnover. Work an ssk (see p.38). Knit 2 stitches. Repeat from * until the end. **Row 2:** Purl 1 stitch. Work an ssp: *slip 2 stitches by inserting the RHN into the first stitch from left to right. Slip both stitches from the RHN back to the LHN by inserting from left to right.*

2 *With the RHN starting at the back of the work, insert from left to right into the second stitch then the first stitch on the LHN. Purl these 2 stitches together.*

3 Work a purl to purl yarnover (see p.43). Purl 3 stitches. Work a purl to purl yarnover. Work a purl 2 together (see p.39). Repeat from * until the last stitch. Purl 1 stitch. **Row 3 and 4:** Repeat Rows 1 and 2 once. **Rows 5 and 6:** Work 2 rows in stocking stitch; one row of knit followed by one row of purl.

Miniature Leaf

OTHER NAME
Trellis Lace

SKILL LEVEL
Intermediate

MULTIPLES
6 (+2) stitches;
4 (+2) rows

STITCHES INCLUDED
knit, purl, yo, sk2po, k2tog

APPEARANCE
Single-sided

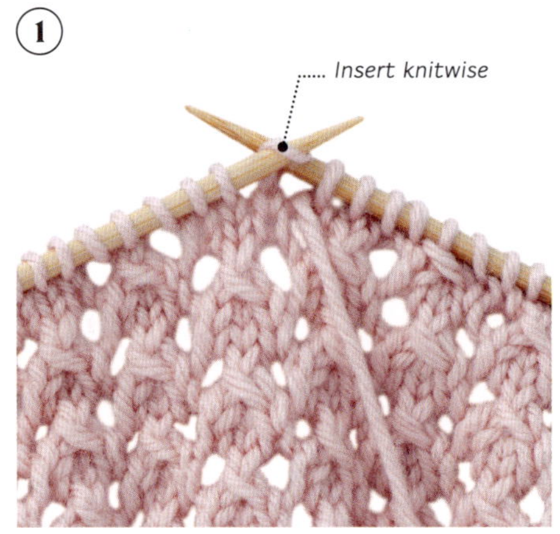

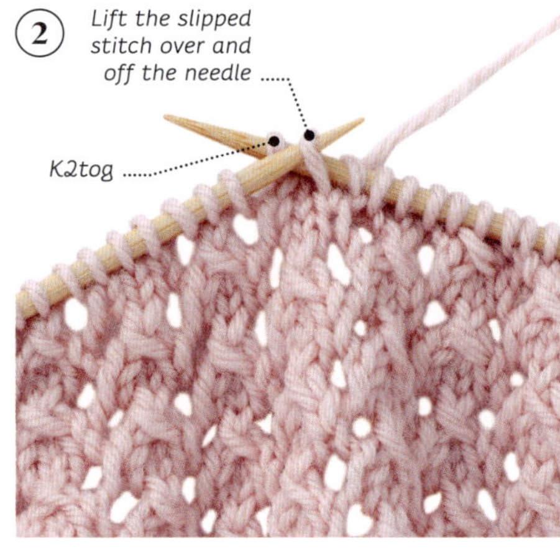

1 **Setup Rows 1 and 2:** Work 2 rows in stocking stitch: 1 row of knit followed by 1 row of purl. **Row 3:** Knit 1 stitch. *Work a yarnover (see p.42). Work an sk2po: *slip the first stitch on the LHN by inserting from left to right. Knit two stitches together (see p.38).*

2 *Insert the LHN from left to right into the slipped stitch on the RHN. Pass the slipped stitch over the k2tog and drop from both needles.* Work a yarnover. Knit 3 stitches. Repeat from * until the last stitch. Knit 1 stitch. **Row 4:** Purl all stitches. **Row 5:** Knit 1 stitch. *Knit 3 stitches. Work a yarnover. Work an sk2po. Work a yarnover. Repeat from * until the last stitch. Knit 1 stitch. **Row 6:** Purl all stitches. Repeat only Rows 3–6.

The chart: Miniature Leaf

This chart has 2 setup rows that are just worked once at the start. Only Rows 3–6 are worked for subsequent repeats.

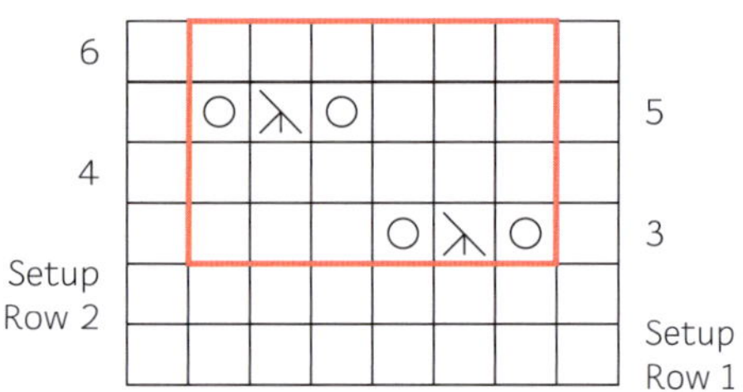

Merinette Eyelet

SKILL LEVEL
Intermediate

MULTIPLES
4 (+1) stitches; 10 rows

STITCHES INCLUDED
knit, purl, yo, s2kpo

APPEARANCE
Single-sided

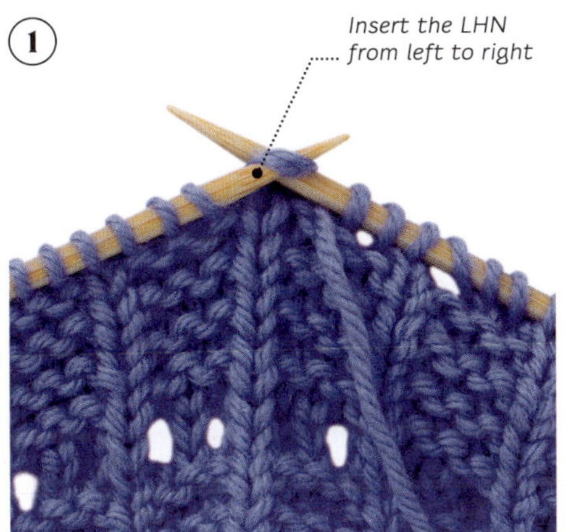

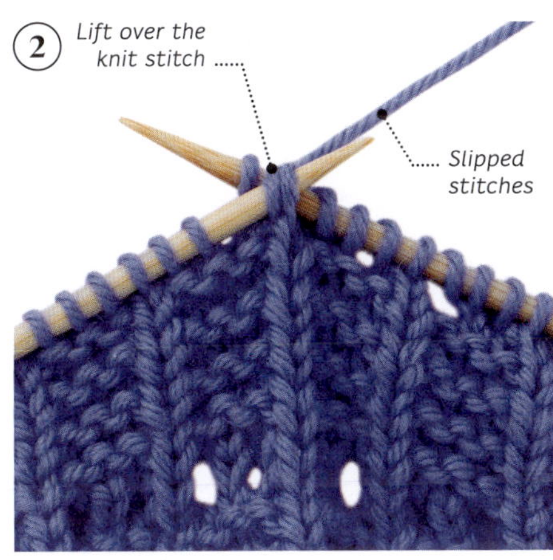

1 **Row 1:** Purl 1 stitch. *Purl 1 stitch. Knit 1 stitch. Purl 2 stitches. Repeat from * until the end. **Row 2:** Knit all stitches. **Rows 3–6:** Repeat Rows 1 and 2 twice more. **Row 7:** Knit 1 stitch. *Work a yarnover (see p.42). Work a s2kpo: *insert the RHN from left to right into the second then first stitch on the LHN. Slip from the LHN. Knit one stitch.*

2 *Insert the LHN from left to right into the first and second slipped stitches. Lift them up and over the knit stitch. Drop the slipped stitches.* Work a yarnover. Knit 1 stitch. **Rows 8–10:** Repeat Row 2 once, then repeat Rows 1 and 2 once more.

The chart: Merinette Eyelet

The vertical knit column is clear to see in the middle of the chart. The s2kpo decrease creates a central knit stitch so that the column can continue uninterrupted.

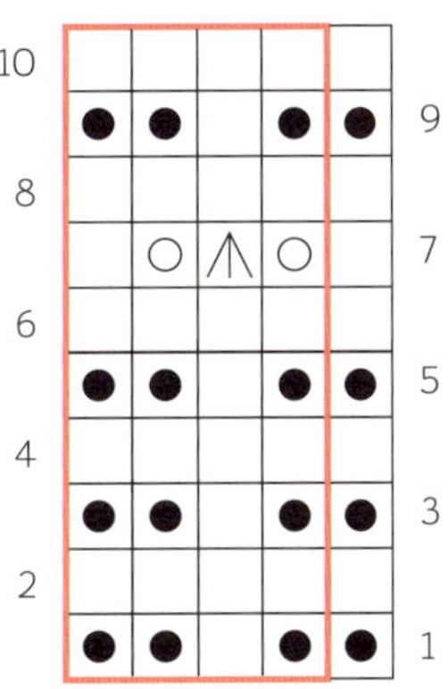

Thistles

SKILL LEVEL
Intermediate

MULTIPLES
8 (+1) stitches; 8 rows

STITCHES INCLUDED
knit, purl, yo, k2tog, ssk

APPEARANCE
Single-sided

Row 1: k1, *ssk, (k1, yo) twice, k1, k2tog, k1, rep from * until the end.
Row 2: purl.
Row 3: k1, *ssk, yo, k3, yo, k2tog, k1, rep from * until the end.
Row 4: purl.
Row 5: k1, *yo, k1, k2tog, k1, ssk, k1, yo, k1, rep from * until the end.
Row 6: purl.
Row 7: k1, *k1, yo, k2tog, k1, ssk, yo, k2, rep from * until the end.
Row 8: purl.

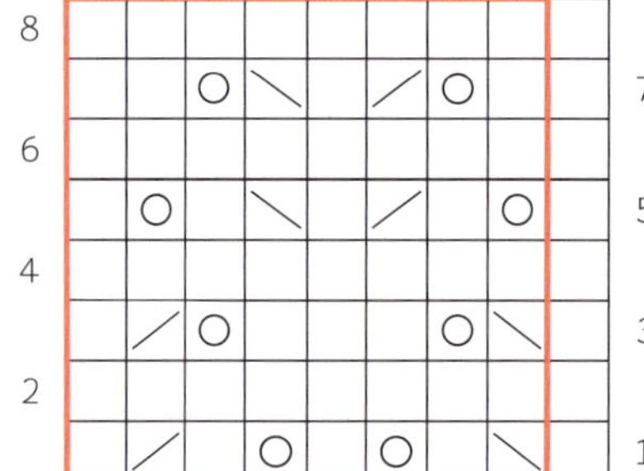

Fine Old Shale

SKILL LEVEL
Intermediate

MULTIPLES
11 stitches; 4 rows

STITCHES INCLUDED
knit, purl, yo, p2tog

APPEARANCE
Single-sided

Row 1: knit.
Row 2: purl.
Row 3: p2tog twice, (yo, k1) three times, yo, p2tog twice.
Row 4: purl.

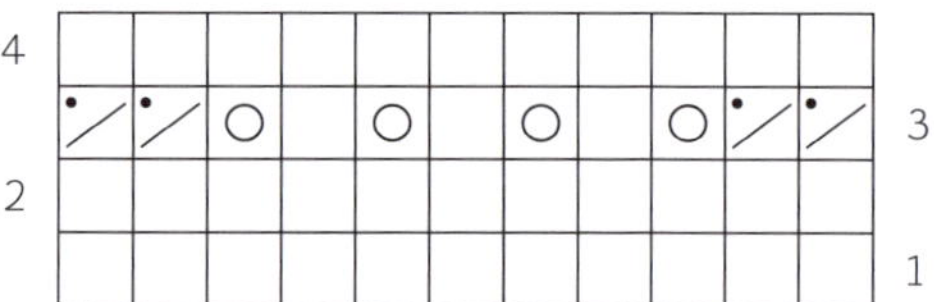

Garter Chevron Lace

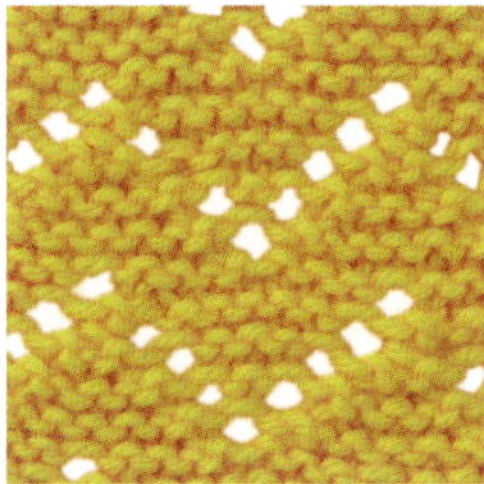

SKILL LEVEL
Intermediate

MULTIPLES
8 (+3) stitches; 10 rows

STITCHES INCLUDED
knit, purl, yo, k2tog, ssk, sk2po

APPEARANCE
Single-sided

Row 1: k1, *yo, ssk, k6, rep from * until last 2 sts, yo, ssk.
Row 2: knit.
Row 3: k1, *k1, yo, ssk, k3, k2tog, yo, rep from * until the last 2 sts, k2.
Row 4: knit.
Row 5: k1, *k2, yo, ssk, k1, k2tog, yo, k1, rep from * until the last 2 sts, k2.
Row 6: knit.
Row 7: k1, *k3, yo, sk2po, yo, k2, rep from * until the last 2 sts, k2.
Row 8: knit.
Row 9: k1, *k3, k2tog, yo, k3, rep from * until the last 2 sts, k2.
Row 10: knit.

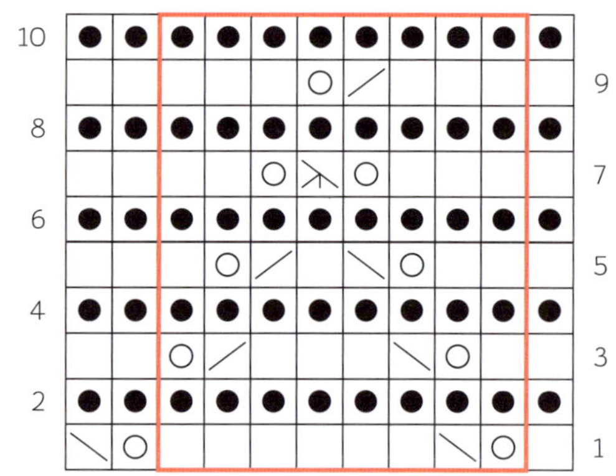

Lattice Lace

SKILL LEVEL
Intermediate

MULTIPLES
4 (+5) stitches; 8 rows

STITCHES INCLUDED
knit, purl, yo, k2tog, ssk, s2kpo

APPEARANCE
Single-sided

Row 1: k2, p2, *p1, k1, p2, rep from * until the last st, k1.
Row 2: purl.
Row 3: k1, ssk, yo, k1, *yo, s2kpo, yo, k1, rep from * until the last st, k1.
Row 4: purl.
Row 5: k1, p1, *p1, k1, p2, rep from * until the last 3 sts, p1, k2.
Row 6: purl.
Row 7: k2, *yo, s2kpo, yo, k1, rep from * until the last 3 sts, yo, k2tog, k1.
Row 8: purl.

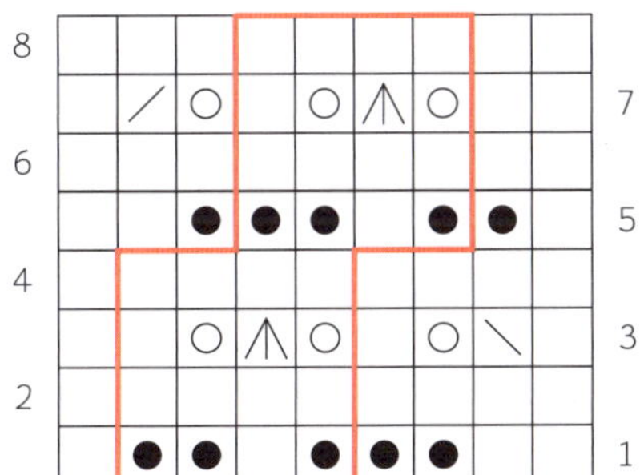

Arrowhead Lace

SKILL LEVEL
Intermediate

MULTIPLES
6 (+2) stitches;
6 rows

STITCHES INCLUDED
knit, purl, yo, k2tog, ssk

APPEARANCE
Single-sided

Row 1: k1, *k1, k2tog, yo twice, ssk, k1, rep from * until the last st, k1.
Row 2: p1, *p3, k1, p2, rep from * until the last st, p1.
Row 3: k1, *k2tog, yo, k2, yo, ssk, rep from * until the last st, k1.
Row 4: purl.
Row 5: knit.
Row 6: purl.

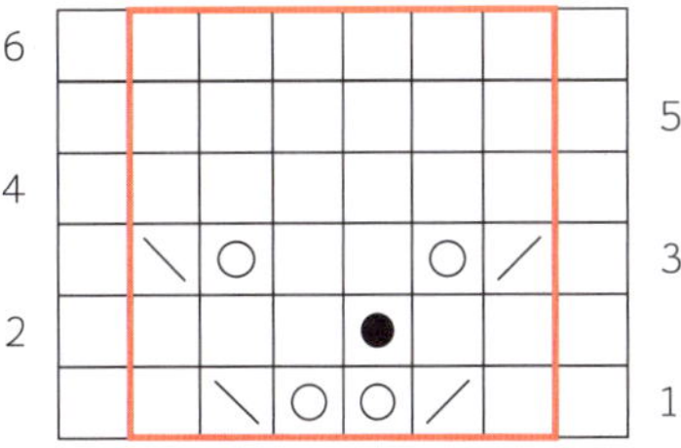

Wandering Leaves

SKILL LEVEL
Advanced

MULTIPLES
8 stitches;
16 rows

STITCHES INCLUDED
knit, purl, yo, k2tog, ssk, p2tog, ssp

APPEARANCE
Single-sided

Row 1: p1, yo, k1, yo, ssk, k3, p1 (1 st increased).
Row 2: k1, p2, ssp, k3, p1 (1 st decreased).
Row 3: p1, (k1, yo) twice, k1, ssk, k1, p1 (1 st increased).
Row 4: k1, ssp, k5, p1 (1 st decreased).
Row 5: p1, k6, p1.
Row 6: k1, p6, k1.
Row 7: Repeat Row 5.
Row 8: Repeat Row 6.
Row 9: p1, k3, k2tog, yo, k1, yo, p1 (1 st increased).
Row 10: k1, p3, p2tog, p2, k1 (1 st decreased).
Row 11: p1, k1, k2tog, (k1, yo) twice, k1, p1 (1 st increased).
Row 12: k1, p5, p2tog, k1 (1 st decreased).
Row 13: Repeat Row 5.
Row 14: Repeat Row 6.
Row 15: Repeat Row 7.
Row 16: Repeat Row 8.

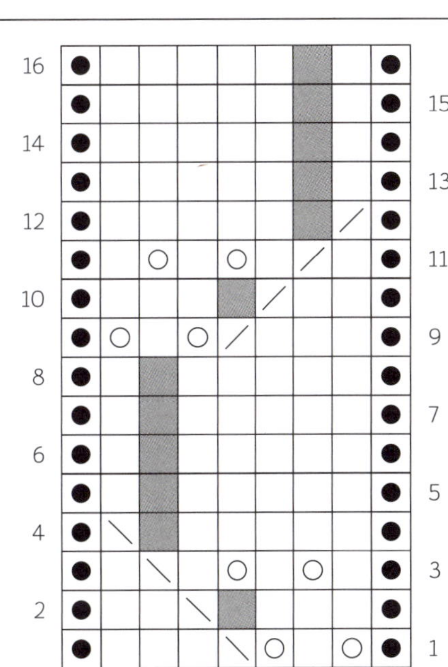

Cables, Twists, and Textures

Twists and Cables

Cable stitches use a separate needle (see p.15) to swap the position of the stitches, creating an interwoven fabric with deeper relief. Twist stitches are a similar type of stitch, but don't need a separate needle to work as they are only worked over two stitches; although they can be worked with a cable needle, if preferred.

Twists and cables use basic knit and purl stitches. However, the addition of the cable needle makes it a more intermediate skill, although there are patterns that only use cable stitches intermittently and would be a good starting point to try cabling (see Shadow Plaiting, p.132). Both twists and cables will pull in the fabric and create a dense and textured material ideal for warm winter garments and accessories. Cable knitting can be called Aran knitting and is named for the Aran Islands in Ireland, which are synonymous with the heavily cabled sweaters.

Left Twist

OTHER NAME
1/1 LC

SKILL LEVEL
Intermediate

MULTIPLES
4 stitches; 4 rows

STITCHES INCLUDED
knit, purl, LT

APPEARANCE
Single-sided

1 **Row 1:** Purl 1 stitch. Knit 2 stitches. Purl 1 stitch. **Row 2:** Knit 1 stitch. Purl 2 stitches. Knit 1 stitch. **Row 3:** Purl 1 stitch. Take the yarn to the back. Work the LT: *slip 2 stitches from the LHN to the RHN by inserting the needle from left to right one at a time. Insert the LHN from left to right into these 2 stitches and slip back onto the LHN.*

2 *From the back of the work, insert the RHN from right to left into the 2nd stitch on the needle and knit without dropping from the LHN.*

3 *Insert the RHN from right to left into the first stitch, then the second stitch on the LHN, towards the back then knit both stitches together. Remove from the LHN.* Purl 1 stitch. **Row 4:** Repeat Row 2.

The chart: Left Twist

The LT symbol in row 3 shows the stitches swapping position, with the right stitch passing over the left. The symbol represents both of the stitches used to create the LT.

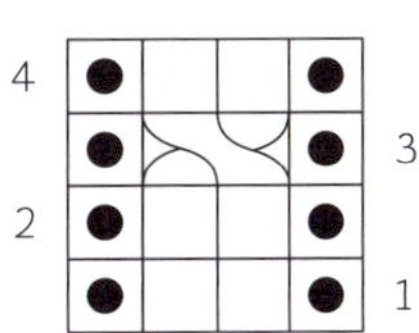

Right Twist

OTHER NAME
1/1 RC

SKILL LEVEL
Intermediate

MULTIPLES
4 stitches; 4 rows

STITCHES INCLUDED
knit, purl, RT

APPEARANCE
Single-sided

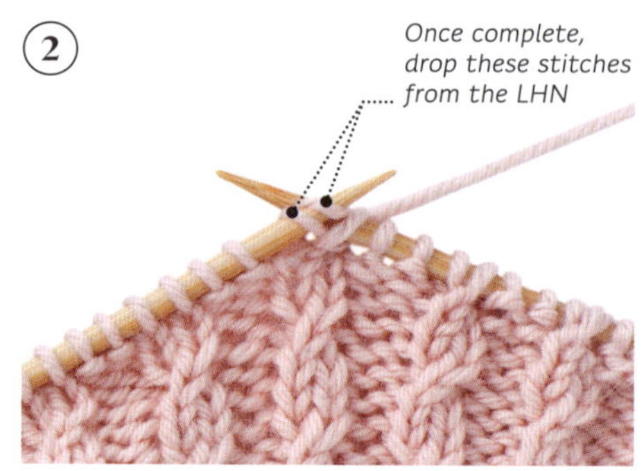

1 **Row 1:** Purl 1 stitch. Knit 2 stitches. Purl 1 stitch. **Row 2:** Knit 1 stitch. Purl 2 stitches. Knit 1 stitch. **Row 3:** Purl 1 stitch. Take the yarn to the back. Work the RT: *insert the RHN from left to right into the second stitch and then the first stitch on the LHN and knit these 2 stitches together but do not remove from the LHN.*

2 *Insert the RHN from left to right into the first stitch only and knit this stitch. Remove from the LHN.* Purl 1 stitch. **Row 4:** Repeat Row 2.

Twisted Ladder

SKILL LEVEL
Intermediate

MULTIPLES
5 (+3) stitches; 4 rows

STITCHES INCLUDED
knit, purl, RT, wyib sl, wyif sl

APPEARANCE
Single-sided

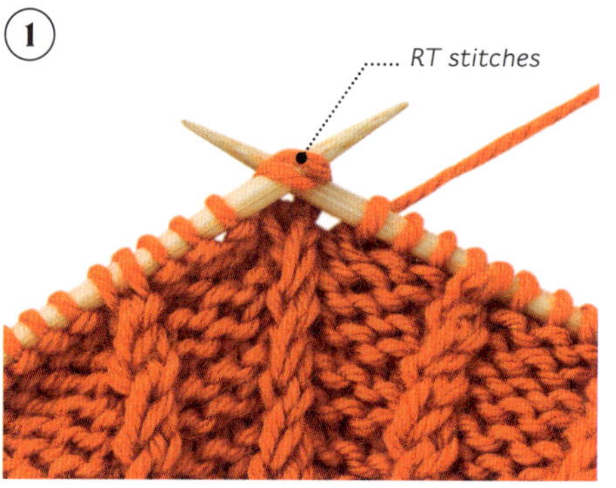

1 **Row 1:** Knit 3 stitches. *Work the RT: *insert the RHN from left to right into the second stitch and then the first stitch on the LHN and knit these 2 stitches together but do not remove from the LHN. Insert the RHN from left to right into the first stitch only and knit this stitch. Remove from the LHN.* Knit 3 stitches. Repeat from * until the end. **Row 2:** Knit 3 stitches. Purl 2 stitches. Repeat until the last 3 stitches. Knit 3 stitches.

2 **Row 3:** Knit 3 stitches. *Work a wyib sl 2 (see p.45). Knit 3 stitches. Repeat from * until the end. **Row 4:** Knit 3 stitches. Bring the yarn to the front between the needles. Slip 2 stitches. Take the yarn to the back between the needles. Repeat until the last 3 stitches. Knit 3 stitches.

Right Cross

OTHER NAMES
2/2 RC, C4B

SKILL LEVEL
Intermediate

MULTIPLES
6 stitches; 4 rows

STITCHES INCLUDED
knit, purl, 2/2 RC

APPEARANCE
Single-sided

ADDITIONAL TOOLS
Cable needle

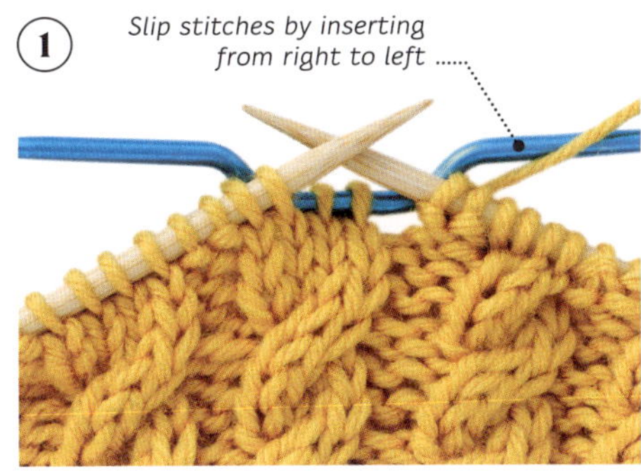

1 **Row 1:** Purl 1 stitch. Knit 4 stitches. Purl 1 stitch. **Row 2:** Knit 1 stitch. Purl 4 stitches. Knit 1 stitch. **Row 3:** Purl 1 stitch. Work a 2/2 RC: *slip the next 2 stitches purlwise to the cable needle. Leave the cable needle at the back.*

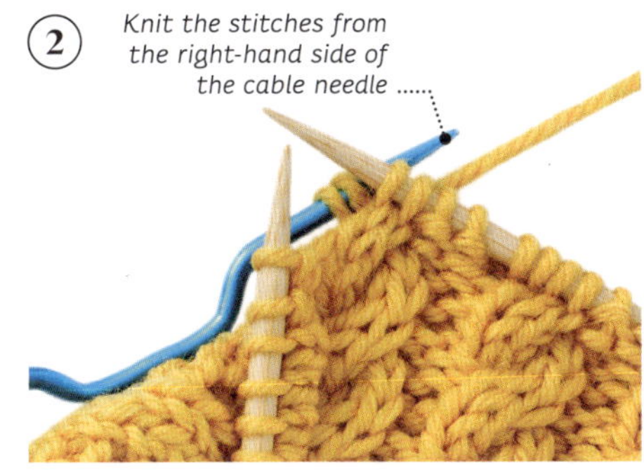

2 *Knit the next 2 stitches on the LHN. Knit 2 stitches from the cable needle.* Purl 1 stitch. **Row 4:** Repeat Row 2.

Left Cross

OTHER NAMES
2/2 LC, C4F

SKILL LEVEL
Intermediate

MULTIPLES
6 stitches; 4 rows

STITCHES INCLUDED
knit, purl, 2/2 LC

APPEARANCE
Single-sided

ADDITIONAL TOOLS
Cable needle

1 **Row 1:** Purl 1 stitch. Knit 4 stitches. Purl 1 stitch. **Row 2:** Knit 1 stitch. Purl 4 stitches. Knit 1 stitch. **Row 3:** Purl 1 stitch. Work a 2/2 RC: *slip the next 2 stitches purlwise to cable needle. Leave the cable needle at the front of the work.*

2 *Knit the next 2 stitches on the LHN. Knit 2 stitches from the cable needle.* Purl 1 stitch. **Row 4:** Repeat Row 2.

The chart: Left Cross

The 2/2 LC symbol in row 3 uses 4 stitches. It shows the first 2 stitches swapping positions with the second 2 stitches.

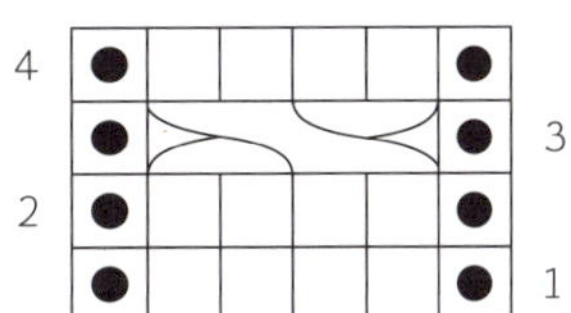

Meandering Purl Cross

SKILL LEVEL
Advanced

MULTIPLES
12 stitches; 4 rows

STITCHES INCLUDED
knit, purl, 2/1 LPC, 2/1 RPC

APPEARANCE
Single-sided

ADDITIONAL TOOLS
Cable needle

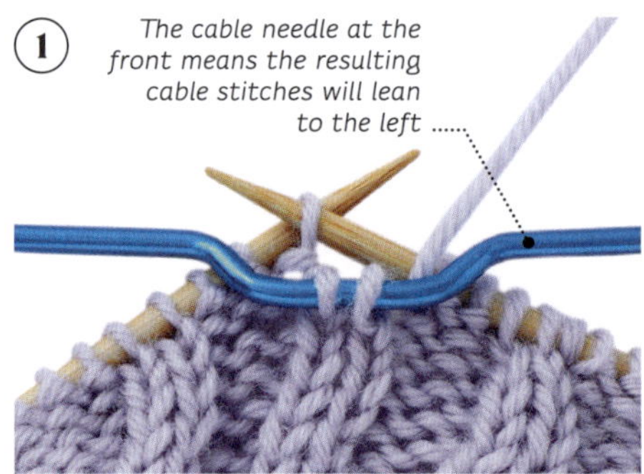

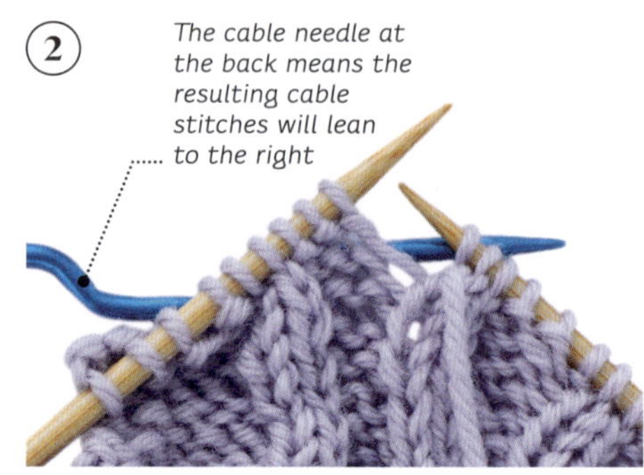

1 **Row 1:** Purl 1 stitch. *Knit 2 stitches. Purl 3 stitches. Repeat from * until the end. **Row 2:** *Knit 3 stitches. Purl 2 stitches. Repeat from * until the last stitch. Knit 1 stitch. **Row 3:** Purl 1 stitch. *Work a 2/1 LPC: *slip the next 2 stitches to the cable needle by inserting it from right to left into each stitch. Leave the cable needle at the front. Purl the next stitch on the LHN. Knit 2 stitches from the cable needle.* Purl 2 stitches. Repeat from * until the end. **Row 4:** *Knit 2 stitches. Purl 2 stitches. Knit 1 stitch. Repeat from * until the last stitch. Knit 1 stitch. **Row 5:** Purl 1 stitch. *Purl 1 stitch. Work a 2/1 LPC. Purl 1 stitch. Repeat from * until the end. **Row 6:** Knit 1 stitch. Purl 2 stitches. Knit 2 stitches. Repeat from * until the last stitch. Knit 1 stitch. **Row 7:** Purl 1 stitch. *Purl 2 stitches. Knit 2 stitches. Purl 1 stitch. Repeat from * until the end. **Row 8**: Repeat Row 6.

2 **Row 9:** Purl 1 stitch. *Purl 1 stitch. Work a 2/1 RPC: *slip the next stitch to the cable needle by inserting it from right to left into the stitch. Leave the cable needle at the back. Knit the next 2 stitches on the LHN.* Purl 1 stitch from the cable needle. Purl 1 stitch. Repeat from * until the end. **Row 10:** Repeat Row 4. **Row 11:** Purl 1 stitch. *Work a 2/1 RPC. Purl 2 stitches. Repeat from * until the end. **Row 12:** Repeat Row 2.

Wide Horseshoe

SKILL LEVEL
Intermediate

MULTIPLES
10 stitches; 4 rows

STITCHES INCLUDED
knit, purl, 1/3 RC, 1/3 LC

APPEARANCE
Single-sided

ADDITIONAL TOOLS
Cable needle

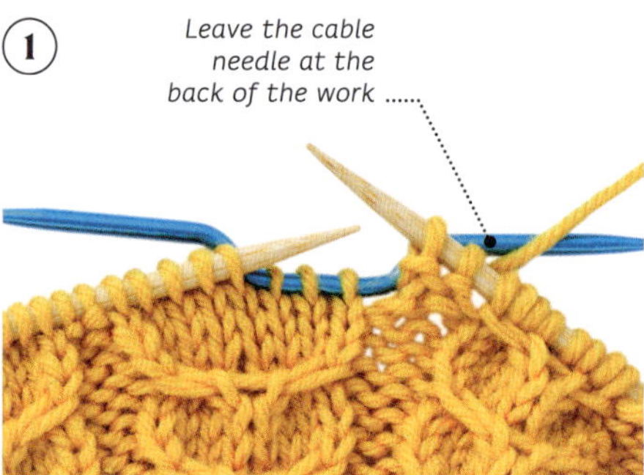

1 **Row 1:** Purl 1 stitch. Knit 8 stitches. Purl 1 stitch. **Row 2:** Knit 1 stitch. Purl 8 stitches. Knit 1 stitch. **Row 3:** Purl 1 stitch. Slip the next 3 stitches to the cable needle by inserting it from right to left into the stitch. Knit the next stitch on the LHN. Knit 3 stitches from the cable needle.

2 Slip the next stitch to the cable needle by inserting it from right to left. Knit the next 3 stitches on the LHN. Knit 1 stitch from the cable needle. Purl 1 stitch. **Row 4:** Repeat Row 2.

Crossed Rib

SKILL LEVEL
Intermediate

MULTIPLES
4 (+2) stitches; 8 rows

STITCHES INCLUDED
knit, purl, 1/1 RPC, 1/1 LPC

APPEARANCE
Reversible

ADDITIONAL TOOLS
Cable needle

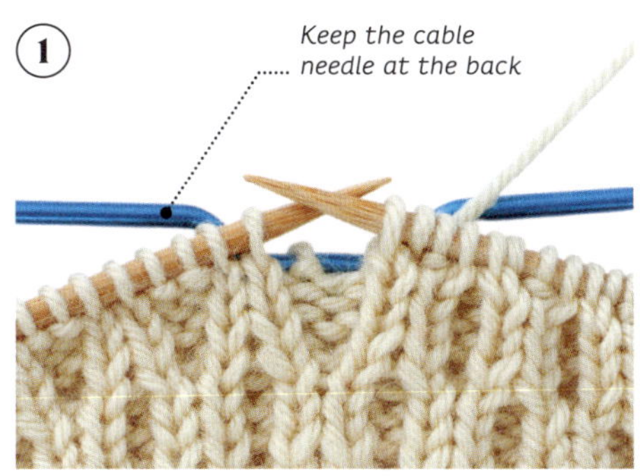

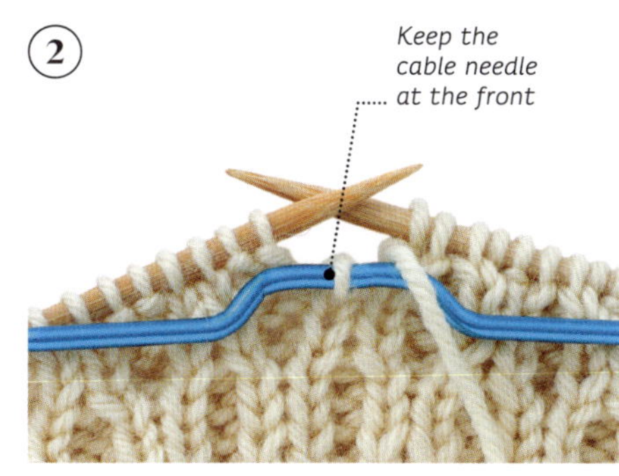

1 **Row 1:** Purl 1 stitch. *Purl 1 stitch. Knit 2 stitches. Purl 1 stitch. Repeat from * until the last stitch. Purl 1 stitch. **Row 2:** Knit 1 stitch. *Knit 1 stitch. Purl 2 stitches. Knit 1 stitch. Repeat from * until the last stitch. Knit 1 stitch. **Row 3:** Purl 1 stitch. *Work a 1/1 RPC: *slip the next stitch to the cable needle by inserting it from right to left into the stitch. Leave the cable needle at the back. Knit the next stitch on the LHN. Purl 1 stitch from the cable needle.*

2 Work a 1/1 LPC: *slip the next stitch to the cable needle by inserting it from right to left into the stitch. Leave the cable needle at the front. Purl the next stitch on the LHN. Knit 1 stitch from the cable needle.* Repeat from * until the last stitch. Purl 1 stitch. **Row 4:** Knit 1 stitch. *Purl 1 stitch. Knit 2 stitches. Purl 1 stitch. Repeat from * until the last stitch. Knit 1 stitch. **Row 5:** Purl 1 stitch. *Knit 1 stitch. Purl 2 stitches. Knit 1 stitch. Repeat from * until the last stitch. Purl 1 stitch. **Row 6:** Repeat Row 4. **Row 7:** Purl 1 stitch. *Work a 1/1 LPC. Work a 1/1 RPC. Repeat from * until the last stitch. Purl 1 stitch. **Row 8:** Repeat Row 2.

The chart: Crossed Rib

The cables in this pattern use both knit and purl stitches. This is represented by the small purl dot in the background of the cable symbol. The knit stitches pass in front of the purl stitch background.

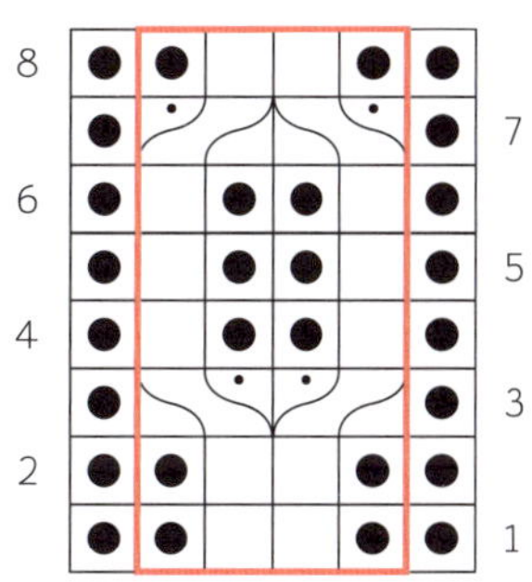

Wave of Honey

Row 1: RT, LT.
Row 2: purl.
Row 3: LT, RT.
Row 4: purl.

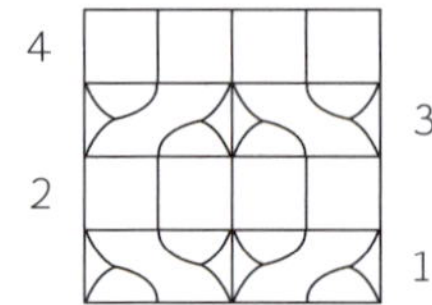

SKILL LEVEL
Easy

MULTIPLES
4 stitches; 4 rows

STITCHES INCLUDED
purl, LT, RT

APPEARANCE
Single-sided

Lightning

Row 1: k1, *k1, RT, k2, rep from * until the end.
Row 2: purl.
Row 3: k1, *RT, k3, rep from * until the end.
Row 4: purl.
Row 5: k1, *k1, LT, k2, rep from * until the end.
Row 6: purl.
Row 7: k1, *k2, LT, k1, rep from * until the end.
Row 8: purl.

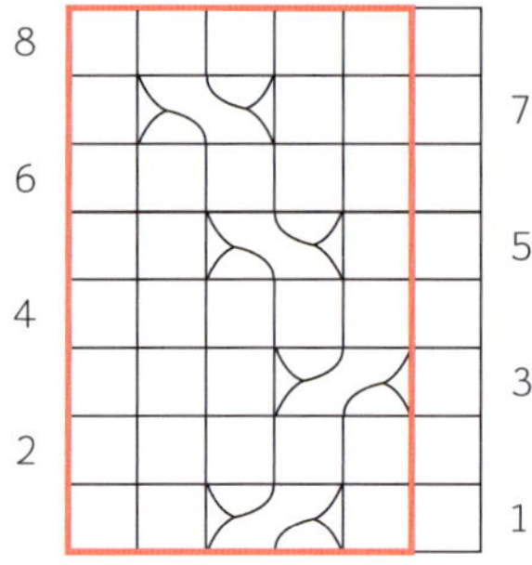

SKILL LEVEL
Intermediate

MULTIPLES
5 (+1) stitches; 8 rows

STITCHES INCLUDED
knit, purl, LT, RT

APPEARANCE
Single-sided

Simple Twisted Braid

Row 1: p1, LT, RT, p1.
Row 2: k1, p4, k1.
Row 3: p1, k1, RT, k1, p1.
Row 4: k1, p4, k1.

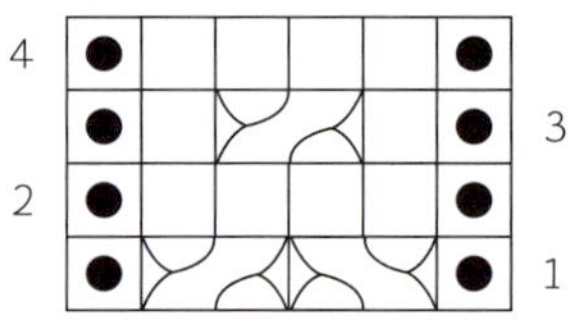

SKILL LEVEL
Easy

MULTIPLES
6 stitches; 4 rows

STITCHES INCLUDED
knit, purl, LT, RT

APPEARANCE
Single-sided

Chain Twist

SKILL LEVEL
Intermediate

MULTIPLES
6 stitches; 8 rows

STITCHES INCLUDED
knit, purl, LT, RT

APPEARANCE
Single-sided

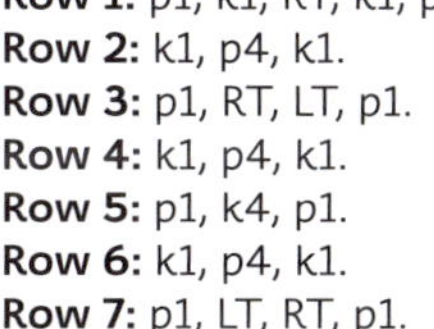

Row 1: p1, k1, RT, k1, p1.
Row 2: k1, p4, k1.
Row 3: p1, RT, LT, p1.
Row 4: k1, p4, k1.
Row 5: p1, k4, p1.
Row 6: k1, p4, k1.
Row 7: p1, LT, RT, p1.
Row 8: k1, p4, k1.

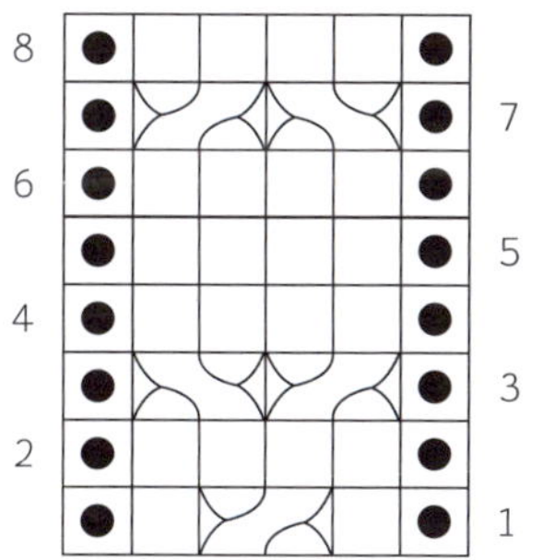

Honeycomb Column Twist

SKILL LEVEL
Intermediate

MULTIPLES
5 (+1) stitches; 16 rows

STITCHES INCLUDED
knit, purl, LT, RT

APPEARANCE
Single-sided

Row 1: p1, *k4, p1, rep from * until the end.
Row 2: *k1, p4, rep until the last st, k1.
Row 3: Repeat Row 1.
Row 4: Repeat Row 2.
Row 5: Repeat Row 1.
Row 6: Repeat Row 2.
Row 7: p1, *RT, LT, p1, rep from * until the end.
Row 8: Repeat Row 2.
Row 9: p1, *LT, RT, p1, rep from * until the end.
Row 10: Repeat Row 2.
Row 11: Repeat Row 7.
Row 12: Repeat Row 2.
Row 13: Repeat Row 9.
Row 14: Repeat Row 2.
Row 15: Repeat Row 1.
Row 16: Repeat Row 2.

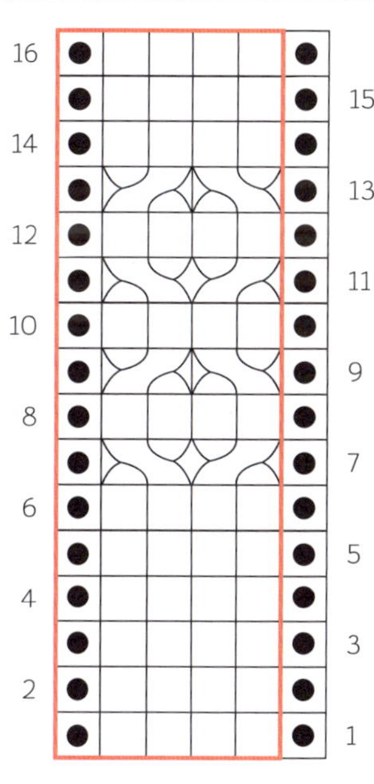

Honeycomb

OTHER NAMES
Cells

SKILL LEVEL
Intermediate

MULTIPLES
8 stitches; 8 rows

STITCHES INCLUDED
knit, purl, 2/2 LC, 2/2 RC

APPEARANCE
Single-sided

Row 1: 2/2 RC, 2/2 LC.
Row 2: purl.
Row 3: knit.
Row 4: purl.
Row 5: 2/2 LC, 2/2 RC.
Row 6: purl.
Row 7: knit.
Row 8: purl.

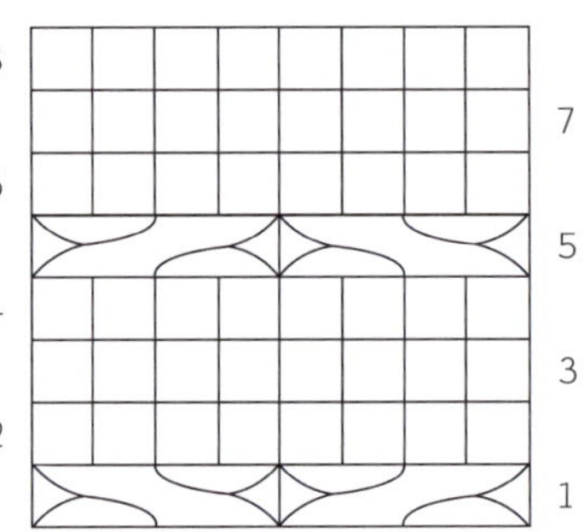

Shadow Plaited

SKILL LEVEL
Intermediate

MULTIPLES
8 stitches; 8 rows

STITCHES INCLUDED
knit, purl, 2/2 LC, 2/2 RC

APPEARANCE
Single-sided

Row 1: knit.
Row 2: purl.
Row 3: 2/2 LC, k4.
Row 4: purl.
Row 5: knit.
Row 6: purl.
Row 7: k4, 2/2 RC.
Row 8: purl.

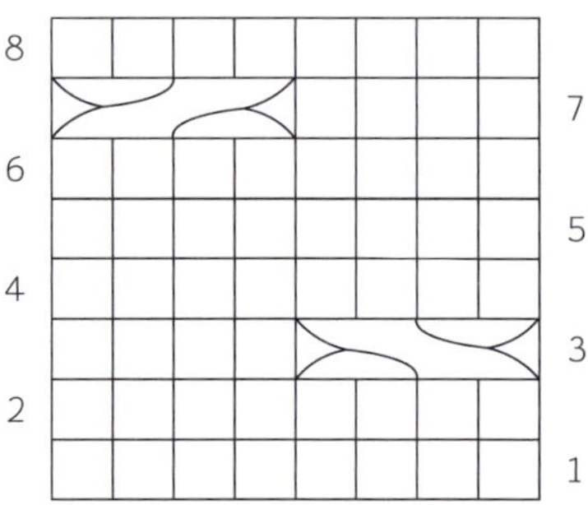

Small Horseshoe Cable

SKILL LEVEL
Intermediate

MULTIPLES
10 stitches; 6 rows

STITCHES INCLUDED
knit, purl, 2/2 LC, 2/2 RC

APPEARANCE
Single-sided

Row 1: p1, k8, p1.
Row 2: k1, p8, k1.
Row 3: p1, 2/2 LC, 2/2 RC, p1.
Row 4: k1, p8, k1.
Row 5: p1, k8, p1.
Row 6: k1, p8, k1.

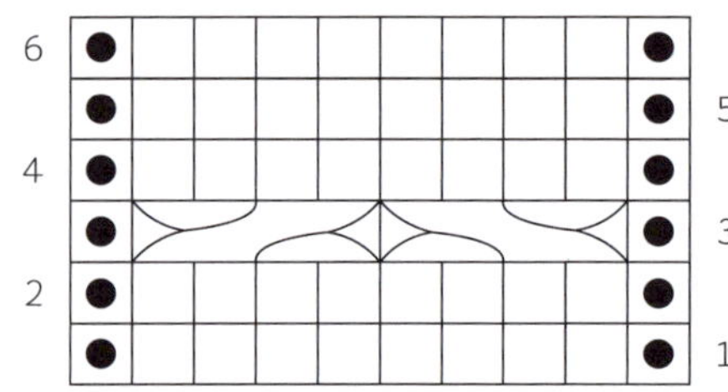

Large Cable with Garter

SKILL LEVEL
Intermediate

MULTIPLES
9 (+1) stitches; 8 rows

STITCHES INCLUDED
knit, purl, 3/3 LC

APPEARANCE
Single-sided

3/3 LC – slip the next 3 stitches purlwise to cable needle and leave at the front of the work, k3, then k3 from the cable needle.

Row 1: knit.
Row 2: *k2, p6, k1, rep from * until the last st, k1.
Row 3: k1, *k1, 3/3 LC, k2, rep from * until the end.
Row 4: *k2, p6, k1, rep from * until the last st, k1.
Row 5: knit.
Row 6: *k2, p6, k1, rep from * until the last st, k1.
Row 7: knit.
Row 8: *k2, p6, k1, rep from * until the last st, k1.

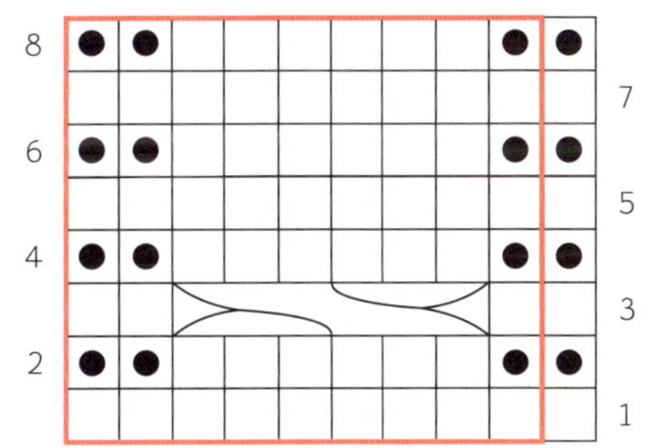

Wandering Cable

SKILL LEVEL
Intermediate

MULTIPLES
6 stitches; 8 rows

STITCHES INCLUDED
knit, purl, 2/2 LC, 2/2 RC

APPEARANCE
Single-sided

Row 1: p1, k4, p1.
Row 2: k1, p4, k1.
Row 3: p1, 2/2 RC, p1.
Row 4: k1, p4, k1.
Row 5: p1, k4, p1.
Row 6: k1, p4, k1.
Row 7: p1, 2/2 LC, p1.
Row 8: k1, p4, k1.

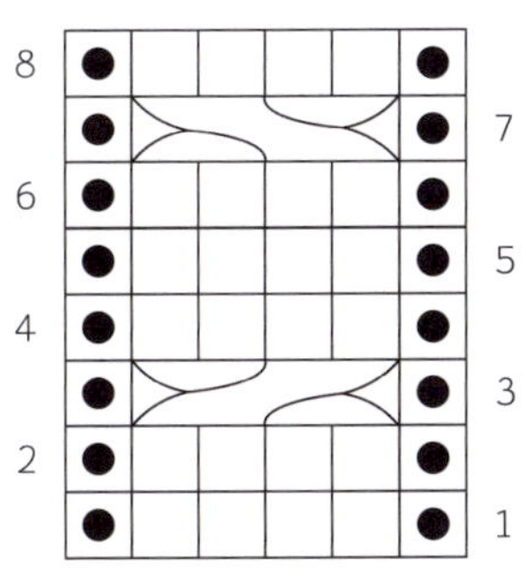

Basketweave Cable

SKILL LEVEL
Intermediate

MULTIPLES
4 (+2) stitches; 4 rows

STITCHES INCLUDED
knit, purl, 2/2 LC, 2/2 RC

APPEARANCE
Single-sided

Row 1: *2/2 LC, rep from * until the last 2 sts, k2.
Row 2: purl.
Row 3: k2, *2/2 RC, rep from * until the end.
Row 4: purl.

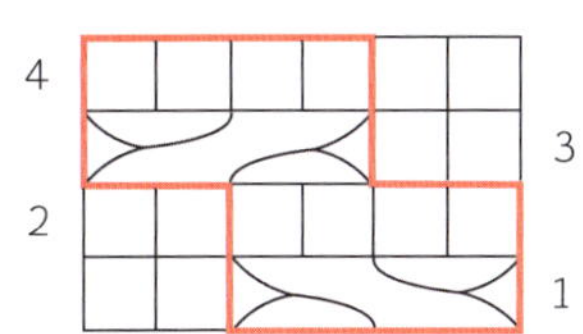

Bold Textures

The patterns in this section use texture in a more profound way, creating dramatic shapes on the surface of the fabric. These are unique stitches, all created in different ways, so they are more suited to an experienced knitter.

The bolder textures use more yarn and take longer to create, so they tend to be used more sporadically within a fabric rather than as all-over textures. For example, the Popcorn and Bobble stitches (see pp.135–36) create rounded dots on the fabric and can be used with cables to add extra texture. The Loop stitch (see p.137), which can be time-consuming to work, is mainly used to replicate fluffy texture and is often used for toys; for example, as doll hair or a lion's mane.

Basic Popcorn Stitch

SKILL LEVEL
Intermediate

MULTIPLES
6 (+1) stitches; 8 rows

STITCHES INCLUDED
knit, purl, kfbfb, p4tog

APPEARANCE
Single-sided

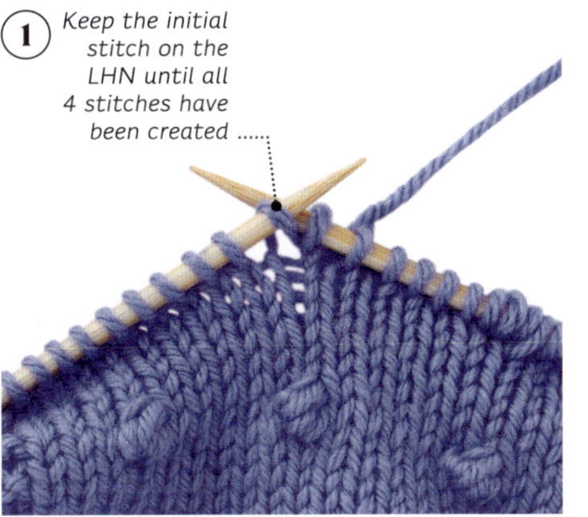

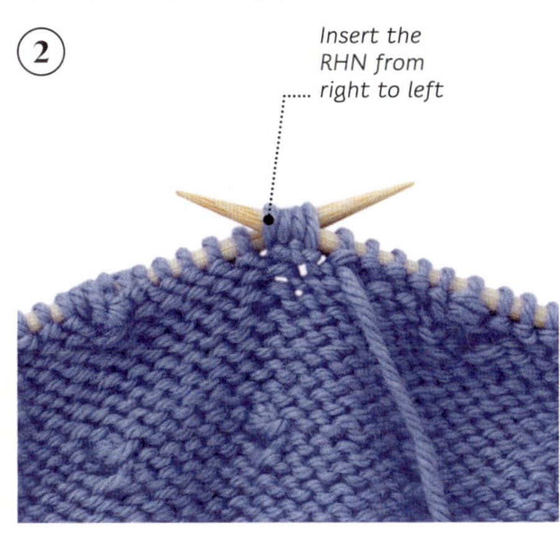

1 **Rows 1–6:** Starting with a knit row, work 6 rows of stocking stitch (see p. 36). **Row 7:** Knit 1 stitch. *Knit 2 stitches. **While keeping the first stitch on the LHN until 4 stitches have been created, knit one stitch by inserting into the first stitch on the LHN from left to right. Insert the RHN into the back loop of the stitch on the LHN from right to left and knit 1 stitch. Repeat from ** once more. Knit 3 stitches. Repeat from * until the end.

2 **Row 8:** *Purl 3 stitches. Insert the RHN into the first, second, third, then fourth stitch on the LHN. Purl these 4 stitches together. Purl 2 stitches. Repeat from * until the last stitch. Purl 1 stitch.

Cluster Stitch

SKILL LEVEL
Advanced

MULTIPLES
6 (+2) stitches; 8 rows

STITCHES INCLUDED
knit, purl, cluster stitch

APPEARANCE
Single-sided

ADDITIONAL TOOLS
Cable needle

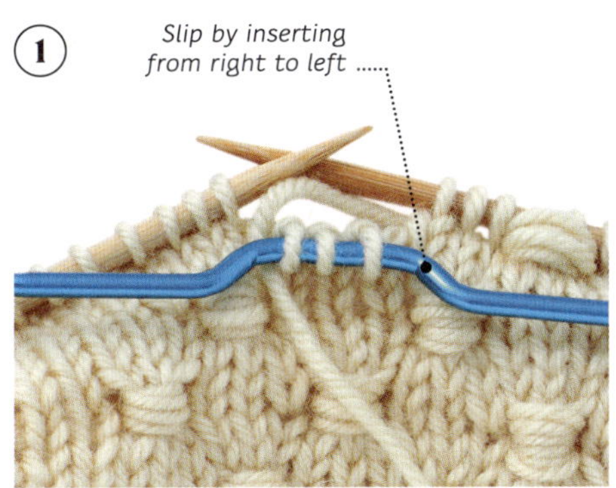

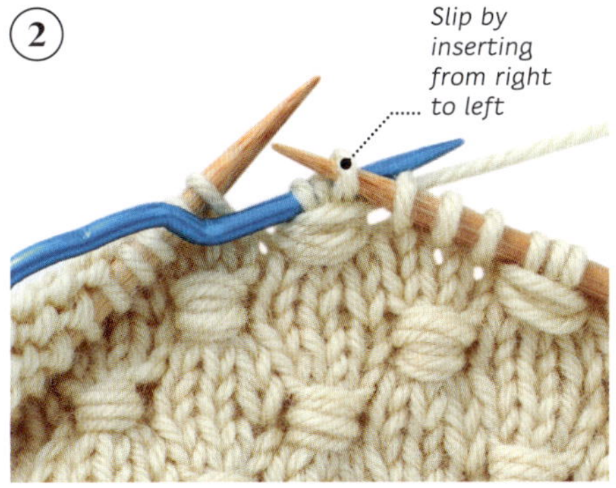

1 **Rows 1 and 2:** Work 2 rows of stocking stitch: 1 row of knit followed by 1 row of purl. **Row 3:** Knit 1 stitch. *To begin working the cluster stitch, *slip the next three stitches onto the cable needle. Wrap the yarn anticlockwise around the stitches on the cable needle six times; end with the yarn at the back.*

2 *Slip these 3 stitches onto the RHN.* Knit 3 stitches. Repeat from * until the last stitch. Knit 1 stitch. **Rows 4–6:** Work 3 rows of stocking stitch, starting with a purl row. **Row 7:** Knit 1 stitch. *Knit 3 stitches. Work a cluster stitch. Repeat from * until the last stitch. Knit 1 stitch. **Row 8:** Purl all the stitches.

Basic Bobble

SKILL LEVEL
Intermediate

MULTIPLES
6 (+1) stitches; 8 rows

STITCHES INCLUDED
knit, purl, make bobble (mb)

APPEARANCE
Single-sided

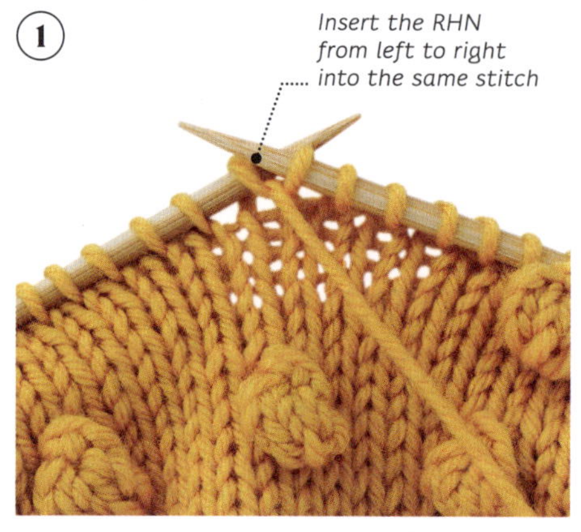

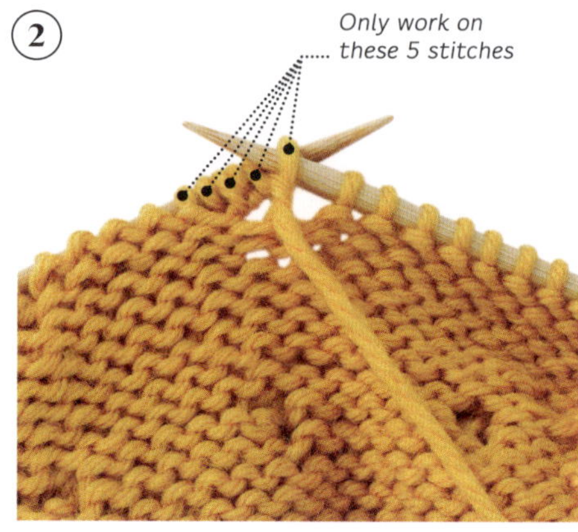

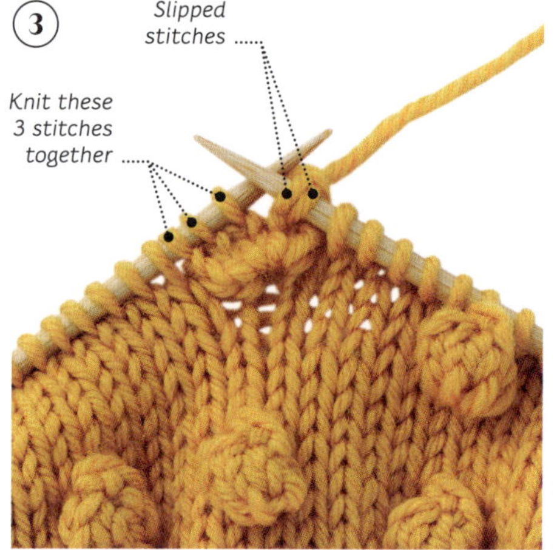

1 **Rows 1–6:** Starting with a knit row, work 6 rows of stocking stitch (see p.36). **Row 3:** Knit 1 stitch. *Knit 2 stitches. Work the bobble: *insert the RHN into the first stitch on the LHN from left to right. Knit 1 stitch, keeping the stitch on the LHN. **Bring the yarn to the front between the needles, then insert the RHN from left to right into the same stitch. Take the yarn over the top of the RHN and knit the next stitch. Repeat from ** once more. Turn the work.*

2 *Purl five stitches. Turn the work. Knit five stitches. Turn the work. Purl five stitches. Turn the work.*

3 *Slip 2 stitches to the RHN by inserting it from left to right into the second stitch and then the first stitch on the LHN (as if to k2tog). Insert the RHN from left to right into the third, second, then first stitch on the LHN. Knit these 3 stitches together.*

4 *Insert the LHN from left to right into the 2 just-slipped stitches on the RHN (the second and third stitches from the tip of the RHN). Lift these over the top of the first stitch, dropping them from both needles.* Knit 3 stitches. Repeat from * until the end. **Row 4:** Purl all the stitches.

Alternating Bobbles

Bobbles can be used in a variety of ways. The background texture can be changed to reverse stocking stitch and the bobbles placed in an alternating pattern, as in this variation. Bobbles can be introduced into any stitch pattern.

Loop Stitch

OTHER NAME
Fur stitch

SKILL LEVEL
Advanced

MULTIPLES
2 stitches; 2 rows

STITCHES INCLUDED
purl, loop stitch

APPEARANCE
Single-sided

1. **Row 1:** Starting on a wrong-side row, purl all the stitches. **Row 2:** Knit 1 stitch, but leave the initial stitch on the LHN. Bring the yarn to the front between the needles.
2. Place your thumb over the yarn, creating a loop over the thumb.
3. Take the yarn to the back between the needles. Knit the same stitch again and remove from the LHN.
4. Insert the LHN into the first then second stitch on the RHN from left to right. Knit these two stitches together and drop from the LHN. Repeat as needed along the row, making sure to keep an even tension on all of the loops you create.

Trinity Stitch

OTHER NAME
Bramble stitch

SKILL LEVEL
Advanced

MULTIPLES
4 stitches; 2 rows

STITCHES INCLUDED
purl, p3tog, (k, p, k) in 1 stitch

APPEARANCE
Single-sided

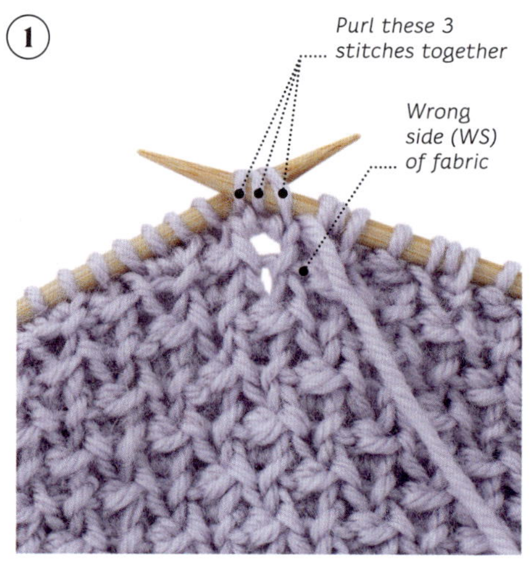

1 **Row 1:** Purl all the stitches. **Row 2:** Work a p3tog: *insert the RHN from right to left into the first, second, and third stitch on the LHN. Purl these 3 stitches together.* Take the yarn to the back.

2 (k, p, k) in 1 stitch: *knit 1 stitch, leaving the initial stitch on the LHN.*

3 *Bring the yarn to the front. Purl 1 stitch into this same stitch, leaving the initial stitch on the LHN.*

4 *Take the yarn to the back. Knit 1 more stitch into this same stitch and remove from the LHN.* **Row 3:** Purl all the stitches. **Row 4:** (k, p, k) in 1 stitch, purl 3 stitches together.

Tuck Stitch

OTHER NAME
Tuck Fold

SKILL LEVEL
Intermediate

MULTIPLES
1 stitch; 16 rows

STITCHES INCLUDED
knit, purl, p3tog, knit together with row below

APPEARANCE
Single-sided

OTHER MATERIALS
Contrast colour, extra knitting needle

1

2

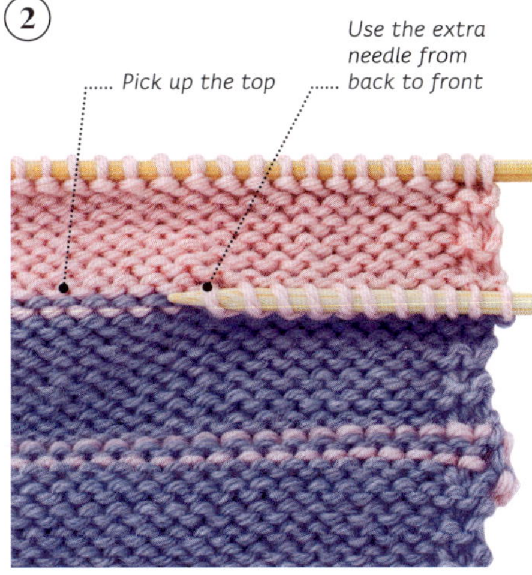

3

4

1 **Rows 1–6:** Using the main colour (MC), work six rows of stocking stitch (see p.36) starting with a knit row. **Rows 7–14:** Using the contrast colour (CC), work 8 rows of stocking stitch, starting with a knit row.

2 **Row 15:** Using a separate needle and working on the wrong side, thread the purl bumps from the top of Row 7 onto the extra needle by inserting it from back to front into each stitch. There should be the same number of stitches as on the main needle.

3 Hold the needle with the purl bumps parallel with the working needle at the back of the work. This will create a fold in the CC row on the right side of the work.

4 Work a knit together with row below: *insert the RHN from left to right into the first stitch on the working needle. Insert the RHN from left to right into the first stitch on the extra needle. Using the MC, knit these 2 stitches together.* **Row 16:** Purl all the stitches.

Specialized Stitches

All the stitch patterns in this section include specialized stitches to create the fabrics: tuck stitches, brioche, knot stitches, and beading. Since they have novel stitches, these tend to be more advanced techniques, though the Tuck Rib Column (see p.145) would suit an adventurous beginner.

Tuck stitches and brioche can create quite similar-looking fabrics but are knitted with very different techniques. Fisherman's Rib and One-colour Brioche are identical fabrics, but the Brioche needs two passes for every row to create the same fabric as Fisherman's Rib creates in one. This difference in technique allows Brioche to easily use extra colours, such as the two-colour version (see p.144).

There are two different methods for beading: one where the beads are threaded onto the yarn prior to knitting, and the other where they are attached with a crochet hook. The crochet hook version allows the bead to be seen from both sides of the knitting, so is ideal for projects where both sides could be seen, such as a shawl or scarf.

Fisherman's Rib

SKILL LEVEL
Intermediate

MULTIPLES
2 (+3) stitches; 2 (+1) rows

STITCHES INCLUDED
knit, purl, k1b

APPEARANCE
Reversible

1 **Setup Row 1:** Starting on the wrong side of the work, purl 2 stitches. *Knit 1 stitch. Purl 1 stitch. Repeat from * until the last stitch. Purl 1 stitch. **Row 2:** Knit 1 stitch. *Knit into the row below: *insert the RHN from front to back into the centre of the stitch on the row below the first stitch on the LHN.*

2 *Wrap the yarn anticlockwise around the needle. Scoop the yarn back through. Drop the first stitch from the LHN.* Purl 1 stitch. Repeat from * until the last 2 stitches. Knit into the row below. Knit 1 stitch. **Row 3:** Purl 2 stitches. *Knit into the row below. Purl 1 stitch. Repeat from * until the last stitch. Purl 1 stitch. Repeat only Rows 2 and 3.

The chart: Fisherman's Rib

Fisherman's Rib requires a setup row that is only worked once, as the knit one below (k1b) is worked into the row below the needles.

The setup row pattern repeat is shown with a blue line and is only repeated across the row and not on any other repeats. Only repeat Rows 2 and 3.

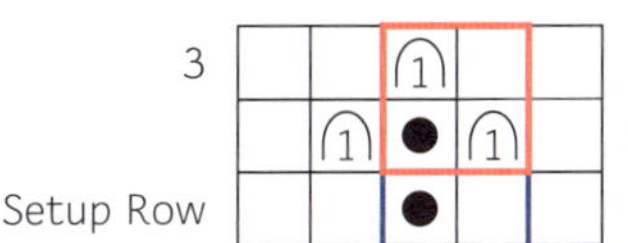

Bee Stitch

SKILL LEVEL
Intermediate

MULTIPLES
2 (+3) stitches; 4 rows

STITCHES INCLUDED
knit, purl, k1b

APPEARANCE
Single-sided

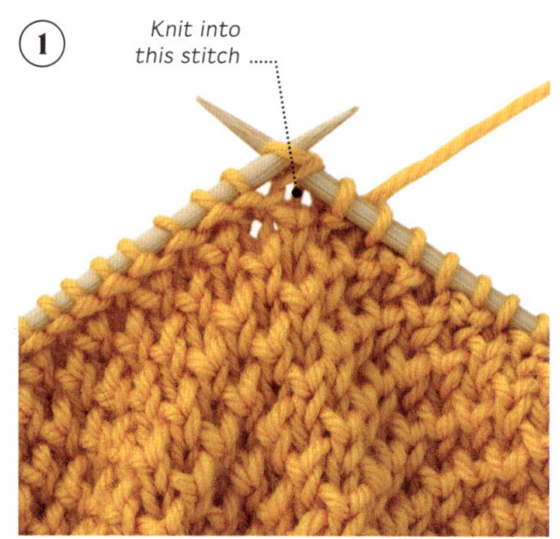

1 **Row 1:** Starting on the wrong side, knit all stitches. **Row 2:** Knit 1 stitch. *Knit into the row below (see p.141). Knit 1 stitch. Repeat from * until the last 2 stitches. Knit into the row below. Knit 1 stitch.

2 **Row 3:** Knit all stitches. **Row 4:** Knit 1 stitch. *Knit 1 stitch. Knit into the row below. Repeat from * until the last 2 stitches. Knit 2 stitches.

The chart: Bee Stitch

The Bee Stitch chart starts on the wrong side (WS). This is shown by the number 1 placed on the left-hand side, so that row is read from left to right. A purl dot on the wrong side is a knit stitch.

			(1)			4
3	●	●	●	●	●	
		(1)		(1)		2
1	●	●	●	●	●	

One-colour Brioche

SKILL LEVEL
Intermediate

MULTIPLES
2 (+2) stitches; 2 (+1) rows

STITCHES INCLUDED
knit, purl, brk, yfsl1yo

APPEARANCE
Reversible

Fisherman's Rib

Though this creates the same fabric as Fisherman's Rib (see p.141), brioche is created by working each row twice.

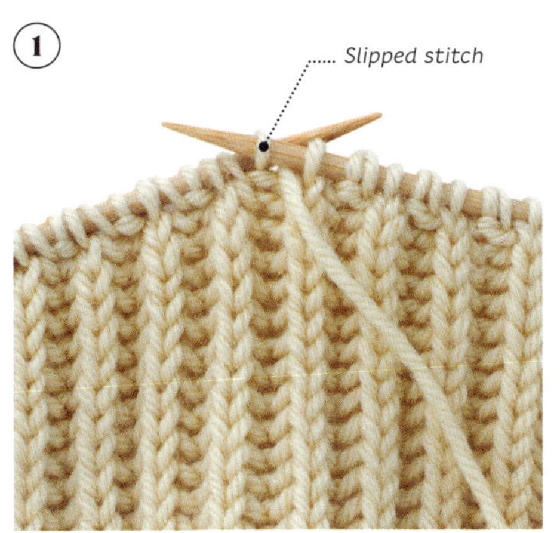

1 **Setup Row:** Work a yfsl1yo: *bring the yarn to the front. Insert the RHN into the first stitch from right to left. Slip to the RHN. Take the yarn over the top of the needle as you work the next stitch.* Knit 1 stitch. **Row 1:** Work a yfsl1yo.

2 Work a brioche knit: *insert the RHN from left to right into the stitch and yarnover from the previous row. Knit both strands together.* **Row 2:** Repeat Row 1. Repeat only Rows 1 and 2.

The chart: One-Colour Brioche

The symbols used in brioche knitting are unique and not used in other types of knitting. There is a setup row that is worked only once, as a brioche stitch is worked into both a slipped stitch and yarnover from the previous row, so this needs to be created first.

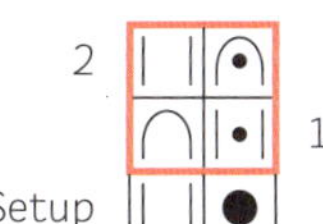

Two-colour Brioche

SKILL LEVEL
Advanced

MULTIPLES
2 (+3) stitches;
4 (+2) rows

STITCHES INCLUDED
knit, purl, brk, brp, yfsl1yo, sl1yo

APPEARANCE
Reversible

OTHER MATERIALS
Circular knitting needle, contrasting yarn

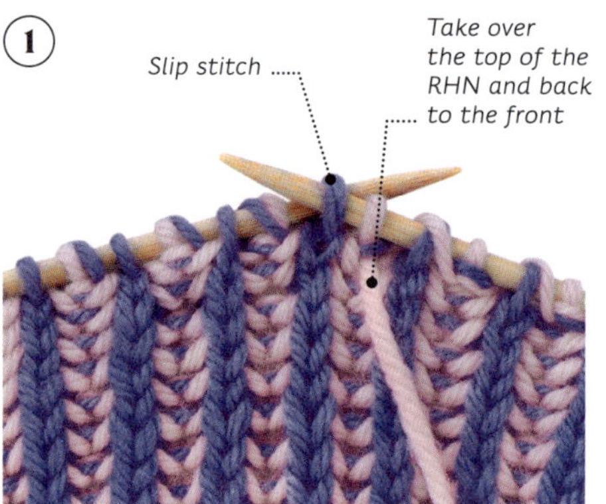

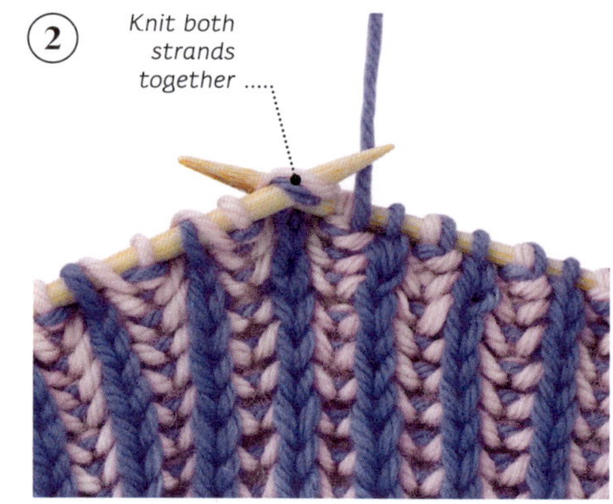

1 **Setup Light Colour (LC) Row:** *Using LC and starting with a WS row, purl 1 stitch. Work a sl1yo: *insert RHN into first stitch from right to left. Slip to RHN. Take the yarn over the top of the RHN and back to the front between the needles.* Repeat from * until the last stitch. Purl 1 stitch. Do not turn work. **Setup Dark Colour (DC) Row:** Slide the stitches to the other end of the needle. Join the DC, leaving a tail at least 15cm (6in) long; this can be sewn in later. Knit 1 stitch.

2 Work a brk: *insert the RHN from left to right into the stitch and yarnover from the previous row. Knit both these strands together.*

3 *Work a yfsl1yo: *bring the yarn to the front. Insert the RHN into the first stitch from right to left. Slip to the RHN. The yarn travels over the needle as you work the next stitch.* Work a brk. Repeat from * until the last stitch. Knit 1 stitch. Turn the work. **LC Row 1:** Using LC, knit 1 stitch. *Work a yfsl1yo. Work a brk. Repeat from * until the last 2 stitches. Work a yfsl1yo. Knit 1 stitch. Do not turn the work. **DC Row 1:** Slide the stitches to the other end of the needle. Using DC, purl 1 stitch.

4 *Work a brp: *insert the RHN from right to left into the stitch and yarnover from previous row. Purl both these strands together.* Work a sl1yo. Repeat from * until the last 2 stitches. Work a brp. Purl 1 stitch. Turn work.
LC Row 2: Using LC, purl 1 stitch. Work a sl1yo. *Work a brp. Work a sl1yo. Repeat from * until the last stitch. Purl 1 stitch. Do not turn work.
DC Row 2: Repeat Setup DC Row. Repeat only LC/DC Rows 1 and 2.

Tuck Rib Column

SKILL LEVEL
Intermediate

MULTIPLES
3 stitches; 4 (+1) rows

STITCHES INCLUDED
knit, purl, k3b

APPEARANCE
Single-sided

1 **Setup Row 1:** Starting with a WS row, knit 1 stitch. Purl 1 stitch. Knit 1 stitch. **Row 2:** Purl 1 stitch. Knit 1 stitch. Purl 1 stitch. **Row 3:** Knit 1 stitch. Purl 1 stitch. Knit 1 stitch. **Row 4:** Purl 1 stitch. Knit into 3 rows below: *insert the RHN from front to back into the centre of the stitch on the third row below the first stitch on the LHN.*

2 *Wrap the yarn anticlockwise around the needle. Scoop the yarn back through. Drop the first stitch from the LHN.* Purl 1 stitch. **Row 5:** Repeat Row 3. Repeat only Rows 2–5.

The chart: Tuck Rib Column

Tuck stitch symbols are shown with an arch and a number. The number indicates how many rows below the needle to work into. Tuck Rib Column has a wrong side setup row that is only worked once.

Row				Row
5	●		●	
	●	(3)	●	4
3	●		●	
	●		●	2
Setup Row 1	●		●	

Knot Stitch

SKILL LEVEL
Intermediate

MULTIPLES
6 (+2) stitches; 8 rows

STITCHES INCLUDED
knit, purl, knot stitch

APPEARANCE
Single-sided

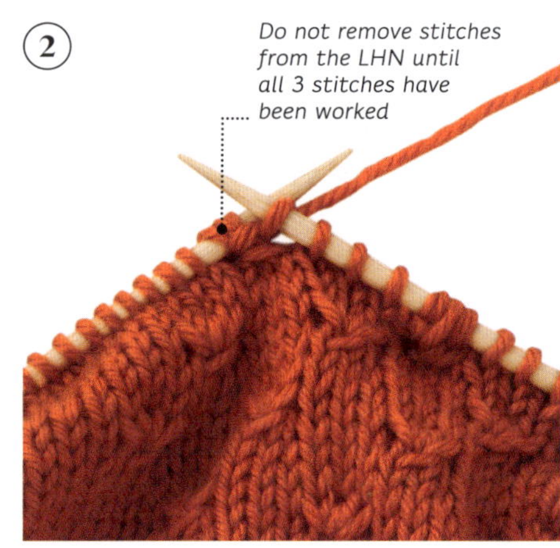

1 **Rows 1 and 2:** Work 2 rows of stocking stitch: 1 row of knit followed by 1 row of purl. **Row 3:** *Knit 1 stitch. Work a knot stitch: *bring the yarn to the front and insert the RHN from right to left into the first, second, and third stitches on the LHN. Purl these 3 stitches together but do not remove from the LHN.*

2 *Take the yarn to the back. Insert the RHN from left to right into the third, second, then first stitches on the LHN. Knit these 3 stitches together but do not remove from the LHN. Bring the yarn to the front. Purl these 3 stitches together again. Remove from the LHN. Take yarn to the back.* Knit 2 stitches. Repeat from * until the last 2 stitches. Knit 2 stitches. **Rows 4–6:** Work 3 rows of stocking stitch, starting with a purl row. **Row 7:** Knit 2 stitches. *Knit 2 stitches. Work a knot stitch. Knit 1 stitch. Repeat from * until the end. **Row 8:** Purl all stitches.

The chart: Knot stitch

Charts can be useful to double-check your placement. The chart shows that the knot stitches don't overlap at all. The knot stitch should sit in the same stitch columns as the knit 3 from the previous pattern row.

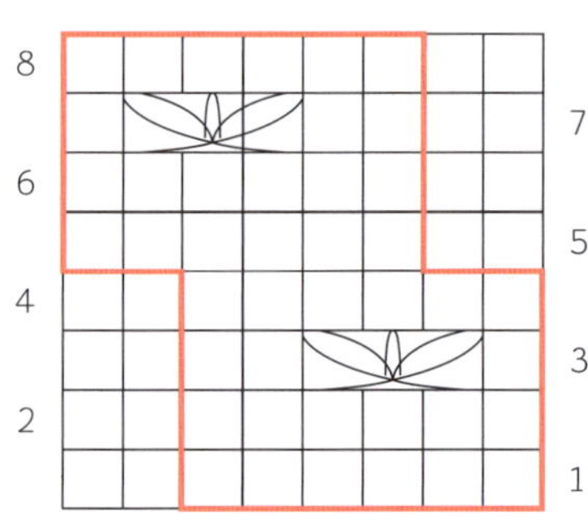

Star Stitch

SKILL LEVEL
Advanced

MULTIPLES
4 (+1) stitches; 4 rows

STITCHES INCLUDED
knit, purl, 3-to-3

APPEARANCE
Single-sided

1 **Row 1:** Knit 1 stitch. *Knit 1 stitch. Work a star stitch: *insert the RHN into the third, second, then first stitches on the LHN.*

2 *Knit these 3 stitches together, but do not remove from the LHN. Bring the yarn to the front.*

3 *Insert the RHN from left to right into the third, second, then first stitches on the LHN. Taking the yarn over the top of the needle first, knit these 3 stitches together. Remove from the LHN.* Repeat from * until the last stitch. **Row 2:** Purl all stitches. **Row 3:** *Work a star stitch. Knit 1 stitch. Repeat from * until the last stitch. Knit 1 stitch. **Row 4:** Purl all stitches.

The chart: Star Stitch

The lower number on the star stitch symbol shows the starting number of stitches. The top number is the final number of stitches. This means that there is no change in stitch count. The star stitch is an Estonian lace stitch and there are variations that do change the stitch count such as the 3-to-9 star stitch.

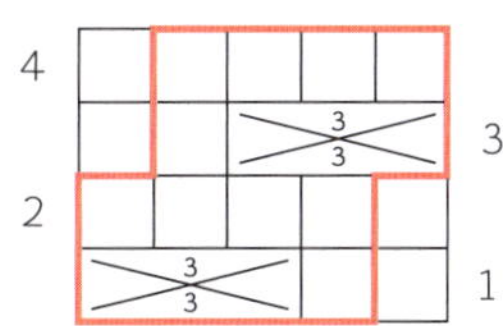

Lice Stitch Beading

SKILL LEVEL
Intermediate

MULTIPLES
4 (+1) stitches; 8 rows

STITCHES INCLUDED
knit, purl, place bead

APPEARANCE
Single-sided

OTHER MATERIALS
6/0 seed beads (2 per full repeat), sewing thread, fine needle to go through centre of beads

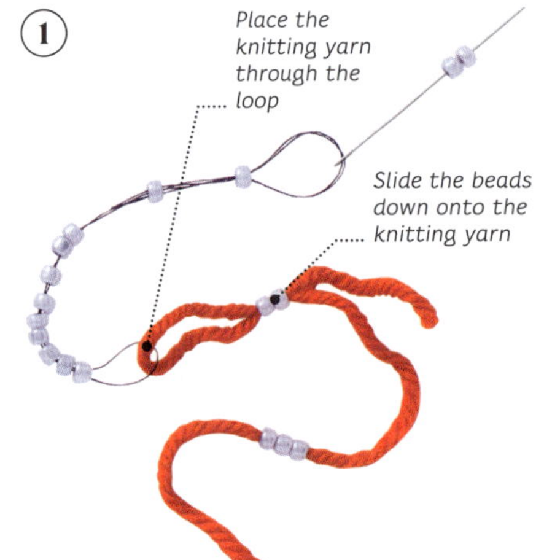

1 Thread all the beads onto the knitting yarn: cut 30cm (12") of sewing thread and fold in half. Thread both cut ends onto the fine needle. Place the knitting yarn through the loop created by the sewing thread. Place the required number of seed beads on the sewing needle and push down onto the knitting yarn. Keep the beads pushed up the yarn and away from the needles until the beads are needed.

2 **Rows 1 and 2:** Work 2 rows of stocking stitch: 1 row of knit followed by 1 row of purl. **Row 3:** Knit 1 stitch. *Place the bead: *bring the yarn to the front. Slide a bead down to the needles. Insert the RHN from right to left into the next stitch. Slip to the RHN.*

3 *Take the yarn to the back*. Knit 3 stitches. Repeat from * until the end. **Rows 4–6:** Work 3 rows of stocking stitch, starting with a purl row. **Row 7:** Knit 1 stitch. *Knit 2 stitches. Place bead. Knit 1 stitch. Repeat from * until the end. **Row 8:** Purl all the stitches.

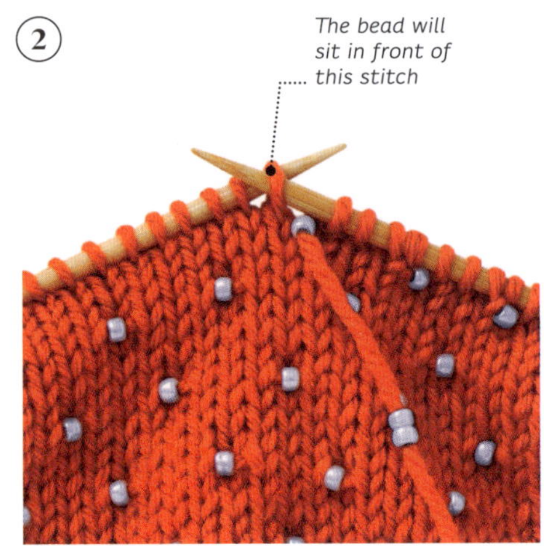

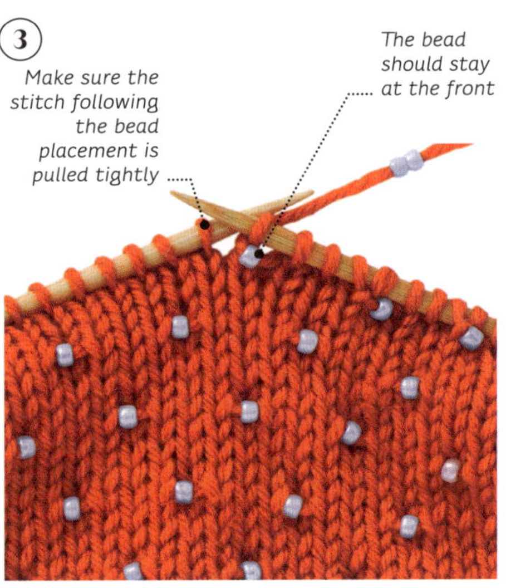

The chart: Lice Stitch Beading

The round symbol indicates where the bead is worked in. However, it will look as if it's sitting on the row below when complete.

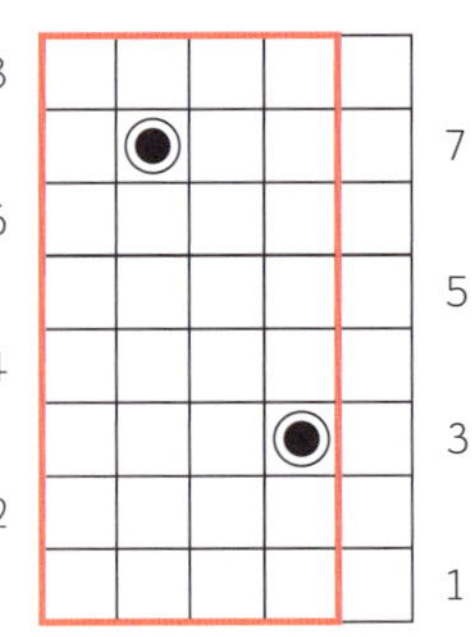

Beaded Row

SKILL LEVEL
Intermediate

MULTIPLES
2 (+1) stitches; 4 rows

STITCHES INCLUDED
knit, purl, place bead

APPEARANCE
Single-sided

OTHER MATERIALS
6/O seed beads (1 per full repeat), sewing thread, fine needle to go through centre of beads

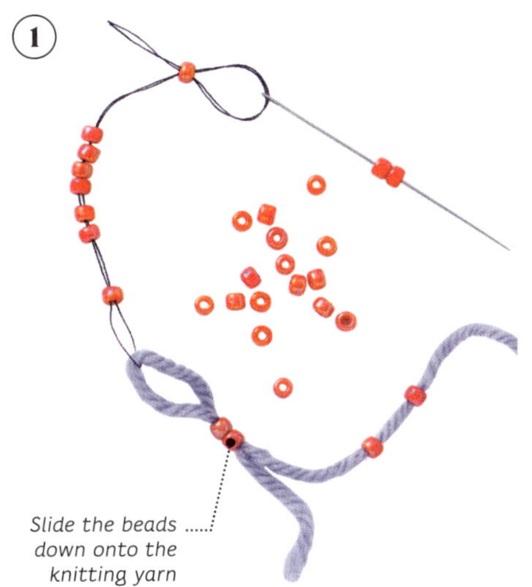

Slide the beads down onto the knitting yarn

Make sure the bead stays at the front

1 Thread the beads onto the knitting yarn (see opposite). **Rows 1 and 2:** Work 2 rows of stocking stitch: 1 row of knit followed by 1 row of purl.

2 **Row 3:** Knit 1 stitch. *Place the bead. Knit 1 stitch. Repeat from * until the end. **Row 4:** Purl all the stitches.

Beaded Column

SKILL LEVEL
Intermediate

MULTIPLES
4 (+1) stitches;
2 (+2) rows

STITCHES INCLUDED
knit, purl, place bead

APPEARANCE
Single-sided

OTHER MATERIALS
6/O seed beads (1 per full repeat), sewing thread, fine needle to go through centre of beads

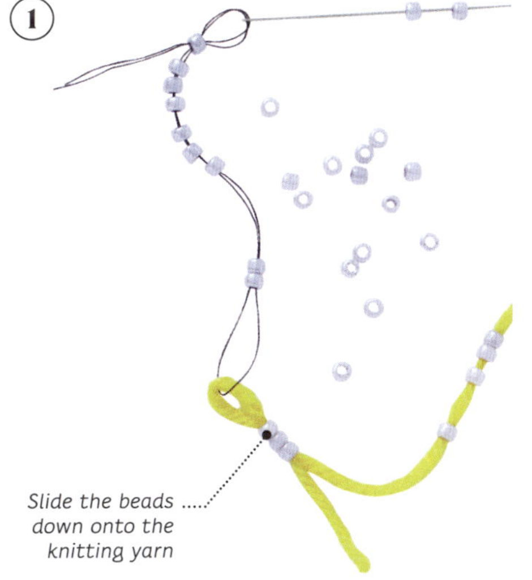

Slide the beads down onto the knitting yarn

Make sure the bead stays at the front

1 Thread the beads onto the knitting yarn (see opposite). **Setup Rows 1 and 2:** Work 2 rows of stocking stitch: 1 row of knit followed by 1 row of purl. **Row 3:** Knit 1 stitch. *Knit 1 stitch.

2 Place the bead. Knit 2 stitches. Repeat from * until the end. **Row 4:** Purl all the stitches. Repeat only Rows 3 and 4.

Crochet Beading

SKILL LEVEL
Intermediate

MULTIPLES
6 (+1) stitches; 2 rows

STITCHES INCLUDED
knit, purl, crochet bead, yo, k2tog, ssk

APPEARANCE
Single-sided

OTHER MATERIALS
6/0 seed beads (1 per full repeat), 0.5mm crochet hook, yarn needs to be DK weight or finer

1

2

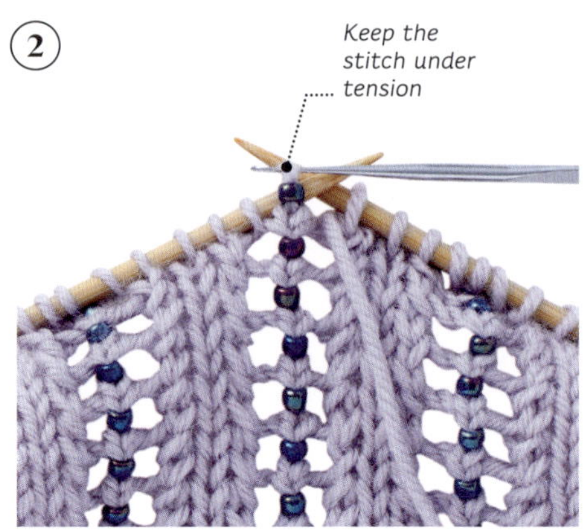

3

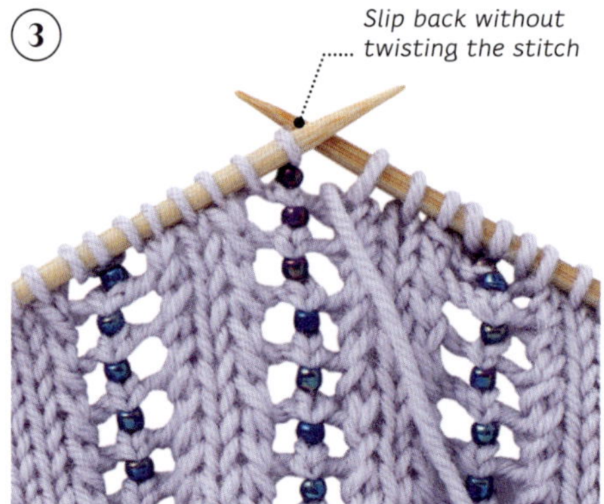

4

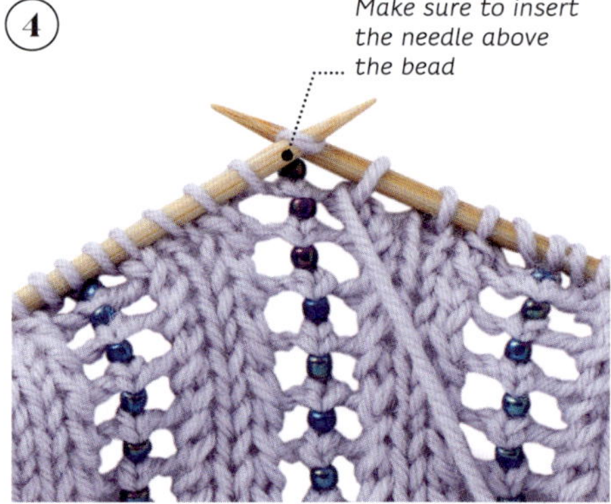

1 **Row 1:** Knit 1 stitch. *Knit 2 stitches together (see p.38). Work a yarnover (see p.42). Place a bead onto the crochet hook. Insert the hook into the stitch on the LHN. Drop from the LHN.

2 Slide the bead down onto the stitch.

3 Place the stitch back on the LHN, above the bead.

4 Insert the RHN into the beaded stitch on the LHN and knit. Work a yarnover. Work an ssk (see p.38). Knit 1 stitch. Repeat from * until the end. **Row 2:** Purl all the stitches.

The chart: Crochet Beading

The chart shows the hooked beadin the centre of the chart. Using the crochet method allows yarnovers to be used next to the bead. This method also allows the bead to be visible on both sides - ideal for scarves and shawls.

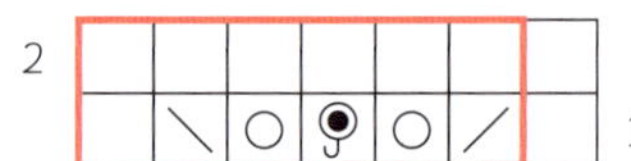

Smock Ribbing

SKILL LEVEL
Intermediate

MULTIPLES
8 (+6) stitches; 8 rows

STITCHES INCLUDED
knit, purl, smock stitch

APPEARANCE
Single-sided

OTHER MATERIALS
Cable needle

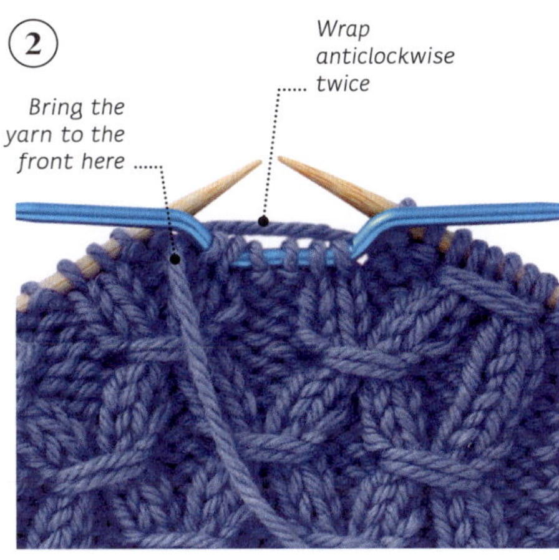

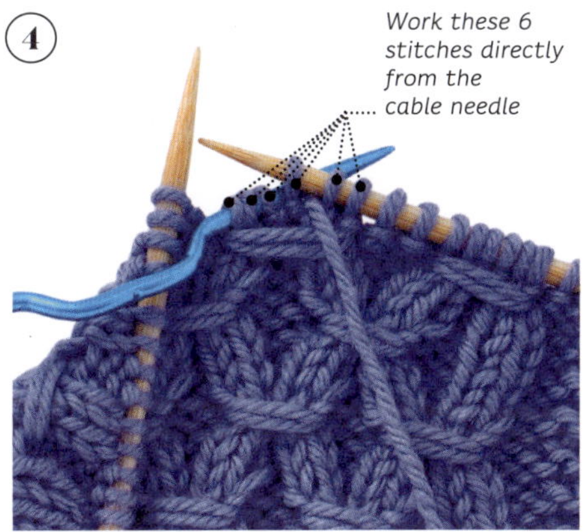

1 **Row 1:** Purl 2 stitches. *Knit 2 stitches. Purl 2 stitches. Repeat from * until the end. **Row 2:** Knit 2 stitches. *Purl 2 stitches. Knit 2 stitches. Repeat from * until the end. **Row 3:** Purl 2 stitches. Take the yarn to the back. *Work a smock stitch: *insert from right to left, and slip the next six stitches to the cable needle.*

2 *Bring the yarn to the front at the left of the cable needle. Wrap the yarn anticlockwise twice around the cable needle.*

3 *Take the yarn to the back at the right of the cable needle.*

4 *From the cable needle, knit 2 stitches, then purl 2 stitches, then knit 2 stitches.* Purl 2 stitches from the LHN. Repeat from * until the last 4 stitches. Knit 2 stitches. Purl 2 stitches. **Rows 4–6:** Repeat Row 2 then repeat Row 1 followed by another Row 2. **Row 7:** Purl 2 stitches. Knit 2 stitches. Purl 2 stitches. *Work a smock stitch. Purl 2 stitches. Repeat from * until the end. **Row 8:** Repeat Row 2 once.

Indian Cross Stitch

SKILL LEVEL
Intermediate

MULTIPLES
8 (+2) stitches; 6 rows

STITCHES INCLUDED
knit, purl, elongated knit stitch, Indian cross stitch

APPEARANCE
Single-sided

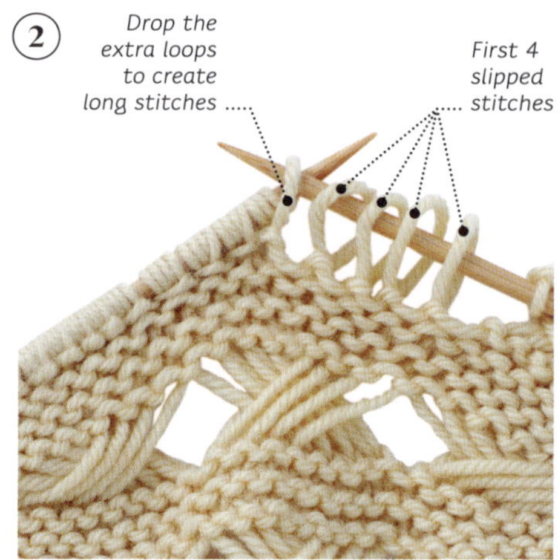

1 **Rows 1–4:** Work 4 rows of garter stitch: knit every row. **Row 5:** Knit 1 stitch. *Work an Elongated Knit Stitch: *insert from left to right into the next stitch on the LHN. Wrap the yarn anticlockwise 4 times around the RHN. Knit 1 stitch with these 4 wraps.* Repeat from * until the last stitch. Knit 1 stitch.

2 **Row 6:** Knit 1 stitch. Work an Indian Cross Stitch: **slip the next 8 stitches by inserting the RHN from right to left and dropping the extra wraps.*

3 *Insert the LHN from right to left into the fifth, sixth, seventh, and then eighth stitch on the RHN. Lift them over the first 4 stitches and off the RHN.*

4 *Slip the first, second, third, and then fourth stitch on the RHN to the LHN by inserting from left to right. Knit all 8 elongated stitches.* Repeat from * until the last stitch. Knit 1 stitch.

Armour Stitch

SKILL LEVEL
Intermediate

MULTIPLES
2 (+3) stitches; 2 rows

STITCHES INCLUDED
knit, purl, k-tbl, p-tbl

APPEARANCE
Single-sided

OTHER MATERIALS
Two different sized needles – approximately 8 sizes apart

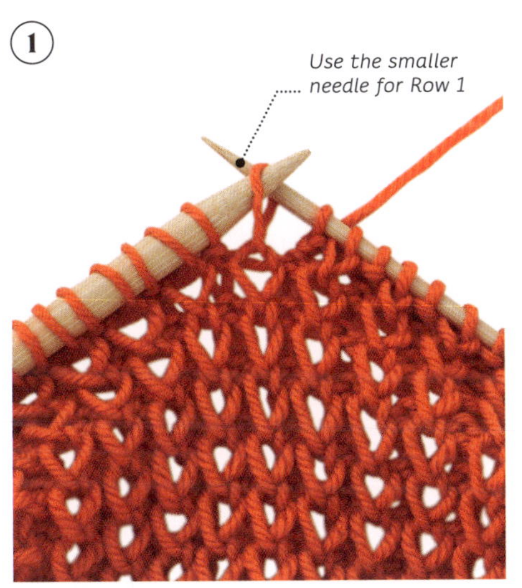

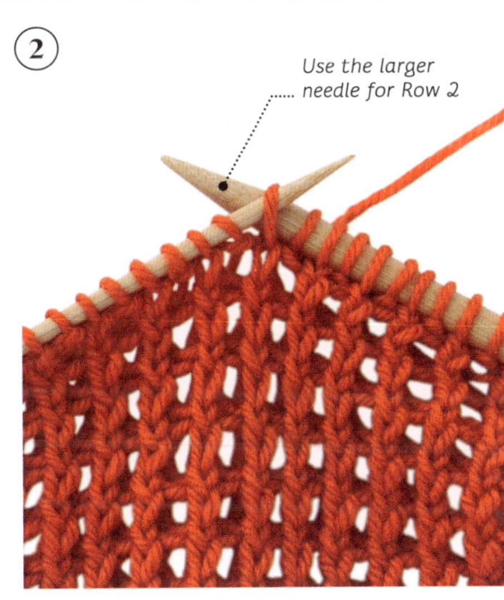

1 **Row 1:** Using the smaller needle, purl 2 stitches. *Knit 1 through the back loop: *insert from right to left and into the back loop.* Knit this stitch. Purl 1 stitch. Repeat from * until the last stitch. Purl 1 stitch.

2 **Row 2:** Using the larger needle, purl 1 stitch. *Knit 1 through the back loop. Purl 1 stitch. Repeat from * until the last 2 stitches. Knit 1 through the back loop. Purl 1 stitch.

The chart: Armour Stitch

The Armour stitch is a relatively simple stitch that uses twisted stitches in a checkerboard pattern. However, changing the needle size every row creates a dramatically different fabric.

2
Larger needle

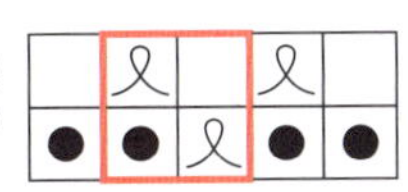

1
Smaller needle

Index

D

E

F

G

H

O

P, Q

R

S

T

Author's acknowledgments

I'd like to thank all the team at DK, especially Amy Slack and Emma Hill for their guidance and editing skills. Ruth Jenkinson and Nigel Wright for their photography and styling expertise, and wonderful company for the photo shoots. As well as Krystyna Egleton for her technical knitting skills at the shoots that I couldn't attend.

A big thank you to Sybil Izzard, who provided those first set of needles and sock yarn and started my knitting journey. Loraine McClean, who tutored me through my City and Guilds Level 3 Hand Knit Textiles. An extra thanks to both my husband, Jim, and Mum, Viv, whose assistance allowed me the time to work on this book. As always a special thanks to my cheerleading team, friends and fellow knitters, Dawn, Julie and Kate.

Finally, to all those knitters that buy my patterns, books and attend my classes. Thank you for your support.

Publisher's acknowledgments

DK would like to thank Tina Egleton for assistance as knitting technician at the photoshoots, Dan Crisp for illustrations, Rushil Pradhan for design assistance, Francesco Piscitelli for proofreading, and Vanessa Bird for indexing.

About the author

Jo Shaw is a knitwear designer and the creative mind behind Hardybarn Designs, based in Lincolnshire, UK. She follows in the footsteps of generations of her family who have worked in the textile trade, including her father, whose skills as a lace designer inspire her own knitting patterns. Jo has a Level 3 City and Guilds qualification in Hand-Knit Textiles, and regularly teaches knitting workshops, including regular sessions as part of A Good Yarn on Tour.

To find out more about Jo, find her on Instagram @hardybarn, or visit her website at hardybarn.co.uk.

DK UK
Project Editor Amy Slack
Senior Designer Glenda Fisher
Production Editor Tony Phipps
Production Controller Luca Bazzoli
Jackets Co-ordinator Abi Gain
Senior Acquisitions Editors Zara Anvari, Becky Alexander
Art Director Maxine Pedliham
Publisher Katie Cowan

Editorial Emma Hill
Design Tessa Bindloss
Photography Ruth Jenkinsons
Photography Art Direction Nigel Wright

DK India
Editor Ankita Gupta
Senior Art Editors Ira Sharma, Nidhi Mehra
Managing Art Editor Neha Ahuja Chowdhry
DTP Coordinator Pushpak Tyagi
DTP Designers Anurag Trivedi, Vikram Singh
Pre-production Manager Balwant Singh
Production Manager Pankaj Sharma
Creative Head Malavika Talukder

First published in Great Britain in 2023 by
Dorling Kindersley Limited
DK, One Embassy Gardens, 8 Viaduct Gardens,
London, SW11 7BW

The authorised representative in the EEA is
Dorling Kindersley Verlag GmbH. Arnulfstr. 124,
80636 Munich, Germany

10 9 8 7 6 5 4 3 2 1
001–336817–Oct/2023

A CIP catalogue record for this book
is available from the British Library.
ISBN: 978-0-2416-3414-1

Printed and bound in China

For the curious
www.dk.com